BUTLER'S
LIVES OF THE SAINTS

NEW

FULL EDITION

APRIL

BUTLER'S
LIVES OF THE SAINTS

NEW FULL EDITION

Patron

H. E. CARDINAL BASIL HUME, O.S.B.
Archbishop of Westminster

BUTLER'S LIVES OF THE SAINTS

NEW
FULL EDITION

APRIL

Revised by
PETER DOYLE

BURNS & OATES

THE LITURGICAL PRESS
Collegeville, Minnesota

First published 1999 in Great Britain by
BURNS & OATES
Wellwood, North Farm Road,
Tunbridge Wells, Kent TN2 3DR

First published 1999 in North America by
THE LITURGICAL PRESS
St John's Abbey, Collegeville,
Minnesota 56321

ISBN 0 86012 253 0   Burns & Oates
ISBN 0-8146-2380-8   The Liturgical Press

The emblems appearing at the foot of some pages are taken from W. Ellwood Post,
Saints, Signs and Symbols: A Concise Dictionary. © Copyright 1962, 1974 by
Morehouse Publishing, with the permission of the publishers.

Library of Congress Catalog Card Number: 95–81671

Typeset by Search Press Limited
Printed in the United States of America

CONTENTS

(Entries in capital letters indicate that the feast or saint is commemorated throughout the Roman Catholic Church with the rank of Solemnity, Feast, Memorial, or Optional Memorial, according to the 1969 revised Calendar of the Latin [Roman] Rite of the Catholic Church, published in the Roman Missal of 1970, or that the saint is of particular importance for the English-speaking world. These entries are placed first on their dates. All others are in chronological order.

Contents

Contents

PREFACE

"To look on the lives of those who have faithfully followed Christ is to be inspired with a new reason for seeking the city which is to come. . . . God shows in a vivid way his presence and his face in the lives of those companions of ours who are more perfectly transformed into the image of Christ." In these words the Second Vatican Council reminds us of the role of the saints: they both inspire us to greater spiritual effort and show how the "most perfect maxims of the gospel" may be "reduced to practice," as Alban Butler put it in his preface to the first edition of his *Lives of the Saints*. In the Church's liturgical year the month of April is usually dominated by the celebration of Holy Week and Easter, with consequently little attention being given to its saints. Yet it is a month as rich as any other in providing us with both inspiration and example. It has its Fathers, Doctors, and founders; its martyrs, missionaries, educationalists, and musicians; its bishops, builders, and mystics; and, with the inclusion of those recently beatified or canonized, they lived or worked in every corner of the Old World and several of the New.

Changes made in the Church's universal Calendar since 1969 have affected the month of April in different ways. The celebration of Cletus and Marcellinus (formerly 26th) has been dropped, while those of other saints formerly held in April have been transferred to different months to coincide with the the the dates of their deaths, or *dies natalis* into heaven. The practice of assigning saints and blessed to the dates of their death follows that adopted by the Roman Martyrology, the Church's official complete list of recognized saints and blessed, a new edition of which for the month of April is in preparation. St Peter Canisius is now to be found in December; St Paul of the Cross in October; SS Robert of Molesmes and Stephen Harding, and St Turibius, in March; St Justin Martyr in June; St Marianus Scotus in February, and the Martyrs of the Vikings under St Edmund in November. St Simeon of Jerusalem has moved from February to 27 April, and St Pius V from May to 30 April, while St Julie Billiart is now celebrated on 8 April instead of in May. In a few cases the traditional date of the feast-day has been kept here, despite a change in the new

ix

Roman Martyrology, because the exact date of death is not known or because the feast seems to fit better where it is—as, for example, with St Eva of Liège and Bd Juliana on 5 April.

Since the last full edition of Butler in the 1950s the number of saints and blessed in the Calendar has increased substantially, and the month of April has nearly thirty new entries. Just three of the blessed may be mentioned here to show the additional variety they bring to an already rich mixture: Bd Gianna Beretta Molla (28th), medical doctor and mother, who died as recently as 1962; Bd Damien De Veuster (15th), apostle of the lepers on Molokai; and Bd Kateri Tekakwitha (17th), the first native North American to be beatified.

Everyone interested in the lives of the saints is indebted to the monumental *Acta Sanctorum* launched by the Bollandists in the seventeenth century, and to their current bi-annual publication, the *Analecta Bollandiana*. There is also the indispensable Italian *Bibliotheca Sanctorum*, published between 1960 and 1970, with a supplementary volume published in 1987. This multi-volume work is based on authoritative scholarship and has the added attraction of being well illustrated. Pope John Paul II has beatified and canonized a large number of people and it is, perhaps susprisingly, sometimes difficult to find out very much about them beyond their basic biographical details; in these cases it is necessary to consult the official Vatican publications *Notitiae* and *A.A.S.* In English there are David Hugh Farmer's *Oxford Dictionary of the Saints* and J. N. D. Kelly's *Oxford Dictionary of the Popes*, which are both very useful, as is the *Oxford Dictionary of the Christian Church* for background information on people, movements, and events in the Church's history. For the sections on art and iconography I have relied mainly on the *Bibliotheca Sanctorum* and on V. Schauber and M. Schindler, *Heilige und Namenspatrone im Jahreslauf* (1992); while E. G. Tasker, *The Encyclopedia of Medieval Church Art* (ed. J. Beaumont, 1993), has been useful for representations of saints and their iconography in England.

An account of the life of Alban Butler and of the many editions of his work may be found in the January volume of this series. While nothing from his original text survives in this volume, we should not forget the importance of his initiative. The modern reader will find far less of the miraculous and the wonderful and will, I hope, welcome the use of psychological and historical insights to help clarify the conduct of our holy predecessors. Butler hoped his *Lives* would edify his readers and be an aid to devotion, but he still tried to make them as historically accurate as he could; devotion is better fed with the truth than with pious legend. It is, I believe, an advantage that in the process of revision the saints have become more like us, moving from being champions too wonderful and powerful to be imitated to being human models, flawed in many respects but overcoming eventually the temptations and obstacles facing all Christians who try to transform themselves "more perfectly into the image of Christ."

My task has been made lighter by help and encouragement given generously by several people. In particular I wish to thank Fr Paul Allerton, S.M.M., for advice and up-to-date publications on St Louis Marie Grignion de Montfort; Fr Clive Birch, S.M., and Fr Philip Graystone, S.M., for materials on St Peter Chanel; Sr Ann Grogan, Fd.C.C., for literature on St Magdalen of Canossa; Fr Bernard Grogan, S.D.B., for books on Bd Michael Rua; Sr Rosaria Kenny of the Good Shepherd Sisters for information on St Mary Euphrasia Pelletier; Br Robert Moore, O.H., for several works on Bd Benedict Menni; Sr Louanna Orth, S.N.DdN., for an up-to-date bibliography on St Julie Billiart; Sr Teresa Rodrigues, O.S.B., for information on Bd Eva of Liège; Br George van Grieken, F.S.C., for new information on St John Baptist de La Salle; and Dom Henry Wansbrough, O.S.B., for advice on the treatment of St Mark. Christa Pongratz-Lippitt very kindly contributed the entry on Bishop Vilmos Apor (1st), beatified in November 1997. I have benefited from the general editorial advice of David Hugh Farmer and particularly from his suggestions about the canonization of St Isidore. Finally, Paul Burns has been his helpful and encouraging self throughout and has been especially helpful with discussions and materials on Bd Gianna Beretta Molla.

Finally, I must thank my wife, Barbara (unfortunately deprived of her heavenly champion by the 1969 revision of the Calendar), and our son, Matthew, for their unfailing encouragement and patience.

---

18 October 1998, Feast of St Luke, Evangelist

Peter Doyle

Abbreviations and short forms

A.A.S.	*Acta Apostolicae Sedis. Commentarium officiale.* Rome, 1908-.
AA.SS.	*Acta Sanctorum.* 64 vols. Antwerp, also Rome and Paris, 1643-.
A.C.M.	H. Musurillo, S.J. *Acts of the Christian Martyrs.* Oxford, 1972.
Anal.Boll.	*Analecta Bollandiana.* 1882-.
Anal.Eccles.	*Analecta Ecclesiastica.* 1893-.
Anal.Franc.	*Analecta Franciscana.* 1885 -.
Anstruther	G. Anstruther, O.P. *The Seminary Priests*, 4 vols. Ware, Ushaw, and Great Wakering, 1968-77.
Archiv. Fratrum Praed.	*Archivum Fratrum Praedicatorum.* 1931-.
A.S.C.	*The Anglo-Saxon Chronicle,* in *E.H.D.*, 1 and 2.
Baring-Gould and Fisher	S. Baring-Gould and J. Fisher. *The Lives of the British Saints*, 4 vols. London, 1907-13.
Bede, *H.E.*	The Venerable Bede. *Historia Ecclesiastica* (ed. L. Sherley-Price and D. H. Farmer) 1955; revised ed. 1990.
Bibl.SS.	*Bibliotheca Sanctorum,* 12 vols. Rome, 1960-70; Suppl. 1, *Prima Appendice,* Rome, 1987.
B.T.A.	H. Thurston and D. Attwater (eds.). *Butler's Lives of the Saints,* 4 vols. London & New York, 1953-4; the previous edition of this work.
Catholic Encyclopaedia	C. Herbermann (ed.). *The Catholic Encyclopaedia,* 17 vols. New York, 1907-14.
Catholicisme	G. Jacquemet *et al.* (eds.). *Catholicisme: hier, aujourd'hui, demain,* Paris, 1948-.
C.R.S.	Publications of the Catholic Record Society. London, 1905-.
D.A.C.L.	H. Cabrol and H. Leclerq (eds.). *Dictionnaire d'archéologie chrétienne et de liturgie,* 15 vols. Paris, 1907-53.
D.C.B.	W. Smith and H. Wace (eds.). *Dictionary of Christian Biography,* 4 vols. London, 1877-87.
Dict.Sp.	M. Viller, S.J., *et al.* (eds.). *Dictionnaire de spiritualité.* Paris, 1937-.

Diz. dei Papi	B. Mondin. *Dizionario enciclopedico dei Papi: storia e insegnamenti.* Rome, 1995.
D.H.G.E.	A. Baudrillart *et al.* (eds.). *Dictionnaire d'Histoire et de Géographie Ecclésiatiques.* Paris, 1912-.
D.N.B.	L. Stephen and S. Lee (eds.). *Dictionary of National Biography,* 63 vols. London, 1885-1900.
D.T.C.	A. Vacant, E. Mangenot, and E. Amman (eds.). *Dictionnaire de Théologie Catholique,* 15 vols. Paris, 1903-50.
E.E.C.	*Encyclopaedia of the Early Church,* 2 vols. 1992.
E.H.D.	D. C. Douglas *et al.* (eds.). *English Historical Documents.* London, 1953-.
Eusebius, *H.E.*	Eusebius of Caesarea. *Historia Ecclesiasticaa.* Various editions.
Gillow	J. Gillow (ed.). *A Literary and Biographical History, or Bibliographical Dictionary of the English Catholics From the Breach with Rome, in 1534, to the Present Day.* 5 vols. London, 1885-1902.
The Irish Saints	D. D. C. Pochin Mould. *The Irish Saints.* Dublin and London, 1964.
Jedin-Holland	A three-vol. abridgement (New York, 1993) of H. Jedin and J. Dolan (eds.). *History of the Church,* Eng. trans., 10 vols. London & New York, 1965-81.
J.E.H.	*Journal of Eccelsiastical History,* 1950-.
K.S.S.	A. P. Forbes (ed.). *Kalendar of Scottish Saints.* Edinburgh,1872 .
L.E.M.	E. H. Burton and J. H. Pollen (eds.). *Lives of the English Martyrs,* 2d series. London, 1915.
Léon	Léon de Clary, O.F.M. *Auréole Séraphique.* Eng. trans., *Lives of the Saints and Blessed of the Orders of St Francis,* 4 vols. Taunton, 1887.
M.G.H.	G. Pertz *et al.*(eds.). *Monumenta Germaniae Historiae.* 64 vols., Hanover, 1839-1921. The *Scriptores* series is split into sub-series: *Auctores antiquissimi*; *Scriptores rerum merovingicarum*; *Poetae Latini*; *Epistolae*; *Scriptores.*
M.M.P.	R. Challoner. *Memoirs of Missionary Priests.* London 1741-2; new ed. by J. H. Pollen, 1924.
N.C.E.	*The New Catholic Encyclopedia,* 14 vols. New York, 1967.

N.D.S.	D. Attwater. *A New Dictionary of Saints,* rev. ed. by John Cumming. Tunbridge Wells and Collegeville, Minn., 1993.
Notitiae	*Congregatio de Cultu Divino et Disciplina Sacramentorum. Notitiae,* Rome, 1965-.
N.P.N.F	P. Schaff and H. Wace (eds.). The Nicene and Post-Nicene Christian Fathers. 1887-1900; 2d series rp., Grand Rapids, Michigan, 1979.
N.S.B. 1	T. Lelièvre. *100 nouveaux saints et bienheureux de 1963 à 1984.* Paris, 1983.
N.S.B. 2	T. Lelièvre. *Nouveaux saints et bienheureux de 1984 à 1988.* Paris, 1989.
O.D.C.C.	F. L. Cross and E. A. Livingstone (eds.). *The Oxford Dictionary of the Christian Church.* Oxford, New York, and Toronto, 1957; 2d. ed., 1974; 3d. ed., 1997.
O.D.P.	J. N. D. Kelly. *The Oxford Dictionary of Popes.* Oxford, 1986.
O.D.S.	D. H. Farmer. *The Oxford Dictionary of Saints.* Oxford and New York, 3d ed., 1993; 4th ed., 1997.
Office of Readings	*The Divine Office. The Liturgy of the Hours according to the Roman Rite,* 3 vols. London, Sydney, and Dublin, 1974.
Pastor	L. Pastor. *The History of the Popes from the Close of the Middle Ages.* London, 1891-1953.
P.G.	J. P. Migne (ed.). *Patrologiae Cursus Completus. Series Graeca,* 162 vols. Paris, 1857-66.
P.L.	J. P. Migne (ed.). *Patrologiae Cursus Completus. Series Latina,* 221 vols. Paris, 1844-64.
Procter	J. Procter (ed.). *Short Lives of the Dominican Saints.* London, 1900.
Propylaeum	*Propylaeum ad Acta Sanctorum Decembris.* Brussels, 1940.
R.H.	*Recusant History,* the journal of the C.R.S., 1951-.
S.C.	*Sources chrétiennes.* Paris, 1940-.
S.C.H.	*Studies in Church History.* London, Leiden, Oxford, 1964-.
Stanton	R. Stanton. *A Menology of England and Wales.* 1892.
Vies des Saints	J. Baudot et P. Chaussin (eds.). *Vies des Saints et des Bienheureux,* 13 vols. Paris, 1935-59.

V.S.H.   C. Plummer (ed.). *Vitae Sanctorum Hiberniae*, 2 vols. 1910; 2d. ed., 1968.

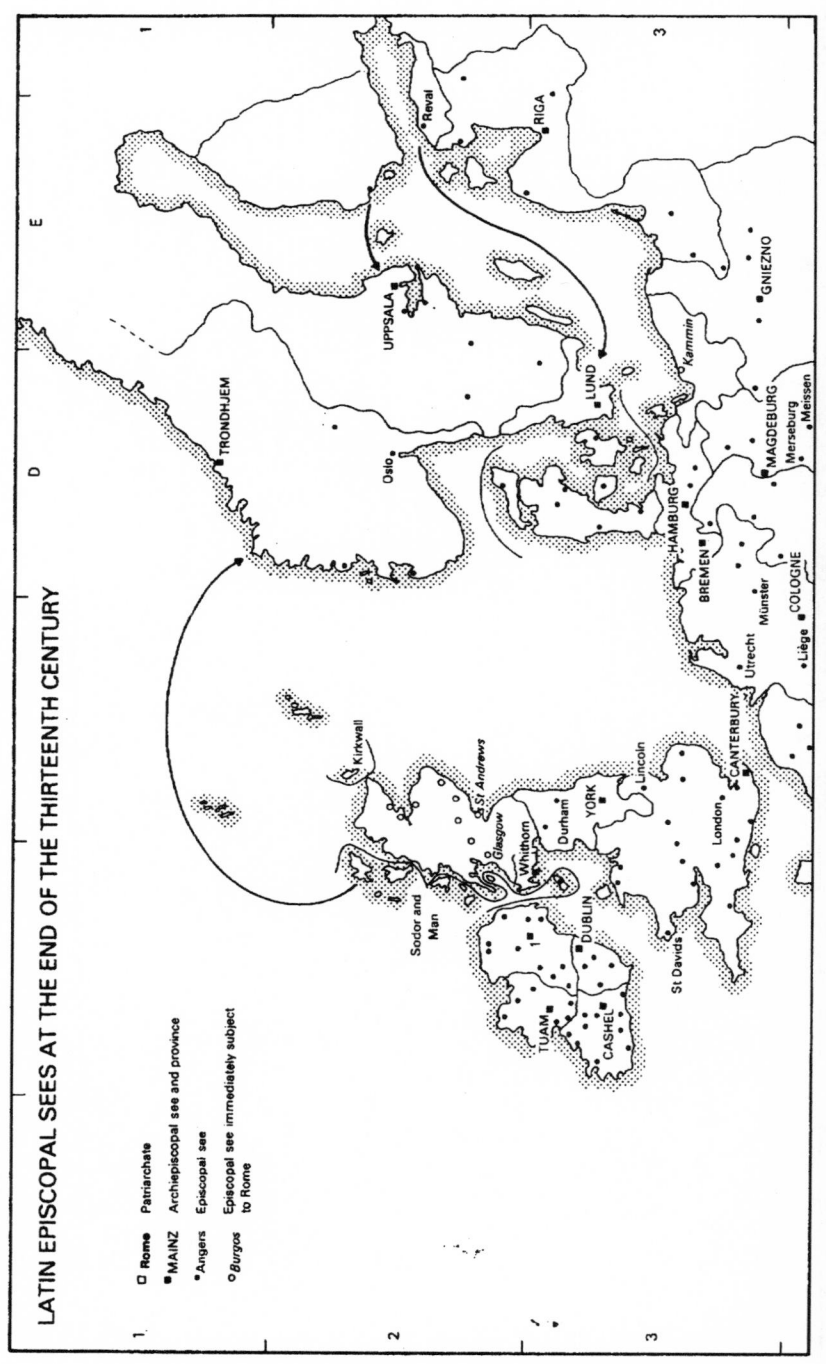

LATIN EPISCOPAL SEES AT THE END OF THE THIRTEENTH CENTURY

□ **Rome** Patriarchate

■ **MAINZ** Archiepiscopal see and province

● *Angers* Episcopal see

○ *Burgos* Episcopal see immediately subject to Rome

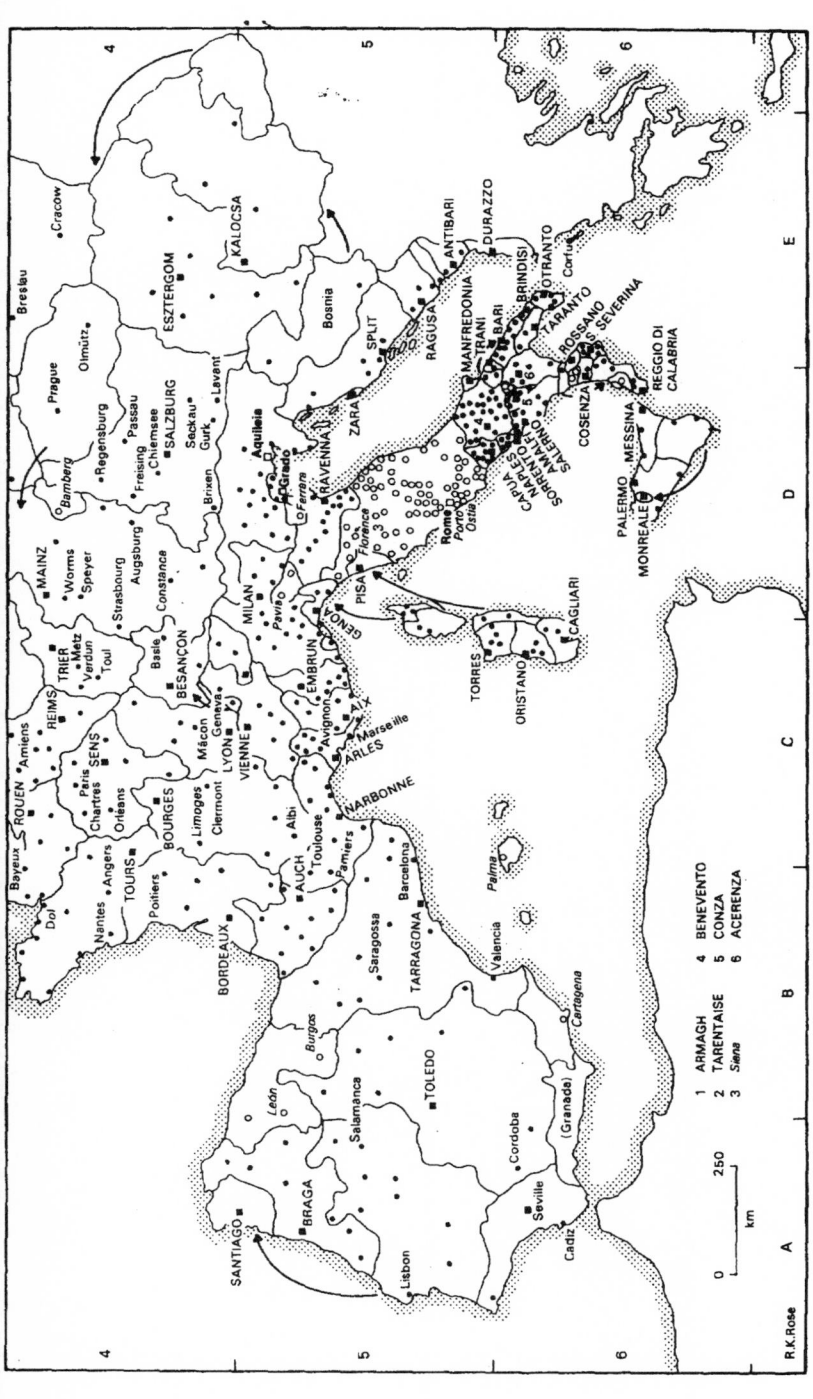

Bishops of the Latin Church—of various dates—featured in the April volume include: St Gilbert of Caithness (p. 7); St Fulbert (p. 70); St Stanislaus of Cracow (p. 77); St Celsus (p. 80); St Lambert (p. 97); St Fructuosus (p. 109); St Galdinus (p. 126); St Alphege of Canterbury (p. 134); St Marcellinus of Embrum (p. 138); St Anselm (p. 146); St John I of Valence (p. 156); St Gerald of Toul (p. 165); St Adalbert of Prague (p. 166); St Mellitus (p. 174); St Maughold of Man (p. 191); St Erkenwald (p. 223).

Map copyright © R. K. Rose, from Atlas of Medieval Europe, *ed. A. Mackay with D. Ditchburn (Routledge: London and New York, 1997), reproduced by permission.*

xvii

1

SS Agape, Chionia, and Irene, *Martyrs* (304)

In the year 303 the emperor Diocletian issued a decree making it a capital offence for anyone to possess copies of the Christian scriptures. One of the charges against the three sisters traditionally commemorated today was that they contravened this decree by hiding copies of the scriptures and refusing to give them up to the authorities. The three, Agape, Chionia, and Irene, were natives of Saloniki in Macedonia who retired to the mountains to avoid the persecution and continue their lives of prayer. They were arrested, however, and ordered to eat the meat used in sacrifices to the pagan gods. This they refused to do, telling the governor they would rather suffer death than agree to such an order. Agape is reported to have said, "I believe in the living God and I will not lose all the merit of my past life by one evil action." They were also interrogated about copies of the scriptures, some of which had been found in their house. They refused to give any information about where other copies might be found. The governor condemned Agape and Chionia to death by burning, but Irene was just imprisoned; perhaps the authorities hoped that the death of her elder sisters would persuade her to conform.

A few days later Irene was cross-examined again. She admitted having possessed copies of the scriptures but refused to implicate anyone else in hiding them and lamented that the law had prevented them from reading them "day and night as we had been accustomed to." The governor condemned her to perpetual imprisonment for having gone against the imperial decree and ordered her to be detained in a soldiers' brothel. As the soldiers refused to molest her she was later executed, perhaps by burning or, more likely, by being shot in the neck with arrows.

There is some doubt whether Irene's name should be included here or not, since she is not venerated in the Greek Church; the new Roman Martyrology omits her name.

The Greek text of the authentic *acta* of these martyrs was discovered and edited in 1902 by Pio Franchi de' Cavalieri in *Studi e Testi*; English versions may be found in A. J. Mason, *Historic Martyrs of the Primitive Church* (1905), pp. 341-6, and in *A.C.M.*, pp. xlii-xliii, 280-93. See also *O.D.S.*, p. 6; *Bibl.SS.*, 1, 303-4.

St Mary of Egypt (? Fifth Century)

The legend of St Mary was very popular for a long time in both East and West. She lived for many years as a hermit in the Palestinian desert beyond the Jordan, apparently entirely solitary and subsisting on next to no food. Her hair grew so long that she was able to use it to cover herself when her clothes rotted away. Eventually she was discovered by two monks and told them that she had been a cantoress in the church of the Anastasis in Jerusalem; she had been very beautiful and had fled the world to avoid being a temptation to men and to do penance. She died shortly afterwards and the monks buried her in a nearby cave.

This basic story is told by Cyril of Scythopolis in his Life of Cyriacus; Cyril claims to have visited her tomb. The same story can be found in the *Pratum Spirituale* of John Moschus (*c*. 550-619), who lived for a time in a monastery near Jerusalem. There is no evidence of any early cult connected with Mary, but the story was taken up and embellished by other writers, and a later Greek Life was falsely attributed to Sophronius of Jerusalem (*c*. 560-638) in an attempt to give it some authenticity. In this expanded version, Mary had been a prostitute in Alexandria in Egypt. She accompanied some men who were going to Jerusalem on pilgrimage, plying her trade as they went. In Jerusalem she tried to enter a church on the feast of the Exaltation of the Holy Cross but was held back by an invisible force. She decided this was because of her sinful life, prayed to Our Lady, and was converted. Taking with her just three loaves of bread she went into the desert and lived there in solitude for forty-seven years until found by a priest named Zosimus. He took her Holy Communion—she walked on the waters of the river to reach him—but when he returned the following year to do so again he found she had died. He buried her, with the help of a friendly lion.

There appears to have been some conflation of her story with that of St Mary Magdalen (22 July), who also, in some legends, retired to the desert and used her long hair as covering. Mary of Egypt's story occurs in various collections of saints' Lives, including Aelfric's *Lives of the Saints* (*c*. 1000) and the famous thirteenth-century *Golden Legend*. St John Damascene (4 Dec.) quoted at length from the Life attributed to Sophronius and clearly regarded it as a reliable record.

A scholarly account of the question is given by H. Leclercq, *D.A.C.L.*, 10, 2128-36. See also *The Coptic Encyclopedia* (1991), 5, pp. 1560-1; *O.D.S.*, pp. 330-1; *O.D.C.C.*, p. 884; Peter and Linda Murray, *The Oxford Companion to Christian Art and Architecture* (1996), p. 314.

She is depicted in stained-glass windows, for example, at Chartres, Bourges, and Auxerre, and in a painting by Memling (in Bruges), in which she is shown carrying her three loaves. She appears with the same emblem on the screen in a church at Kenn in Devon. It is only when she is shown in this way, or being buried with the help of the lion, that we can be certain it is her and not Mary Magdalen who is being depicted. A twelfth-century carving in Toulouse shows various scenes from the legend. There is a late medieval wood carving of her in the cathedral of Burgos in Spain. Such widespread artistic and literary references are evidence of the remarkable popularity of a legend that probably had some basis in fact but is now very difficult to disentangle.

St Walaricus, *Abbot (c. 620)*

Walaricus, or Valéry, was born in the Auvergne region of France. Details of his early life are uncertain, but it seems that he worked on his father's farm as a young boy and learned the Psalter by heart while looking after the sheep. He was taken to visit the monastery at Autumo and when it was time to return home insisted on staying there, against the wishes of his father, who was strongly opposed to his son's wish to become a monk. He was too young to join the community but seems to have remained long enough to complete his education. He then entered the abbey of St Germanus at Auxerre, moving on after a short time to join the monastery at Luxeuil in 594. This house was under the direction of St Columban (23 Nov.), and Walaricus was attracted by the fame of the Irish abbot as a spiritual director. Walaricus was reputed to be particularly good at gardening, and when the rest of the abbey's grounds suffered from blight his allotment is said to have flourished in a miraculous way.

When Columban was expelled by King Theodoric, Walaricus left the abbey and became a missionary in the west of France. After a successful period as a preacher, when his miracles and eloquence won over a large number of converts, he wanted to return to a more settled way of life. He chose a secluded spot near the mouth of the river Somme, hoping to lead the life of a solitary, but was soon surrounded by disciples asking for guidance. The settlement later became the famous abbey of Leuconay, which followed the Rule of St Columban in its early years. Walaricus seems to have found it difficult to settle for very long to a single way of life and was soon combining the duties of abbot and missionary. He was credited with having evangelized most of the northern French coast and the Pas-de-Calais region.

Walaricus was said to be tall and ascetic-looking, but with a gentle manner and approach that tempered the strict Rule of St Columban to good effect. He was also said to be kind to animals, with birds perching on his shoulders and eating from his hands. He ruled his monastery for six or seven years and died about the year 620. Several miracles were attributed to his intercession, and his cult spread rapidly, with at least two towns being named after him—Saint-Valéry-sur-Somme and Saint-Valéry-en-Caux.

His relics were much sought after. Charlemagne gave part of them to the monastery of Corbie, near Amiens, and in the tenth century a count of Flanders moved them to Montreuil and then to Saint-Bertin. According to legend, this annoyed Walaricus so much that he appeared in a dream to the king, Hugh Capet, and ordered him to return the remains to Leuconay. William the Conqueror had the saint's remains exposed in public and prayed to him for a favourable wind for his invasion of England, which set off from the town of St-Valéry-sur-Somme. King Richard I of England moved the remains again, but they were later restored to the town and enshrined on the site of the abbey of Leuconay.

Apparently a Life of Walaricus was written shortly after his death by an abbot of Leuconay, but the surviving version of this is a much later composition with elements from other lives than Walaricus'; see *AA.SS.*, Apr., 1, pp. 14-30, and *M.G.H., Scriptores,* 4, pp. 157-75. See also *Bibl.SS.*, 12, 921-4; *O.D.S.*, p. 485; *Vies des Saints,* 4, pp. 9-16.

St Hugh of Grenoble, *Bishop* (1052-1132)

Hugh was born of a noble family at Châteauneuf d'Isère near Valence, in the Dauphiné region of France, in 1052. His father, Odilo, was described by Hugh's first biographer as a "friend of chastity and truth"; he ended his days in the nearby Carthusian monastery that Hugh was to help found. Hugh's mother taught her sons the importance of prayer and almsgiving and did what she could to play down the appeal of a life dedicated to the pursuit of military glory.

After a distinguished academic career that had taken him to some of the leading centres of learning of the day Hugh became a canon of Valence cathedral while still a layman. He was good-looking and talented but very shy, with a humility that led him to try to hide his abilities and learning. The bishop of Die, however, was so impressed by the young man that he made him a member of his household and gave him a leading role in the campaign against simony in his diocese. In 1080 Hugh attended a synod at Avignon, called to deal with the problems of the vacant see of Grenoble, and so impressed the delegates that he was unanimously chosen to be the bishop of that city. He accepted reluctantly, was ordained priest, and went to Rome to be consecrated. He consulted the pope, St Gregory VII (25 May), about particular temptations he had to blasphemy and was assured by Gregory that these did not make him unfit to be a bishop, since God was using them to purify him and make him a stronger character; the temptations remained to trouble Hugh until his death. There is some indication that they were intellectual temptations about matters of faith and may even have involved doubts about the existence of God, but the evidence is debatable.

When the young bishop arrived in Grenoble he was appalled by the state of his diocese: simony and usury were common among the clergy, the obligation to celibacy was largely ignored, the people were ignorant of their religion, and church property had been seized by laymen. The scene was set for the rest of Hugh's life: he was to be an ardent reformer, using an effective mixture of severity and gentleness to improve the state of his diocese. At the same time he was a lover of solitude and had to struggle to overcome his desire to give up the demands of his office and retire from the world. After two years as bishop he was so disheartened by what he saw as his failure to reform his priests and people that he withdrew to an abbey and took the Benedictine habit. He remained there for about a year and, presumably, would have stayed permanently if he had not been ordered back to his diocese by the pope to continue the work of reform. In the last ten years of his life he tried on a number of

4

occasions to resign and retire to the solitude of the Grande Chartreuse, but papal permission was never forthcoming. On one occasion, when he put forward his increasing age and illness as a reason for retiring from his diocese, the pope, Honorius II, replied that the sick man's authority and example would do more for the good of the diocese than the more energetic activity of a healthier man.

Hugh was an active and unbending defender of his own rights as bishop and those of the Church at large, upholding the temporal claims of the papacy against political interference and, in general, implementing in every way he could the reforms inspired by Pope St Gregory. He always took the papal side in conflicts between pope and emperor. He opposed the king of France when the latter had his eye on part of the Papal States, and his own metropolitan archbishop when he tried to take over part of Hugh's diocese. He spoke fearlessly at councils in defence of the papacy and his own rights as bishop, whether his opponents were the emperor Henry V or local nobles and bishops. At one stage he was forced into exile by the emperor, and all the temporalities of his diocese were confiscated, but he returned to his diocese to the acclaim of the people and was able to restore his position and settle local disputes in his favour. This pugnacity, which sometimes had at least a touch of obstinacy about it, was as much part of his make-up as his humility and desire to retire from the world: both witness to his determination to give himself wholly to God's service in whatever walk of life he was ordered to perform.

Hugh was an eloquent and effective preacher, and his reforming work was much more successful than he would ever admit. He set up houses throughout the diocese for reformed priests, and the people were moved to a stricter religious observance. He was ahead of his time in advocating regular Confession by laypeople and was himself renowned as a confessor. His own generous almsgiving inspired the wealthy to give to the poor and support the needs of the diocese. Part of his task as bishop was to look after the civil administration of Grenoble. He repaired roads and bridges, built three hospitals, established a central market in the city, imposed taxes, and in general was as conscientious in these matters as in his religious duties.

Hugh is probably best known for the support he gave to St Bruno (6 Oct.), founder of the Carthusians, and the establishment of what became the great monastery of the Grande Chartreuse. The two men had first met when Hugh was studying at Reims, where Bruno had been a noted teacher. When the latter gave up his career in the world and was searching for a place of sufficient solitude for himself and his disciples, he eventually turned to Hugh and asked to be allowed to settle in the diocese of Grenoble. Hugh had apparently been told of this previously in a dream and gave Bruno a remote valley he himself had sometimes used as a retreat. In 1085 he consecrated the chapel Bruno had built and from then on became the patron and lifelong benefactor of the new foundation. Hugh himself had a cell in the monastery and used it regularly as a place of prayer, sharing whenever he could in the daily life of the monks. On at least one occasion Bruno had to order him to return to Grenoble and not neglect his duties as bishop.

A short time before he died Hugh apparently lost his memory completely except for the psalms and the Lord's Prayer, which he recited continuously. He died on 1 April 1132, surrounded on his death-bed by Carthusian monks; he had been a bishop for fifty-two years. He was canonized two years later by Pope Innocent II. Whatever his inner turmoils, Hugh stands out as a striking example of a reforming bishop—a very capable administrator and conspicuous for his personal holiness.

Guigo, who wrote the first Life, was prior of the Chartreuse at the time of Hugh's death; see M-A. Chomel, *Guiges le Chartreux, vie de Saint Hugues, évêque de Grenoble, ami des moines* (1984), reprinted in *Anal.Cartusiana* 112 (1986), pp. 5-23, and p. 71 for a full bibliography. See also A. Murray, "The Temptation of St Hugh of Grenoble," in L. Smith and B. Ward (eds.), *Intellectual Life in the Middle Ages* (1992), pp. 81-101; *Bibl.SS.*, 12, 759-64; *O.D.S.*, pp. 237-8.

Pictures of Hugh show those parts of his life that were concerned with the foundation of the Grande Chartreuse; see, for example, the series by Zurbarán in Seville. There is a surprising lack of miracles in accounts of the saint—in Guigo's early and very reliable Life only one is recounted, and the writer justifies what must have seemed a strange lack to contemporaries by saying that a person's inner virtues are far more important than any miracles. This lack of miracle stories may account for the relative neglect of Hugh by later artists.

St Hugh of Bonnevaux, *Abbot* (*c.* 1120-94)

Like his uncle, St Hugh of Grenoble, whose feast-day is also celebrated today, Hugh was born at Châteauneuf d'Isère near Valence, in the Dauphiné region of France, about the year 1120. He started out on an ecclesiastical career in Lyons but, after several meetings with a Carthusian, decided to become a monk and took the habit in the nearby Carthusian house at Mézières. His family was totally opposed to his becoming a religious, and when he fell seriously ill during his novitiate he was himself tempted to give up the idea. A letter from St Bernard of Clairvaux (20 Aug.) encouraged him to remain faithful to his vocation, and later on, when his bodily penances became too severe, it was also St Bernard who counselled commonsense and a more balanced approach to the spiritual life.

In 1162 Hugh was elected abbot of the house at Léoncel in Languedoc. He became involved in disputes over the rights of the abbey and managed to obtain a papal Bull confirming and protecting all its properties. In 1166 he was chosen as abbot of Bonnevaux, the motherhouse of Léoncel, and once again was drawn into ecclesiastical disputes and politics. This time the issues were more important in that they concerned the attempts of the emperor, Frederick Barbarossa, to depose Pope Alexander III in favour of an antipope. This dispute was resolved in favour of Alexander at a meeting between him, the emperor, and Hugh at Venice in 1177. The emperor gave much of the credit for the success of the negotiations to the role Hugh had played as mediator between the warring parties.

Hugh died in 1194 and was buried in the church at Bonnevaux. His tomb became a place of pilgrimage, and a number of miracles were reported to have occurred there. An inquiry into his life and miracles was set up about twenty years after he died, but no formal process of canonization was ever started. The long-standing cult was officially recognized in 1907. His tomb was partially destroyed at the time of the Reformation, and his remains were re-buried in a nearby chapel in 1743. A new chapel to house the relics was built on the same spot in 1966.

There is no early Life, and details have to be put together from various sources. See *Bibl.SS.*, 12, 749-51, for a very full bibliography. See also A. Dimier, *St Hugues de Bonnevaux* (1941); *Catholicisme*, 5, 1018-9.

St Gilbert of Caithness, *Bishop* (1245)

Gilbert was born into the noble Scottish family of Moray sometime in the second half of the twelfth century. His father, William, lord of Duffus and Strabrook, owned very extensive estates in the north of Scotland. Gilbert became archdeacon of Moray, an office he held from about 1203 to 1223, when he was nominated bishop of Caithness by King Alexander. He served as bishop for over twenty years, but there is no evidence to support the tradition that he was also high steward of Scotland during that time. No doubt he did carry out royal duties, as all bishops did, and he may have been responsible for administering the royal estates in the north of the country. He is credited with doing a great deal to bring religion and law and order to the territories he administered and seems to have been a popular and respected figure; at least he survived to die a natural death, unlike his two predecessors, who had both been murdered. He built the cathedral at Dornoch and established a Constitution for its clergy. He also set up a number of hospices for the poor. He died on 1 April 1245. He is reported to have said to those who attended him on his death-bed, "Three maxims that I have always tried to follow I now commend to you. First, never to hurt anyone and, if injured, never to seek revenge; second, to bear patiently whatever suffering God may inflict, remembering that he chastises everyone he receives; and finally, to obey those in authority so as not to be a stumbling-block to others."

He is reputed to have written two works, *Exhortationes ad ecclesiam suam* (Exhortations to his church), and *De libertate Scotiae* (On the liberty of Scotland). There is a link between the second of these works and a strongly-held tradition that Gilbert attended the Council of Northampton in England in 1176 as spokesman of the Scottish bishops. He is said to have spoken eloquently and effectively in support of the independence of the Scottish Church.

There was a young canon named Gilbert who spoke at the council, but it is most unlikely that it was the same Gilbert who became bishop of Caithness nearly fifty years later.

K.S.S., pp. 355-6; *D.N.B.*, 21, pp. 317-8, with references.

Bd John Bretton, *Martyr* (1598)

John Bretton (or Britton, according to Challoner) was born at Bretton in the West Riding of Yorkshire. Little is known about his life except that he was a member of the gentry and remained loyal to the Catholic religion during Queen Elizabeth's reign. He was subject to heavy fines for his refusal to conform, and Challoner tells us that he spent long periods away from his wife and children "to keep himself further from danger." When he was sixty-eight years old he was accused, out of malice apparently, of saying treasonable things about the queen. He was condemned to death under the Act of 1571, which had made it treason to deny the queen any of her titles or to accuse her of heresy. He refused to save his life by giving up his Catholicism and was executed at York for high treason on 1 April 1598. His wife, Frances, and daughter Dorothy were named as "old recusants" in a Yorkshire listing of 1604. He was among the group of English martyrs beatified in 1987.

M.M.P., p. 233; Gillow, 1, pp. 304-5.

Bd Vilmos Apor, *Bishop and Martyr* (1892-1945)

Vilmos Apor was born in 1892 at Segesvar in Transylvania. He was the seventh of eight children born to Baron Gabor Apor and his wife, Fidelia, the Countess Palffy. His mother, a very devout Catholic, took special care over the religious education of her children, and Vilmos is said to have been a gentle and religious boy. From the age of ten he attended Jesuit schools, and the seeds of his vocation began to develop early on. In 1910 he went to study theology at Innsbruck University, where he stayed at the Canisianum, a Jesuit college and hall of residence for students studying for the priesthood. He was ordained in 1915 and appointed as curate in Gyula, a Hungarian town two miles from the present Romanian border. He soon became known for his commitment to social work, especially among the poor; when he was sent to the Italian front in 1917 the suffering and misery he saw there had a great impact on him.

After the war Vilmos returned to Gyula and became parish priest there. For a time the town was occupied by Romanian troops, and when Hungarian soldiers were deported to Romania, he hurried to the Romanian capital to intercede—succesfully—with British-born Queen Mary for their release. Other postwar problems were more difficult to deal with. The number of churchgoers was declining, and there was a growing antagonism to religion. Vilmos launched a monthly paper, *The Catholic Church Correspondent of Gyula*, and wrote in its first editorial: "We are not here to deal with a few, we have to look after everyone . . . not only after those who listen to the Church, but also those who are kept away from God's house because of illness, poverty, lack of shoes or decent clothes." When Gyula was badly affected by the economic depression the unemployed and destitute flocked to his door, which remained open day and night. There is a story that an important visitor found Vilmos sitting at his desk in his bare feet because he had given his only good pair of shoes to a destitute father of seven.

As well as his commitment to the poor, Vilmos was known for his ecumenism; he had established excellent relations with the other Christian Churches in Hungary.When he was appointed bishop of Győr in 1940 the dean of the Reformed Church in Gyula made a speech in his honour: "My conscience compels me to speak because it was Bishop Apor's example that, during a twenty-five-year period, created and maintained a golden age of denominational peace in this divided and restless world."

Vilmos took up his appointment as bishop in March 1941 and immediately faced the problem of the treatment of Jews. From the outset he protested against any discrimination against them and offered accommodation to Jewish refugees. When the persecution increased in 1944 and the Jews were being deported to the death camps, Vilmos wrote to the minister of the interior in protest: "As bishop of the ancient city of Győr, I protest before God, Hungary, and the world against these measures, which are in contradiction to human rights. I hold you responsible for all the cases of sickness, humiliation, and death caused by these measures." As soon as the Jews in his own diocese began to be moved to the camps he asked several times for permission to visit them and give them spiritual help, but he was refused. He went to the German headquarters to try to stop their deportation, and when this failed he approached every competent person from the prime minister down to the heads of local authorities to ask for permission to visit the Jews, but he succeeded only in being threatened with imprisonment himself.

On Whitsunday 1944 he preached against what was happening: "He who assumes that men, whether Negroes or Jews, may be tortured, must be regarded as a pagan, even if he boasts of being a Christian. Everyone who approves of, or takes part in, the torturing of human beings, commits a grave sin." He got in touch with former fellow-sudents at the Canisianum who were in Switzerland and informed them of what was happening, and he wrote to a fellow-bishop in Hungary, saying, "One cannot tolerate anti-semitism. It must be condemned from the Pope down to the least of the bishops. . . . One must state openly that nobody must be persecuted for the blood in his veins. What Jews are undergoing is genocide, and he who approves of it may not protest if another class of society, possibly the Church itself, is deprived of its rights." But despite his protests the remaining Jews in the camps around Győr were, in the course of that summer (1944), forced into cattle trucks and deported from the country.

By autumn 1944 the Russian front was rapidly approaching Hungary. In September 1944 Bishop Apor told his priests that it was their duty to stay with their flock, come what may. Many persecuted people and refugees turned to him, and he offered shelter to everyone. As he expected the siege of Györ to last a long time, he laid in stores of non-perishable food and had generators put in the huge cellars of the bishop's palace, built by the Turks in the seventh century. Gradually the cellars filled with people, until some three to four hundred were gathered there. The fighting in Györ between Russian and German troops began on 28 March 1945, the Wednesday of Holy Week. The first Russians came to the cellars after dark that night. Bishop Apor received each Russian soldier personally at the entrance to the cellars. He did not get a wink of sleep until Good Friday, as he refused to leave his post "in case anything happens." After supper on Good Friday, some drunken Russian soldiers started to annoy a young girl. She called to the bishop for help, and so he stood in front of the soldiers and told them to leave. One of the soldiers fired at the bishop and severely wounded him; he could not be taken to hospital quickly because of the street-fighting, and his wounds became infected. He died on Easter Monday, 2 April 1945.

The cathedral was too badly damaged for Vilmos to be buried there, and he was buried in the Carmelite church. Devotion to him spread quickly, especially among refugees in Vienna, Cologne, and Rome. It was not until 1986 that the Communist authorities allowed his remains to be moved to the cathedral. He was beatified in Rome on 9 November 1997.

A large collection of documents about the bishop is in the Canisianum. See David O'Driscoll, *Martyr of Service and Charity. A Life of Baron Vilmos Apor, 1892–1945, Bishop of Györ* (n.d., ? 1997); *Korrespondenzblatt des Collegium Canisianum Innsbruck* (1998).

2

ST FRANCIS OF PAOLA, *Founder* (1416-1507)

Francis was born at Paola in Calabria, southern Italy. His parents, Giacomo Alessio (usually known as Martolilla) and Vienna di Fuscaldo, were small farmers of modest means. They were childless after several years of marriage, and Francis was born after they had made a vow to St Francis of Assisi (4 Oct.) to dedicate any son that might be born in his honour. They paid particular attention to his religious education and took him at the age of twelve to a house of the Conventual Friars to spend a year there in accordance with their vow. His biographers relate a number of miracles worked by him, or in his favour, during the time he spent in the monastery; in particular, he was credited with powers of bilocation so that he could, for example, serve Mass while at the same time be seen to be helping in the kitchens. Whatever the basis for these stories, it is clear that Francis had a reputation for outstanding sanctity while still in his teens and was consulted on spiritual matters by various people. His parents took him to Rome on pilgrimage, but he was horrified by the luxury and worldliness he saw there. On his return to Paola he retired to live as a hermit in a cave not far from the town and adopted a way of life marked by rigorous fasting and penance. He never sought ordination, preferring in his humility to remain a layperson; in this, as in so many other things, he followed the example of his great patron.

By 1436 a group of disciples had gathered around him. They called themselves "the hermits of Brother Francis of Assisi" and were the foundation of his new Order. Later on a church and monastery were built for them with the help of local people who had been greatly impressed by the way of life of the hermits and their adherence to the original Franciscan ideals of poverty and simplicity. While the church and monastery were being built Francis was again credited with a number of miracles designed to hasten the building or save the workmen from injury. The local archbishop granted the Order approval in 1471, and in 1474 the pope, Sixtus IV, placed it directly under his own jurisdiction and protection and gave it all the privileges of other Mendicant Orders. Such was his reputation and the demands made of him that Francis was forced to open a number of other houses in the region and in Sicily.

Penance, charity, and humility were the basis of the Rule drawn up by Francis, and he required his followers to take a fourth vow, to observe a perpetual Lenten fast, with abstinence not just from meat but also from eggs and anything made from milk. He regarded fasting as the chief means of self-conquest and hoped that through it they would also be able to make reparation for the lukewarmness of so many Christians. We have nothing in Francis' own words about his spiritual development or methods of prayer and meditation, but the external picture we have from his contemporaries is of a person wholly devoted to a life of austerity and solitude (he was often compared to John the Baptist), constantly at prayer, with a special devotion to the passion of Our Lord (he recommended devotion to the Five Wounds) and to Our Lady (his houses were almost always dedicated to "Jesus-Maria"). He was deeply concerned by the troubles facing the Church and by the moral laxity in the Church itself. This may explain his constant stress on the need for penance and why there seems to have been little of the joy of his patron in his life or teaching; we should remember that he drew on the austere Desert Fathers for inspiration as well as on St Francis.

In 1483, on the orders of the pope, he accepted very reluctantly an invitation from the king of France to visit his court. He travelled barefoot, refusing any special hospitality en route and praying most of the time; the journey became a sort of humble triumphal march. At court he continued to live as simple and solitary a life as possible. He spent hours at a time in prayer and often seemed to be in ecstasy; he fasted for days at a time, always went about barefoot, and slept on a board. As a result of the contacts he made at the court he was invited to open houses of his Order in France, Spain, and Germany. He revised his Rule four times, the last in 1507, and some of the earlier severity was dropped in the later versions. He also issued a Rule for nuns in 1506 and a version for laypeople who wished to join his Third Order in 1501. In 1492 he changed the name of the Order from the Hermits of St Francis to the Friars Minims to indicate publicly that they were the least (*minimi*) of all religious, and that is the name they have kept since. The Order reached its greatest size in the first half of the sixteenth century, when it had about 450 houses and witnessed to the strength of the Catholic reform movement. It declined from the end of the eighteenth century and is now confined to Italy and Spain.

Francis did not return to Italy and died in France at Plessis-les-Tours on Good Friday, 2 April 1507. His reputation for holiness and as a reformer was widespread, and he was regarded as one of the greatest miracle-workers of the age. He was beatified in 1513 and canonized in 1519. In 1943 he was declared "Patron of Italian Seafarers" by Pope Pius XII because so many of his miracles had been worked at sea or in favour of those at sea, and sailors had testified to the effectiveness of his intercession.

In addition to the various versions of the Rule, some letters written by Francis are extant. They concern mainly business matters, with only an occasional scriptural quotation or piece of spiritual advice. There is also his *Correctorium*, a manual of penances for those who broke the Rule.

AA.SS., Apr., 1, pp. 103-234, gives the material gathered for the process of canonization and a later Life. See also *Dict.Sp.*, 5, 1040-51; G. M. Roberti, *San Francesco di Paola* (1963);

N.C.E., 6, pp. 33-4; *Bibl.SS.*, 5, 1163-82, with a range of illustrations. The *acta* of a conference devoted to St Francis, published as *Fede, pietà, religiosità popolare e S. Francesco di Paola: Atti del II Congresso Internazionale di Studio* (1992), run to a thousand pages and must be the starting point for any study of the saint.

Francis was a very popular saint and was frequently depicted in art, almost always as a bearded, ascetic figure in a monk's habit and hood, carrying a placard or scroll with the word *Charitas* and often holding a rosary; he is sometimes shown meditating before a crucifix. The original of a contemporary portrait by his friend Jean Bourdichon has been lost, but apparently reliable copies exist—for example, in S. Maria della Pace in Rome. A painting by Tiepolo shows him in ecstasy (San Benedetto's, Venice); one by Tintoretto shows Our Lord appearing to Francis and St Justina (Sta Maria del Giglio, Venice), while Murillo painted him at prayer (Prado, Madrid).

SS Apphian and Theodosia, *Martyrs* (306)

These martyrs are known through the writings of the historian Eusebius (*c.* 260-340). In his work *The Martyrs of Palestine* he gives an account of the persecution under the emperor Diocletian, which lasted from 303 to 310; he witnessed many of the executions and knew several of the martyrs personally, including the two whose feast-day is celebrated today.

Apphian (or Apian, or Anphian) was born in Lycia and, after becoming a Christian, went to study with Eusebius in Caesarea in Palestine when he was eighteen. A year or so later a general order was issued that everyone should attend the public sacrifices. Apphian did so but tried to prevent the magistrate from performing the sacrifice, proclaiming that it was an act of impiety to worship idols instead of the true God. He was arrested and tortured but re-fused to change his beliefs, saying, "I confess Christ, the one God, and the same God with the Father" as he was urged to sacrifice to the Roman gods. Eventually he was condemned to death and executed by being thrown into the sea. Eusebius reports that an earthquake immediately shook the area, and the martyr's body, though weighted with stones, was cast up on the shore.

Theodosia suffered a similar fate in 308, also on 2 April. She had gone to Caesarea from Tyre when she was about eighteen and had tried to comfort some prisoners who were awaiting their sentence. They were probably Chris-tians, and she seems to have asked them to remember her when they entered God's presence. She was arrested, tortured cruelly, and executed.

Eusebius' account can be found in *AA.SS.*, Apr., 1, pp. 59-61. See also *Bibl.SS.*, 1, 1181-2, under Anfiano, and 12, 286-8, under Teodosia.

St John Payne, *Martyr* (*c.* 1550-82)

John Payne (or Paine) was born at Peterborough in Huntingdonshire about the year 1550. We know nothing about his early life or where he was educated except that he was brought up a Protestant. He converted to Catholicism at some point and entered the new college at Douai to study for the priesthood in 1574. He was bursar at the college for a period before his ordination in 1576:

the short time between his entering Douai and his ordination may be evidence that he had already studied theology elsewhere.

He left for missionary work in England along with St Cuthbert Mayne (30 Nov.) and established himself in Essex at Ingatestone Hall, the home of the Petres, a strongly recusant family. This gave him a base for his work among the local Catholics. He was arrested in 1577 and imprisoned for a short time. On his release he returned briefly to Douai but was back at Ingatestone Hall by the middle of 1578. In 1581 he was betrayed and arrested while he was working in Warwickshire. After being taken to the Tower of London he was charged with treason against the queen, tortured on the rack, and condemned to be hanged, drawn, and quartered. The evidence against him was provided by a certain George Elliot, but John denied it completely, stating at his trial "that he always, in mind or word, honoured the queen's majesty above any woman in the world; that he would gladly always have spent his life for her pleasure in any lawful service; that he prayed for her as for his own soul; that he never invented or compassed any treason against her majesty, or any of the nobility of England" (Challoner). He was taken to Chelmsford in Essex and executed there on 2 April 1582. He had created a good impression in the area, and the local people who attended the execution insisted that his body should be allowed to hang until he was dead before the gruesome drawing and quartering be carried out. He died with the words "Jesus, Jesus, Jesus" on his lips.

He was canonized as one of the Forty Martyrs of England and Wales in 1970.

M.M.P., pp. 39-44; *O.D.S.*, pp. 375-6; B. Foley, *Blessed John Paine* (1961). See the general entries on the Martyrs of England and Wales under 4 May and 25 October.

Bd Diego de San Vitores, *Martyr* (1627-72)

Diego de San Vitores was born in Burgos, Spain, in 1627. His family belonged to the Spanish nobility, and his father worked in the king's service. Diego was educated by the Jesuits and joined them as a novice while still only fourteen years old. After two years in the novitiate he was still too young to make his vows and so had to spend some time in other studies before he could do so. He was eventually ordained priest in 1651, when still only twenty-four. He had always wanted to work on the foreign missions, if possible in China and Japan, but instead had to teach, first humanities and then theology.

Eventually he was sent to the Philippines in 1660 to work as a missionary. He travelled by way of Mexico and spent two years there, making such an impression on his fellow-Jesuits that they began to compare him with that other great missionary, St Francis Xavier (3 Dec.). When he left for the Philippines the ship called at the Marianas Islands (south of Japan, and including Guam and Saipan), and Diego was struck by the fact that the islanders had never been evangelized. He wrote to his superiors in Rome and Spain asking to be allowed to work on the island of Guam and saying how much it pained him to see the islanders neglected in that way. In the meantime he settled in the Philippines and worked there, first as a missionary in Taytay and then in the Jesuit college in Manila as prefect of studies.

He needed royal permission to work in the Marianas, and when this was granted he went back to Mexico in 1668 to collect funds and supplies for his work on Guam. He finally arrived in the new mission field with a group of fellow-Jesuits later in the same year. At first the work of evangelization went well, and large numbers of the people received baptism. Then opposition from the local leaders grew, as they feared a loss of their influence, and the new Christians came under pressure to give up their faith. Part of Diego's work was to visit the other islands to encourage his fellow-missionaries, and while he was visiting Tumon he went to baptize the newborn baby of a couple where the husband had apostatized. The man objected and began to abuse Diego; when the missionary tried to reason with him he was killed with a spear. The date was 2 April 1672. Diego's life had been ruled by a phrase from the Gospels, "He sent me to preach the good news to the poor," and by St Ignatius' (31 July) injunction to his followers, "Do not be deaf to God's call, but keen and ready to do his holy will." He was beatified in 1985.

The principal source is Juan M. H. Ledesma, S.J., *The Cause of Beatification of Ven. Diego Luis de San Vitores, Apostle of the Marianas* (1981). See also P. Molinari, "Tre Nuovi beati gesuiti" in *Civiltà Cattolica* 136 (1985), 3, pp. 373-87; J. L. Saborido Cursach, *Hasta los confines de la Tierra; Diego Luis de S.V.* (1985); *Bibl.SS.*, Suppl. 1, 1229-31; *N.S.B.* 2, pp. 79-80.

Bd Leopold of Gaiche (1733-1815)

Giovanni Croci was born at Gaiche in the Italian diocese of Perugia in 1733. When he was eighteen he received the Franciscan habit, taking the name of Leopold in religion. He was ordained priest in 1757 and was appointed to teach philosophy and theology. When he was asked to preach the Lenten sermons in local churches he gave the first evidence of his remarkably effective abilities as a preacher, and it is not surprising that he was later chosen to be the principal missioner throughout the Papal States. He carried out this office for ten years, holding annual missions in several dioceses, and even after becoming minister provincial of the Order he continued with this pastoral work. He followed the emotional methods of St Leonard of Port-Maurice (26 Nov.), with intense sermons followed by *svegliarini* designed to awaken the consciences of his hearers. These included displaying penitential instruments to the congregation and having a group of men scourge themselves across the shoulders while the psalm *Miserere* was recited. All his missions included two processions, one penitential, in which people walked barefoot with crowns of thorns on their heads, the other in honour of Our Lady, in which women and children took part dressed in white and wearing crowns of flowers and thorns. As minister provincial he founded a house where preachers and missionaries could go for their annual retreat and for spiritual renewal. He held a number of posts in the Order and was always inflexible with regard to strict observance of the Rule, regarding any easing of it as an abuse.

When French troops invaded Rome in 1808 convents and monasteries were suppressed, and Leopold, then aged over seventy-five, had to flee and take refuge in a hut near Spoleto. Even there he continued his pastoral work, acting as parish priest when the local priest was driven out. He was imprisoned for a time for refusing to take an oath of loyalty to the new government but was soon released and returned to his favourite work, giving retreats and missions wherever he could. He was regarded as having powers of prophecy, and strange phenomena were said to attend his preaching: his head, for example, often seemed to be crowned with thorns. When the French finally left Italy he set about re-establishing the houses of his Order but died on 2 April 1815 after a long life devoted to preaching and other pastoral work. His diary shows that over a period of forty-seven years he preached 330 formal missions, each one usually lasting fifteen days and involving him in giving three or four sermons a day. Again following the example of St Leonard, he set up or restored the Stations of the Cross in over a hundred churches. The numerous miracles reported to have taken place at his grave caused the process of canonization to be introduced soon after his death. He was beatified in 1893.

L. Canonici, *Un faro sul monte, il Beato L. de Gaiche* (1957); *Bibl.SS.*, 7, 1337-40.

3

ST RICHARD OF CHICHESTER, *Bishop* (*c.* 1197-1253)

Richard was born at Wyche, the present-day Droitwich, in Worcestershire, about the year 1197. His parents, Richard and Alice, were well-to-do landowners but died when Richard was young, and the family seems to have fallen into poverty. His elder brother offered to let him have the land, and there may have been an offer of a wealthy lady as a bride as well. Richard refused both. Some accounts (followed by the previous edition of this work) tell how Richard took on the administration of the estate, which had been neglected, and even laboured as a ploughman to help his brother, but there is no trustworthy evidence to support this. He went to study at Oxford and then at Paris. There is a later account which tells of him also studying at Bologna and again refusing an offer of marriage, but this seems to be unlikely. He returned to Oxford, making a reputation for himself as a scholar and a teacher, and became chancellor of the university. The role of the chancellor was in transition, and Richard helped to increase its importance by his able administration and energy. This brought him to the notice of one of his former tutors, St Edmund of Abingdon (16 Nov.), who had become archbishop of Canterbury and who now appointed Richard to be his diocesan chancellor.

This move brought Richard for the first time into the world of politics. Edmund, a keen reformer and upholder of the rights of the Church, was involved in a number of quarrels with King Henry III and eventually went into voluntary exile in France. Richard, who had won praise for his refusal to accept bribes and favours from suitors to the archbishop's court, accompanied him to Pontigny, where the archbishop died in 1240. The ex-chancellor moved on to Orleans and after two years of study with the Dominicans was ordained priest in 1243. He returned to England and worked as a parish priest before being called back to Canterbury by the new archbishop and asked to take up his post again. When the king tried to get his own candidate elected to the see of Chichester, the archbishop refused to accept him and had Richard elected in his place. The enraged king confiscated all the temporalities of the diocese and refused to recognize Richard. Both sides appealed to the pope, and Innocent IV decided in Richard's favour, consecrating him bishop at Lyons in 1245. The king, however, refused to accept the ruling, and decreed that no one should even give the new bishop shelter—as his biographer put it, Richard "was like a stranger in a foreign land." It was at this time that he wrote to the canons of Chichester, who supported him: "Do you not understand what is written in the Acts of the Apostles, how they rejoiced that they were counted worthy to suffer shame for Christ's name? I tell you that God of his grace will turn our tribulation to joy." In the meantime Richard lived in the house of one of his priests and carried out visitations of the diocese as best he could on foot. Eventually, after about two years, the king gave in, and Richard was able to take up his duties fully.

His seven-and-a-half years as bishop were judged by his contemporaries to be a prime example of the work of a reforming bishop. His biographer said of him: "Towards his clergy he desired to be as a master to his disciples, to his household as a father to his children, to the people as a kindly nurse to her infants." Personally he led a blameless life of great austerity marked by almsgiving and other works of mercy. At the same time he was an extremely capable administrator and was personally involved in establishing suitable vicarages for his clergy and also in increasing the revenues of the diocese. He published a set of constitutions for his clergy which drew on the decrees of synods and councils and were a model of their kind. Among other things Richard was concerned that his priests should understand and instruct their people about the meaning of the sacraments, that they should understand the words of the Mass and say them clearly and without rushing, that his arch-deacons should carry out their duties properly and not for personal gain, that the rule of celibacy should be observed, and so on. "Throughout these constitutions is heard the voice of a bishop resolved . . . to instruct the clergy in the fundamental faith and duty of their office, and determined to pass that instruction on to the laity" (Jacob).

Toward the end of his life Richard was involved in preaching a crusade in Sussex and Kent. He described it in spiritual terms, as offering the opportunity for showing devotion to God and allowing pilgrims to visit the Holy Places again. He had some success in raising money and recruits, but he fell ill on reaching Dover and died on 3 April 1253. He was canonized shortly afterwards, in 1262, and his remains moved to a shrine in Chichester Cathedral, which became a favourite place of pilgrimage, although to some extent it was overshadowed by that of St Thomas (29 Dec.) at Canterbury, and Richard did not become a widely popular saint—only one medieval English church was dedicated to him. For some reason he became the patron saint of the coach-man's union in Milan—a reference, perhaps, to his days spent driving carts on his brother's farm.

He was the author of the following prayer: "Thanks be to thee my Lord Jesus Christ for all the benefits thou hast given me, for all the pains and insults thou hast borne for me. O most merciful redeemer, friend, and brother, may I know thee more clearly, love thee more dearly, and follow thee more nearly."

A Life was written by Ralph Bocking, O.P., about 1270, based on plentiful evidence and perhaps on Richard's own reminiscences; see *AA.SS.*, Apr., 1, pp. 276–318. See also *D.N.B.*, 48, pp. 202–4; C. M. Duncan-Jones, *St Richard of Chichester* (1953); E. F. Jacob,

"St Richard of Chichester" in *J.E.H.* 7 (1956), pp. 174-88; D. Jones, "The Medieval Lives of Richard of Chichester," in *Anal.Boll.* 105 (1987), pp. 105-29; *O.D.S.*, pp. 416-7.

Richard is depicted in full episcopal dress, usually with a chalice at his feet—there is a legend that while he was saying Mass one day the chalice fell from the altar but did not spill. There are frescoes of him in Norwich Cathedral and at Black Bourton, Oxfordshire.

St Sixtus I, *Pope* (*c*. 125)

Sixtus, or, more correctly, Xystus, was pope for a period of ten years, from about 116 to 125. We have no certain information about his life or how he died, and the account given in the *Liber Pontificalis* of the disciplinary and liturgical regulations he introduced to the Church in Rome can hardly be true, as they relate to a much more settled time. Traditionally he has been described as of Roman birth, the son of a man named Pastor; the correct form of his name would indicate he was of Greek origin, though he could still have been born in Rome. He died during the reign of the emperor Hadrian (117-38), perhaps as a martyr although it is strange that he is not mentioned by St Irenaeus (28 June) as one in his list of the early popes. The former edition of this work suggests that the Sixtus commemorated formerly in the Canon of the Mass was St Sixtus II (6 Aug.), whose martyrdom was much more widely celebrated, and not today's saint.

D.T.C., 14, 2193-4; *Bibl.SS.*, 11, 1254-6; *O.D.P.*, pp. 9, 22.

St Nicetas, *Abbot* (*c*. 760-824)

Nicetas was born in Caesarea in Bithynia (modern Turkey) about the year 760. His mother died while he was an infant, and his father entered a monastery, leaving Nicetas in the care of a grandmother until he was old enough to go to the monastery himself for his education. He became a monk in the monastery of Medikion on Mount Olympus, was ordained priest in 790, and became head of the monastery in 813. He was responsible for its enlargement to a community of about one hundred monks.

Along with other important monks he was summoned to Constantinople by the emperor, Leo the Armenian (813-20), who had deposed the patriarch, St Nicephorus (13 Mar.), when the latter had refused to support the emperor's Iconoclasm (an attack on the cult of holy statues and pictures as idolatrous). Nicetas and the others also refused to support the emperor and his puppet patriarch, and they were exiled. Nicetas was sent to a fortress where he was kept prisoner in an open cell and had to sleep on the ground exposed to snow and rain. He was taken back to Constantinople and there made peace with the emperor, receiving Holy Communion from the hands of the false patriarch. His friends urged him to withdraw his support for the emperor, and he soon repented of his weakness in giving in, returned to Constantinople, and denounced the emperor's policies in public. He was exiled for a second time and kept confined in a dungeon without proper food and water. When the emperor was assassinated in 820, his successor released all the prisoners of the persecution, and Nicetas lived out the rest of his life in a hermitage close to the imperial city. He refused all requests to return to his monastery because of the guilt he felt at having compromised his views and given scandal to his followers. When he died in 824 his remains were carried in triumph to Medikion.

A Life of Nicetas was written shortly after his death by one of his disciples; see *AA.SS.*, Apr., 1, pp. 253–66. See also *Anal.Boll.* 31, pp. 149–55, and 32, pp. 44–5; *Bibl.SS.*, 9, 890–2.

Bd Gandulf (1260)

Gandulf was born at Binasco near Milan. He joined the Franciscans while St Francis (4 Oct.) was still alive and from then on led a life of remarkable austerity. He went to preach in Sicily (he may have already gone to Sicily before becoming a friar) and won so much praise for his eloquence that he retired with a companion, Brother Pascal, to the more remote parts of the island to lead a life of solitude. From time to time he would leave his hermitage to preach among the local people, working miracles and converting many to a better way of life. He is said to have had a special relationship with animals and birds, similar to that of St Francis, on one occasion getting them to keep silent while he was preaching. Legend says the birds marked his death in 1260 by singing in the church where his body was laid out. There was a feast in his honour from 1320, and the process for his canonization was opened in 1632. His cult, which was especially strong in Sicily, was approved in 1881.

Bibl.SS., 6, 33; A. Russo-Alsi, *Vita di S. Gandolfo da Binasco* (1932).

Bd Aloysius Scrosoppi, *Founder* (1804-84)

Luigi Scrosoppi was born on 4 August 1804 at Udine in Italy. He joined the Congregation of the Oratory in the town, where two of his brothers were already members, and was ordained priest at the age of twenty-three; he took the name Aloysius in religion. About ten years before this two priests had set up a house in rented accommodation to act as a refuge for abandoned orphan girls. As they were already elderly when they started the work, the priests wondered what would happen to it when they had to retire. Aloysius' half-bother, Fr Charles Filaferro, took it over in 1822 and was joined by Aloysius in 1826. Together they enlarged the establishment so that it could accommodate ninety-five boarders and cater for a further 230 non-residents. In 1839 they received official recognition from the town authorities for their work, but financial worries continued, and the two priests faced considerable opposition because of the nature of the work itself.

They were helped by a group of women, and in 1837 seven of these formed a new religious Institute under Aloysius' guidance. They were to become the Sisters of Providence, led by a woman of considerable ability and organizational skill, Sister Lucia de Giorgio, and assisted by a local countess, Franca di Colloredo. The first Sisters received the religious habit in 1845, and the new Congregation received provisional papal approval in 1862 and definitive approval in 1891; its Constitution was drawn up by Aloysius.

In 1854 Aloysius was elected provincial of the Oratorians, a post he held until the suppression of the Congregation in 1866. Among his other concerns and projects were a "providence house" he set up for older children who could not find employment, an apostolate for those who were deaf and dumb, and a free school. He inherited a considerable amount of money and, as well as using it to help the poor, supported a popular newspaper with it and also used it to keep a convent of Poor Clares from financial ruin. He was particularly interested in providing assistance for poor priests, especially those who were elderly or sick, and was largely responsible for setting up a foundation to give practical help. It could be said of him that there was little in the way of charitable and social work undertaken in Udine in those years in which he was not involved, and at the same time he was very active as a preacher and confessor.

His life was built around three great loves: a love of Jesus, a love of the Church, and a love of the poor and abandoned. He wrote that he wanted to be faithful to Jesus and so "pefectly attached to him on the way to heaven as to become a replica of him." Despite his busy apostolate, he lived a life of intense prayer, devoting time every day to meditation, visiting the Blessed Sacrament, making the Stations of the Cross and saying the rosary, and spending part of the night in prayer. He was a living example of the balance that could be achieved between a life of contemplative prayer and an active apostolate. His love of the Church was shown by his complete submission to its laws and an acceptance of whatever authority laid down with regard to his numerous foundations. He was known above all else, however, for his love of the poor. "The poor and the sick," he wrote, "are our patrons and represent the person of Jesus Christ himself." He devoted his life to their service and left behind a number of institutions to continue his work, chief among which are the Sisters of Providence and their work in Italy, Brazil, and Paraguay. After a final illness lasting three months, which he bore with great patience, he died on 3 April 1884. He was beatified on 4 October 1981.

Notitiae, 17 (1981), pp. 641-2; *A.A.S.* 73, pt. 1 (1981), pp. 281-3, for miracles worked through his intercession, and 73, pt. 2 (1981), pp. 663-4, for the beatification. See also P. Colombara, *Un apostolo della carità, Padre Luigi Scrosoppi* (1929); *N.S.B.* 1, pp. 176-7; *Bibl.SS.*, 11, 753-4.

4

ST ISIDORE, *Bishop and Doctor* (*c.* 565-636)

Little is known for certain of Isidore's early life. His father, Severian, probably came from Cartagena in Spain and was of Romano-Spanish and senatorial extraction. Isidore was probably born in Seville, where the family had moved during an invasion of Cartagena. Other members of the family were St Leander (13 Mar.), who became bishop of Seville; St Fulgentius (14 Jan.), who became bishop of Ecija; and St Florentina, abbess of a number of convents. Leander seems to have been responsible for Isidore's education, which may have taken place in one of the monastic or episcopal schools that flourished in Spain at the time. He inherited a rich literary tradition, and whatever form his education took it was highly successful, since he became the most learned person of his generation and a leading authority on a whole range of subjects throughout the Middle Ages: there are more manuscript copies of his works than of any other medieval writer. In his studies and writing he was motivated by two aims, to stop the spread of barbarism in Spain and to combat the Arian heresy that was common among the Visigoths. He welcomed the political and religious unity they brought and regarded them as the successors of the Romans and the saviours of Spain; there was a need for a bringing together of the various strands of thought and culture to serve the new nation, and he tried to provide such a compendium (Fontaine).

He succeeded his brother as bishop of Seville about the year 600. We do not have details of his pastoral work as bishop, but we know from his writings that he believed a bishop should start by overcoming his own desires and continue with integrity and humility, giving good example, preaching the Faith effectively, and behaving as a good shepherd with concern for his flock just as a doctor is concerned with the health of his patients. Pope John XXIII was inspired by Isidore's portrayal of the ideal bishop: "He who is set in authority for the education and instruction of the people for their good must be holy in all things and reprehensible in nothing. . . . Every Bishop should be distinguished as much by his humility as by his authority. . . . He will also preserve that charity which excels all other gifts, and without which all virtue is nothing" (from *De officiis ecclesiasticis*). As bishop he presided over two councils, a provincial one in Seville in 619 and a national one in Toledo (the Fourth Council of Toledo) in 633. Both of these passed important decrees and show Isidore's ability as a thinker and administrator. The creed drawn up in Toledo in 633 was based on his theology of the Trinity and the Incarnation and was accepted as a correct statement of the Faith by succeeding councils. "His influence did much to secure the general acceptance of the *Filioque* clause in the West" (*O.D.C.C.*). The Council of Toledo also fixed a uniform liturgy to be observed throughout Spain—the famous Mozarabic Rite, largely the work of Isidore himself—and laid down that every diocese should have a cathedral school.

While Isidore's work as a bishop was important, it was as a writer that he was revered for almost a thousand years. "He founded a line of clerical scholars in Spain and had a profound impact upon the culture and educational practice of Western medieval Europe. . . . His works became a storehouse of knowledge freely utilized by innumerable medieval authors" (*O.D.C.C.*). His historical writings are still valuable sources for our knowledge of Spain at the time of the barbarian invasions, while his most famous work, the *Etymologiae*, has been described as an encyclopedia of the knowledge of his time, containing information on subjects such as grammar, rhetoric, mathematics, medicine, and history, as well as on the books and offices of the Church, and other theological matters (*ibid.*). His writings are not just of antiquarian interest, however; they show the mind of a man deeply interested in spiritual matters, keen to instruct his clergy and people in the spiritual life. He stressed to them the importance of studying the scriptures: "If anyone wants to be always with God, he ought to pray often and to read often as well. For when we pray, it is we who talk to God, whereas when we read, it is God who speaks to us. . . . The more conscientious one is in becoming familiar with the sacred writings, the richer an understanding one will draw from them, as with the earth—the more it is cultivated, the more abundant is its harvest" (from *The Book of Sentences*). It has been usual to censure Isidore's writings for being mainly derivative and lacking in originality, and it is true that he borrows frequently from earlier writers. The most recent critical studies of his works, however, have tended to re-evaluate them and to stress the original elements he brought to their composition.

There is a detailed and reliable account of Isidore's death in 636, written by one of his disciples who was a deacon in Seville. First of all, Isidore prepared himself for death by giving away all his possessions in alms and publicly asking forgiveness. Then he was carried to the church, dressed in sackcloth by one of his suffragan bishops while another put ashes on his head, and confessed his faults to the assembled people. He received Holy Communion and was taken back to his room, where he died a few days later on 4 April. Although his name appears in a few listings of saints from the ninth century onward, there is no evidence of any widespread veneration of him as a saint until his remains were translated to León in 1063 (where they still are), when panegyrics of him appeared with accounts of the miracles worked through his intercession. The new shrine became very popular as a place of pilgrimage, as it was on the route to Compostela. The comparative lack of reference to his holiness in the centuries after his death may be partly explained by the lowly place given to confessors as opposed to martyrs in the Mozarabic liturgy. He was not included in the Roman Martyrology until the late sixteenth century, and it appears his cult was officially approved in 1598. He was declared a Doctor of the Church by Innocent XIII in 1722, a title already awarded him locally by a Council of Toledo shortly after his death.

The works of Isidore are in *P.L.*, 81-4. For editions of particular works, see bibliography in *O.D.C.C.* (1997), pp. 851-2; recent English translations include C. M. Lawson, *De Officiis Ecclesiasticis* (1989); K. B. Wolf, *Conquerors and Chronicles of Early Medieval Spain* (1990), for the *Historia Gothorum*. See also M. C. Diaz y Diaz (ed.), *Isidoriana* (1961); *D.T.C.*, 8, 98-111; *Bibl.SS.*, 7, 973-82; *O.D.S.*, pp. 245-6. For the most recent research see P. Cazier, *Isidore de Séville et la naissance de l'Espagne Catholique* (1994); J. Fontaine, *Culture et spiritualité en Espagne de IVe au VIIe siècle* (1986), and *Tradition et actualité chez Isidore de Séville* (1988); see also his article in *Dict.Sp.*, 7, pt. 2 (1971). The quotation from *The Sentences* is taken from *The Office of Readings*, 2 (1974), pp.93-4; that from *De officiis* is taken from *The Journal of a Soul* (1965), p. 261.

Most of the sculptures and paintings of Isidore are in León and Seville in Spain. He is usually depicted either as a bishop, holding a book or a pen, or as a holy warrior, and even, in one instance, as a bishop in full episcopal attire on a galloping horse, with a cross in one hand and a sword in the other (in the basilica in León). There is a painting of him dressed as a bishop by Murillo in the cathedral in Seville, and a large statue by Alcoverro in the National Library in Madrid, while the Prado has a painting by Goya of pilgrims visiting the church of St Isidore in Seville.

St Plato, *Abbot* (*c.* 734-814)

Plato was brought up in Constantinople. When he was thirteen his parents died, and he was looked after by an uncle who trained him to enter the imperial service as a treasurer. In his early twenties, however, Plato gave up what seemed to be a promising career to become a monk in the monastery of Symboleon on Mount Olympus in Bithynia (modern Turkey). Here he led an exemplary life and in 770 was chosen as abbot although he was still only thirty-six. It was a time of persecution for those who opposed the imperial policy of Iconoclasm (opposition to the cult of holy pictures and statues), but the remoteness of Symboleon seems to have saved the monastery from its worst effects.

In 775 Plato visited Constantinople and was received with great honour because of his reputation for holiness. He was offered a bishopric but refused and would not even be ordained priest. He did, however, leave Symboleon and become abbot of the Sakkudion, a monastery which had been founded near the city by his nephews and nieces. He remained there for twelve years before resigning in favour of his nephew St Theodore Studites (11 Nov.). Both uncle and nephew became involved in a quarrel with the emperor when he divorced his wife and married another. Plato and Theodore led the monastic opposition party, and as a result Plato was imprisoned and then exiled. On his return he lived mainly as a hermit in the monastery of Studios but continued to oppose the emperor's wrongdoings. He was exiled again and spent four years being moved from place to place despite his age and bad health. In 811 he was finally released by a new emperor and returned to Constantinople, where he was treated with great respect. For the last four years of life he was bed-ridden and lived in almost solitary retirement. He died on 4 April 814.

For biographical details we are reliant on the funeral sermon of St Theodore; see *AA.SS.*, Apr., 1, pp. 46-54. See also *Bibl.SS.*, 10, 961-4. On Iconoclasm see *O.D.C.C.* (1997), pp. 815-6.

St Peter of Poitiers, *Bishop* (1115)

In 1087 Peter was elected bishop of Poitiers. He had already gained a reputation for holiness and firmness as archdeacon of the diocese, traits which were to be the hallmarks of his years as a bishop. He had considerable pastoral ability but was noted chiefly for his determination to oppose the immoral conduct of those in high places. He publicly denounced the French king, Philip I, for having repudiated his wife in favour of another woman. Along with St Ivo of Chartres (23 May) and Bd Robert of Arbrissel (25 Feb.), Peter played a leading part in convening the Council of Poitiers in 1110, called to pass judgment on the king's behaviour. William, count of Poitou, in whose territory Poitiers was, tried to disrupt the council by using his soldiers to intimidate the assembled bishops, but the king was condemned and excommunicated. When William, who had himself taken a second wife illegally, on another occasion publicly insulted the bishop of Angoulême, Peter excommunicated him and refused to withdraw the sentence even when William threatened to use force. William forced Peter to leave his diocese and go into exile at Chauvigny.

Peter encouraged Bd Robert of Arbrissel to found a new monastery in his diocese at Fontevrault and even went to Rome in 1106 to obtain papal approval for it. He was a generous benefactor of the new house and is regarded as a founder of what became one of the most famous monasteries in France.

Peter died at Chauvigny in 1115. His relics were divided between Fontrevault and the church of St Cyprian in Poitiers. His cult does not seem to have ever been officially approved, but his reputation for sanctity was widespread during his life. William of Malmesbury, writing shortly after Peter's death, described him as a "man of eminent holiness" and reproduced some highly praiseworthy verses written in his honour; these praise his austerity, kindness to the poor, and upholding of the law and include the lines:

> ". . . for God his soul possessed
> unmixed: his friendless neighbour had the rest."

There is no early Life of Peter, but information can be found in accounts of Robert of Arbrissel. For William of Malmesbury see J. Stephenson (trans. and ed.), *A History of the Norman Kings* (rp. 1989), section 438, pp. 162-3. See also *Bibl.SS.*, 10, 777-8.

St Benedict the Moor (*c.* 1526-1589)

Benedict was born in the village of San Fratello, near Messina in Sicily, about the year 1526. His parents were African slaves belonging to a landowner named Manasseri and so took that as their surname. The father, Christopher, was promoted to foreman, and Benedict, as his eldest son, was given his freedom. As he grew up he impressed his neighbours by his holiness and was given the nickname *il moro santo* ("the holy Moor," not "the holy black" as in the former edition of this work). He was frequently taunted with his colour and the fact that his parents had been slaves. His patience in the face of these insults convinced a young man named Lanza, the leader of a group of Franciscan hermits, that Benedict had the makings of a religious, and he invited him to join them. When Lanza died Benedict was chosen as superior. Not long afterwards, in 1562, the hermits were ordered by the pope to disband and join an established Order. Benedict chose the Friars Minor of the Observance and joined their house near Palermo as a lay brother. After spending three years in another house he returned and worked there as cook, enjoying the seclusion that the post allowed him but unable to hide his holiness from his brethren.

In 1578 he was chosen as guardian of the house, a surprising post for someone who was illiterate and only a lay brother. He turned out to be an ideal superior, however, with sound judgment and great tact. His reputation for holiness and as a miracle-worker spread throughout Sicily, and he could no longer avoid people's attention and requests for favours. When his period of office as guardian was over, he was made vicar of the house and its novice-master. He seemed to have an infused knowledge of the scriptures and difficult points of theology so that he was able to instruct the novices and other members of the community. Eventually he was allowed to retire from these posts and return to being cook. He was too well known by now to be able to live in the seclusion he wished for, and he was visited every day by the poor asking for alms, the sick seeking to be cured, and the wealthy (including the viceroy of Sicily) wanting advice and spiritual direction. His own life was one of austerity, fasting, and penance. He died in 1589 after a short illness. His cult spread throughout Italy, Spain, and South America, where he was regarded as a special protector of the black population. He was canonized in 1807 and is one of the patron saints of the city of Palermo.

F. G. da Capistrano, *Vita di S. B. da San Fratello* (1908); *Bibl.SS.*, 2, 1103-4.

Bd Joseph Benedict Dusmet, *Bishop and Cardinal* (1818-94)

Giuseppe Benedetto was born in Palermo in Sicily in 1818, the son of a marquis, Luigi Dusmet des Mours, who was of Belgian origin, and his wife, Maria-Gracia Dragonetti-Gorgone. He made his religious profession in 1840 in the local Benedictine monastery of San Martino della Scala, where he had been educated, and was ordained priest in 1842. He taught philosophy and theology in the monastery for five years before being transferred to the monastery of St Flavia at Caltanissetta, apparently because his understanding of the monastic life was considered by his superiors to be too rigorist. In 1850 he was nominated prior of San Severino in Naples, and two years later he was chosen by the general chapter to be prior and administrator back at Caltanissetta. He restored the monastery and gained a reputation locally as a helper of the poor, especially during an outbreak of cholera in 1854. Finally, in 1858, he became abbot of San Niccolò at Catania in Sicily, where he was successful in implementing his ideas for monastic reform; these concentrated on regular observance of the Rule and the development of the spiritual life of the monks. In 1866, however, he had to leave the monastery, as the religious Orders had been suppressed throughout the recently united Italian States. A year later he was appointed archbishop of Catania and consecrated in Rome. Because he was known to be a supporter of the royal family of the former kingdom of Naples and Sicily, who had lost their power in the new Italy, he was not recognized as archbishop by the Italian government and for several years was not allowed to touch any of the income or funds of the diocese. He worked successfully to have a number of churches that had been confiscated by the civil authorities returned to their proper use.

Joseph played a leading part in the Vatican Council in 1870. He spoke warmly in favour of the definition of papal infallibility, arguing that it was necessary and opportune, given the liberal scepticism of the day. He also presented a petition in favour of the definition of the Assumption of Our Lady. In his diocese he arranged for exposition of the Blessed Sacrament in all churches every Sunday in reparation for the the amount of blasphemy in the modern world, and he dedicated the diocese to the Sacred Heart, to which he had a strong personal devotion. He restored over sixty churches throughout the diocese and opened seventeen new ones. He reformed the clergy, restored the seminary, set up a number of pious institutes, and built schools. He was involved in developing work to help the poor, especially in the aftermath of a number of natural disasters, such as the eruptions of Mount Etna and an epidemic of cholera, that struck Sicily in his last years as bishop. In 1889 he was created a cardinal by Pope Leo XIII.

Despite the work involved in restoring and reforming his diocese, the bishop remained involved in Benedictine affairs. Indeed, it has been said that he remained at heart a Benedictine monk, making his episcopal palace like a monastery and trying to adhere to a monastic life style as much as possible. In 1886 he presided over the general chapter of the Cassinese Benedictines, which had been convened by the pope, and was given the task of introducing a degree of centralization into the Congregation. A year later he was put in charge of founding the Benedictine College of St Anselm in Rome and made its first director.

In his diocese he was respected for his pastoral concern, his personal charity, and his willingness to defend the rights of religion, and was spoken of as a Sicilian St Charles Borromeo (4 Nov.). He followed an austere way of life and had so few possessions and so little money when he died that not even a spare sheet could be found to use as a shroud: he had given everything to the poor. He died on 4 April 1894. At his beatification in 1988 the pope presented him as an example of genuine conformity to the spirit of the gospel and positive acceptance of the demands of his vocation as monk and bishop.

The fullest and most balanced Life is T. Leccisotti, *Il Cardinale Dusmet* (1962). See also G. Amadio, *A Sicilian Borromeo* (1938); R. Aubert in *D.H.G.E.*, 14 (1960), 1208-9; *N.S.B.* 2, pp. 180-1.

Bd Gaetano Catanoso, *Founder* (1879-1963)

He was born at Chorio di San Lorenzo in the Reggio Calabria region of Italy on 17 February 1879, studied for the priesthood at the diocesan seminary, and was ordained in 1902. Two years later he was appointed parish priest of Pentedattilo, in the east of the region, where he remained till 1921. He was then appointed to Reggio Calabria itself, where he served as parish priest at the church of the Purification till 1940. He was made a cathedral canon in 1930 and penitentiary in 1940.

His guiding spiritual impetus was to spread devotion to the Holy Face of Jesus and to make reparation for offences done to Jesus under this title. To this end he had established the Pious Union of the Holy Face at Pentedattilo in 1919, and he transferred its seat to Reggio Calabria in 1950. This became a formal foundation in 1934, as the Institute of Veronican Sisters of the Holy Face, whose work was to be the establishment of refuges and catechetical centres in the most remote rural areas of the region. He pursued this aim through many difficulties with dogged determination to the end of his life. It was given practical expression in the publication of a small but effective newsletter, called "The Holy Face," and finally in the construction of a sanctuary in honour of the Holy Face next to the motherhouse of the Veronican Sisters on the outskirts of Reggio Calabria.

The decisive influence in his life was Don Luigi Orione (Bd Aloysius Orione; 12 Mar.) and his "Little Work of Divine Providence," designed to bring help to the neediest whoever and wherever they were: slum-dwellers, orphans, earthquake victims. . . . The "Little Work" provided the inspiration for the Veronican Sisters and their mission to the most abandoned areas of the country and of society. Before his death Gaetano had also sketched out the idea for a Congregation of priests, to be known as "Cyreneans" after Simon of Cyrene, who would simply be available for posting to the most remote areas of a diocese at the direction of the bishop.

He died at Reggio Calabria on 4 April 1963, and his reputation for holiness quickly gathered pace. The beatification process was begun in 1981, and he was beatified by Pope John Paul II in 1998.

Bibl.SS., 3, 282-4, with photograph. A selection from his writings was issued in 1964 as *Parole del Venerato P. Gaetano Catanoso* (1964); the beatification process led to the re-issue of B. Guzzo, *P. Gaetano Catanoso* (1963, 1981). See also V. Lembo, *Spiritualità di P. Catanoso* (1981); special number of *Il Volto Santo* on the twentieth anniversary of his death (1983).

5

ST VINCENT FERRER (c. 1350-1419)

Vincent Ferrer was born in Valencia, probably in 1350, the son of William Ferrer, an Englishman who had settled in Spain, and his Spanish wife, Costanza Miguel. He showed early signs of academic brilliance and unusual devoutness and joined the Dominicans in 1367. Before he was twenty-one he taught philosophy at Lérida, the most famous university in Catalonia. He was ordained about 1374 and taught at Barcelona, before moving to Toledo, where he studied theology and Hebrew. In 1379 he became prior of the Dominican house in Valencia, the only office he was to hold throughout his life. He was a man of strong personality, with clear convictions and totally dedicated to the good of his Order and of the Church. As well as building a reputation as a theologian and writer, he was becoming known as an accomplished preacher with considerable success in moving sinners to repentance and also in converting Jews to Christianity, his most famous convert being a certain Rabbi Paul, who became bishop of Cartagena.

It was the time of the Great Schism (1378-1417), and Vincent supported the Avignon popes against their rivals in Rome. He became involved actively in the church politics of the day through his friendship with Cardinal Peter de Luna, whom he accompanied on a number of legatine missions in Spain and Portugal aimed at raising support for Clement VII at Avignon. When Peter de Luna, became the antipope Benedict XIII at Avignon in 1394 he appointed Vincent as his adviser and confessor, and at first Vincent was happy in both roles. He came to believe, however, that it was Benedict who was hindering moves for unity between the two parties. He tried to convince him to negotiate with Urban VI in Rome but was unsuccessful and left Avignon in 1399 to take up work as a preacher and roving missioner, inspired by a vision of Our Lord flanked by St Francis (4 Oct.) and St Dominic (8 Aug.) and the command to evangelize the whole world.

From 1399 to 1412 he worked in various parts of France, Spain, and Italy with considerable success; one of his early biographers says he also worked in England and Scotland, but there is no evidence to support this. His sermons stressed the need for repentance and the fear of hell, and some of his hearers were moved to excessive forms of penance. His brother was prior of the Grande Chartreuse and received a number of well-known postulants as a result of Vincent's preaching. Large crowds flocked to hear him, and he was credited with working a very large number of miracles. His own life was one of great austerity and penance to atone for what he regarded as his own evil life. "I am a plague-spot in soul and body," he wrote in a treatise on the spiritual life, "everything in me reeks of corruption because of the abomination of my sins and injustice."

Toward the end of his life Vincent was once again involved in trying to heal the Great Schism. After 1409 there were three rival popes, and when a council was called at Constance in 1414 to deal with the problem, Vincent tried once more to persuade Benedict to resign. He preached a famous sermon before him and a great crowd of assembled bishops and nobles, beginning, "You dry bones, listen to the word of the Lord," and condemned their pointless pride, urging the necessity of unity in the Church. When this failed, he turned his attention to King Ferdinand of Aragon and persuaded him to stop supporting Benedict. This finally convinced Benedict he would have to resign; he did so, and the council was eventually able to restore unity.

Vincent spent the last three years of his life preaching in Normandy and Brittany and died at Vannes in Brittany in 1419. He was immediately venerated as a saint and his cult spread very quickly, with reports of miracles worked in many parts of Europe through his intercession. He was canonized in 1455.

Vincent's surviving writings include two treatises on philosophy, a book on the sacrifice of the Mass, and a treatise on the schism in the Church. We have many of his sermons and some letters, a treatise on the spiritual life and on how to obtain consolation in times of temptations against the Faith. There is also a "new and very full" treatise against the "perfidy of the Jews," which shows him to have been, unfortunately, a man of his time in that respect.

An early biography written about thirty years after Vincent's death is unreliable and full of incredible detail; unfortunately it was used uncritically by later authors. For modern accounts and bibliographies see *Bibl.SS.*, 12, 1168-76; *O.D.S.*, p. 482; *D.T.C.*, 15, 3033-45. See also H. Gorce, *Saint Vincent Ferrer* (1935); H. Ghéon, *Saint Vincent Ferrer* (Eng. trans., 1940); J. M. de Garganta, O.P., and V. Forcada, O.P., *Biografía y escritos de San Vicente Ferrer* (1956).

In art Vincent is usually shown preaching in his Dominican habit, holding a book or sometimes a lily or a cross. There is a painting of him by Giovanni Bellini (1464) in the church of SS John and Paul in Venice, and one by Francesco del Cossa (1472/3) in the National Gallery, London, while the cathedral in Vannes has a series of seventeenth-century murals showing scenes from his life.

St Gerald of Sauve-Majeure, *Abbot (c. 1025-95)*

Gerald was born about the year 1025 at Corbie near Amiens in northern France, the site of a famous monastery which had been founded in the seventh century. Gerald studied there and then joined the community as a monk. For some years he suffered from a painful illness (now thought to have been a severe form of shingles) and was unable to concentrate at prayer or other monastic duties, so he took on the care of three poor people as a practical way of serving God. His abbot took him to Rome hoping that the pilgrimage would bring about a cure. He visited the tombs of the apostles and was ordained priest by the pope, St Leo IX (19 Apr.). His illness suddenly left him, a fact Gerald attributed to the intercession of St Adelard (30 Jan.), a former abbot of Corbie whose Life Gerald had written. In thanksgiving he increased his austerities. In 1073 he went on a pilgrimage to Jerusalem.

On his return to Corbie his first task was to restore the abbey church, which had been badly damaged by fire. He was then chosen by the monks of a monastery at Laon to be their abbot, but he was too strict for their liking and resigned after about five years. He set out with a small group of companions to look for a site for a new monastery and settled near Bordeaux, where they were given a piece of land by the local count. Here Gerald established the monastery of Sauve-Majeure (or Grande-Sauve) in 1079 and became its first abbot. The monks took on the task of evangelizing the neighbouring district, and Gerald became famous as a preacher and confessor. He is credited with having started the custom of offering Mass and saying the office for thirty days after the death of a member of the community and, during that time, of giving bread and wine to the poor. The custom spread to other monasteries and to some parish churches, but after a time the offerings were not given to the poor but to the local priest. He also set up an Order of knights and monks to help in the fight against the Moors in Spain. Gerald died in 1095 and was canonized in 1197. His relics are in the parish church of Sauve-Majeure.

There is an anonymous contemporary Life, and a later one by a monk named Christian, in *AA.SS.*, Apr., 1, pp. 407-31. See also *Bibl.SS.*, 6, 172-4; *Vies des Saints*, 4, pp. 106-9.

Bd Juliana of Mount Cornillon (1192-1258)

Juliana was born at Retinnes, near Liège, in 1192. Her parents died while she was young, and she was brought up in a nearby Augustinian double monastery at Mount Cornillon, where the nuns ran a hospital for lepers. She is sometimes known as Juliana of Mount Cornillon and sometimes as Juliana of Liège. She entered the community as a nun in 1206 and developed a strong devotion to the Blessed Sacrament. At the same time she began to have a recurring vision of a bright moon crossed by a single black band. She could not see the significance of this until she had a dream or vision of Our Lord explaining to her that the moon stood for the Church's Calendar of feasts which was marred by the absence of a day to celebrate the Blessed Sacrament. When she was elected prioress about 1225 she told some of her friends about the earlier visions and said that she felt she had a mission to have such a feast inaugurated. She was encouraged to confide in a local canon, John of Lausanne, and asked him to consult some theologians about the idea. One of these was James Pantaléon, archdeacon of Liège and the future Pope Urban IV. Although he and several others gave their support, she met with opposition from those who were suspicious of her as a visionary, including some within her own community who also objected to her strict interpretation of the Rule. She was accused of falsifying the accounts of the hospital and using the money to further her scheme for the feast-day and was forced to leave the monastery. The local bishop reinstated her and in 1246 established the new feast throughout the diocese. When he died later in the same year, however, she was forced to leave for good, and the feast was abolished despite the fact that it had proved popular with the people of the region, who had a strong devotion to the presence of Christ in the Eucharist. It continued to be celebrated by the Dominicans in their church in Liège. Juliana lived for a time in a monastery at Namur and then as a hermit at Fosses, where she died on 5 April 1258, having apparently failed to achieve her mission.

When James Pantaléon became pope in 1261 he was approached by some of Juliana's friends to establish a feast-day in honour of the Blessed Sacrament (see the entry below for Bd Eva of Liège). He agreed, partly because of his memory of Juliana and partly because he was impressed by reports of a miraculous event at Bolsena, where a priest was supposed to have seen blood issuing from the host at Mass. In 1264 he ordered the new feast to be included in the universal Calendar of the Church, the first time apparently that a feast had been imposed in that way, although it was not universally observed until the early years of the next century. This was the origin of the feast of Corpus Christi, celebrated today throughout the Church, generally on the Thursday after Trinity Sunday, but in North America on the following Sunday as the feast of the Body and Blood of Christ.

Juliana's cult was approved in 1869.

The principal source for Juliana's life is a contemporary French account that John of Lausanne translated into Latin; this is fairly reliable though too ready to see the supernatural in everything she did—see *AA.SS.*, April, 1, pp. 443-75. See also *Bibl.SS.*, 6, 1172-6, with very full bibliography; *O.D.C.C.*, p. 767; M. Walsh, *A Dictionary of Devotions* (1993), pp. 77-8.

St Eva of Liège (*c.* 1205-65)

Eva, or Heva, was born between 1205 and 1210. She seems to have become a recluse at the suggestion of Bd Juliana (5 Apr., above) and spent the rest of her life in a cell attached to St Martin's church in Liège—hence the other name by which she is sometimes known, Eva of St Martin. She and Juliana became close friends, and it was with her that Juliana took refuge when she was forced to leave her convent for the first time. The former edition of this work says that when Juliana died Eva continued her work for the establishment of a feast in honour of the Blessed Sacrament, and it was to her that Pope Urban IV sent a copy of his Bull establishing the feast along with a copy of the office composed for it by St Thomas Aquinas (28 Jan.). There is some evidence, however, that at first Eva and not Juliana was credited with being the main promoter of the idea for the feast-day, and certainly her importance in getting it established must not be overlooked. She died about the year 1265 and was buried in St Martin's church. A cult grew up rapidly around her tomb and was much more popular than that attaching to Juliana. A formal recognition of her relics took place in 1622 at the request of the infanta Isabella, governor of The Netherlands, and in 1746 they were ensrined above the high altar in the church. The cult was approved in 1902, but her name did not appear in the Roman Martyrology until the new draft, which assigns her to 14 March, but she is noticed here in view of her inseparability from Juliana.

The main source for Eva's life is the Life of Juliana; some writers have claimed this was based on an earlier Life of Juliana writen by Eva herself. See *Bibl.SS.*, 5, 353-6, with full bibliogrpahy of relevant articles; *Vies des Saints*, 4, p. 114.

Bd Christopher Robinson, *Martyr* (1597)

Christopher Robinson was born at Woodside, near Carlisle. He studied for the priesthood at the English College at Reims in northern France (where it had moved temporarily from Douai). He was ordained in 1592 after only three years in the college, such was the shortage of priests to work in England, and later that same year went to work as a priest in his native county of Cumberland. He was present at the trial and execution of a fellow-priest, Bd John Boste (24 July), and wrote a vivid account of the procedings. He himself was taken prisoner on 4 March 1597 while staying at Johnby Hall near Penrith in Cumberland, the home of Leonard Musgrave.

A Protestant minister, also named Robinson and later to be bishop of Carlisle, held a number of discussions with him on points of theology and was impressed by his learning and general good nature. Christopher, however, refused to accept the offer of pardon in return for giving up the Catholic faith and was hanged, drawn, and quartered at Carlisle shortly afterwards. The charge against him was that he was a seminary priest in England in contravention of the 1585 Act, which made the presence of such priests and Jesuits a treasonable offence. The Musgraves were later pardoned, for according to the Act they were also guilty of treason for having sheltered him. Fr Garnet, the Jesuit superior in England, reported his death to Rome and said the hangman's rope broke twice and Christopher rebuked the sheriff for his cruelty, for although "he meant no way to yield, but was glad of the combat, yet flesh and blood was weak, and therefore he showed little humanity to torment a man so long. . . . But it is no matter, I am very willing to suffer all." The bishop of Carlisle claimed that his death had "terrified a great sort of our obstinate recusants," but Catholic accounts say the martyr's meekness and "the constancy and cheerfulness with which he died" had won over many to Catholicism. There is some dispute about the date of his death, but as the date of Garnet's letter is 7 April 1597 the execution must have taken place a few days before, at the end of March or in the first few days of April. Christopher was beatified in 1987.

M.M.P., p. 235, where Challoner gives the altogether wrong date of 19 August 1598; Anstruther, 1, p. 293. For a full account see J. E. Bamber, "The Venerable Christopher Robinson," in *R.H.* 4 (1957-8), pp. 18-35.

Bd Mary Crescentia (1682-1744)

Anna Höss was born in Kaufbeuren in Bavaria in 1682, the daughter of poor wool-weavers. From an early age she used to visit the chapel of a local Franciscan convent to pray on her own, and one day she seemed to hear a voice from the crucifix say to her, "This shall be your home." Her father took her there as a postulant but was told the house was so poor that Anna would have to have a dowry before she could enter, and her parents could not afford this. When she was twenty-one, however, the Protestant mayor of the town, impressed by Anna's holiness, persuaded the nuns to accept her in return for his help in getting rid of a noisy inn that had been annoying them. She became a member of the Third Order Regular of St Francis, taking the name Mary Crescentia in religion.

Crescentia was treated badly for the first few years of her religious life. The mother superior and the other nuns would not let her forget her humble origins nor the fact she had not brought a dowry with her. She was not given a cell of her own but slept on the floor in one of the other nuns' cells. She was given only menial jobs to do, and when she was eventually given a cell it was small and damp. Some of the younger nuns sympathized with her and tried to intercede on her behalf, but Crescentia refused to support their protests. After some years, in 1707, a new mother superior accepted her as a full member of the community and, after she had spent sixteen years as door-keeper and gained a reputation for kindness to the poor, appointed her to the important post of novice-mistress. In 1726 she was elected mother superior by the community. Her prayer life had developed to such a high degree that she experienced visions and ecstasies, and on Fridays suffered a mystical sharing in Our Lord's passion that lasted from nine o'clock until three in the afternoon, often rendering her unconscious.

As mother superior she was known for her gentleness toward the nuns, although she was reputed to be very rigorous in testing the vocations of postulants. Her favourite message to them was also a summary of her own life: "The practices most pleasing to God are those which He himself imposes—to bear meekly and patiently the adversities He sends or which our neighbours inflict on us." She became known outside the convent as a wise and prudent spiritual director and was consulted by people in many walks of life. After her death in 1744 her tomb became a place of pilgrimage. She was beatified in 1900, and the cause of her canonization was re-opened in the 1950s.

The decree of beatification gives a summary of her life; see *Anal.Eccles.*, 8 (1900), pp. 455-7. See also G. Gatz, *Leben der seligen Creszentia von Kaufbeuren* (2d ed., 1953); *Bibl.SS.*, 7, 601-3.

6

St Prudentius, *Bishop* (861)

Prudentius was by birth a Spaniard, christened Galindo. It is probable that his family was of some importance socially. He received a good education and became a chaplain at the court of Louis the Pious (778-840), the third son of Charlemagne, who became king of Aquitaine in 781 and then joint emperor in 813. Prudentius became bishop of Troyes, south-east of Paris, about the year 843. He tells us in one of his sermons that he was busy hearing Confessions and giving the Last Sacraments as well as carrying out his strictly episcopal duties. He also had a reputation as a writer and wrote a number of important works, including a continuation of the *Annales Bertiniani* for the years 835-61, which is a valuable source for the history of the Frankish Empire. His main writings, however, were scriptural and theological. He produced a *Florilegium* (a collection of extracts) of the scriptures for the use of his clergy, which included moral and doctrinal instruction. A sermon he wrote as a panegyric survives and tells us something of his own character: he was a man of deep faith, learning, and apostolic energy. He was also something of a rigorist, and this may explain in part the stance he took in one of the most important theological controversies of his day.

A monk named Gottschalk had been condemned for teaching that Christ had died only for the elect while the majority of human beings had been doomed to hell by God from all eternity, and had been tortured, imprisoned, and excommunicated by Hincmar, bishop of Reims. Prudentius wrote to the bishop to say that he thought the sentence was too severe and claimed that Gottschalk had St Augustine (28 Aug.) on his side. He seems to have been among those who suspected Hincmar of himself being heretical in allowing human beings too much of an active role in their salvation. He later wrote a book against the views of John Scotus Erigena, whom Hincmar had quoted with approval, attacking point by point Erigena's work on predestination and adopting a strictly Augustinian point of view. In 853 a synod held at Quiercy under Hincmar issued four statements summing up the more orthodox Catholic position on this very difficult subject. Prudentius seems to have accepted these at first, intimidated, perhaps, by the presence of the emperor at the synod, but then in 857 he issued his own counter-propositions. By now, however, he was old and in bad health and appears not to have taken any further part in the controversy. How far his views should be considered unorthodox is difficult to assess, given the complexities of the issues and the lack of theological sophistication in the writings of all the people involved. What is clear is that Prudentius was regarded by his contemporaries as being among the most learned theologians of his day.

He attended several important councils and played a leading role in their deliberations. As an active, pastorally-minded bishop he was interested in the reform of clerical discipline and in improving the morals of his people, and he established two monasteries in his diocese. He died on 6 April 861. There does not appear to have been a cult in Troyes before the thirteenth century, but his name occurs in a number of martyrologies, though it was not included in the Roman Martyrology, presumably because of doubts about his doctrinal orthodoxy.

There is no early Life. For his writings see *P.L.*, 115, 965-1458. See also *D.T.C.*, 13, pt. 1 (1936), 1079-84; *Bibl.SS.*, 10, 1231-34. On the predestination controversy see *O.D.C.C.*, pp. 1117-8, and 584-5, 651, 1138, with ample bibliographies.

Bd Notker (912)

Notker was born about the year 840 and educated in the great abbey of Saint-Gall in Switzerland. He was a delicate child and had a stammer that earned him the nickname "Balbulus." His main interest was in studying music, which he did under an Irish monk named Marcellus along with two companions, Radpert and Tutilo; all three became teachers at the abbey and did much to develop it as a centre for the proper performance of church music. Notker became a monk and was appointed librarian and guest-master in addition to his work as a teacher. His last post was master of the monastic school. He was often consulted by people outside the abbey for advice on spiritual and temporal matters and was a favourite counsellor and friend of the emperor, Charles the Fat (877-87). Notker was probably the author of a biography in verse of Charlemagne undertaken at the request of the emperor. He also continued the "Breviary of the Frankish Kings" and wrote a verse Life of St Gall (16 Oct.), the founder of the abbey. Because there were a number of monks at Saint-Gall named Notker it is not always easy to be definite about the authorship of some of these works.

It is in the field of liturgical music, however, that Notker is best known. His most important work here is his *Liber Hymnorum* of 884. It used to be thought that he was the inventor of the sequence, a type of hymn sung or recited on important feast-days before the Gospel; for example, the "Veni, sancte Spiritus" on Whitsunday and the "Dies Irae" on All Souls' Day. It is now accepted that these existed in one form or another long before his time; what Notker did was collect them together, compose about forty new ones, and generally popularize their use north of the Alps. From the technical point of view his compositions are important for determining the structure of the earlier sequences, and his careful use of Latin and understanding of the relationship between words and music show considerable ability and sophistication. He made vivid use of imagery drawn from a wide range of classical, biblical, and patristic sources, and his texts "have an individuality and occasionally an originality worthy of first-rate literature" (Crocker). He also played an important part in introducing the Roman method of singing the chant to France and Germany. One of the monks of the abbey later described him as "weakly in body but not in mind, stammering of tongue but not of intellect, pressing forward boldly in things divine—a vessel filled with the Holy Ghost without equal in his time . . . assiduous in prayer, reading and copying, versed in knowledge [and] a master of the chant."

Notker died in 912. His cult began straightaway and was approved in 1512.

Notker's works are in *P.L.*, 131, pp. 993-1178; for a modern edition of his poetical works, see W. von den Steinen, *Notker der Dichter und seine geistige Welt*, 2 vols. (1948). See also *D.A.C.L.*, 11, 1615-23, and 12, 1727-32; *Bibl.SS.*, 9, 1075-6; *O.D.C.C.*, p. 983; R. L. Crocker in S. Sadie (ed.), *New Grove Dictionary of Music and Musicians* (1980), 13, p. 428.

St William of Eskill, *Abbot* (*c.* 1125-1203)

William was born about the year 1125 in Saint-Germain-Crépy-en-Valois in France and became a canon of the collegiate church of St Genevieve in Paris. In 1148 Suger, abbot of Saint-Denis, established a house of canons regular at St Genevieve's, and William was one of those who accepted the new, more austere way of life. His reputation for holiness and observance of the Rule spread, and in 1170 he was invited by the bishop of the Danish diocese of Roskilde to carry out a reform of monastic life in that country. William accepted and with three companions started his work with the canons regular at Eskilsoe, who did not follow any Rule and observed very little in the way of religious discipline. He was abbot there for many years and succeeded in reforming the community, despite opposition both from them and from powerful lay patrons. In 1175 the monastery was transferred to the island of Zealand and became a centre for reform throughout the country. William took on the reform of other religious houses, again in the face of active resentment and opposition, and soon controlled, at least in practice, all the Danish monasteries, even those of other Orders.

He became involved in political affairs over the marriage of King Philip-Augustus of France with a Danish princess in 1193. The king wanted to repudiate his wife very shortly after the wedding, and the French bishops agreed to this. William took the case to Rome to try to get justice for the queen. On his way back he was taken prisoner in France by the duke of Burgundy but was released and allowed to return to his abbey. He did not live to see the reconciliation of Philip-Augustus and his wife, which took place ten years later, for he died on 6 April 1203. He was canonized soon afterwards, in 1224, and his cult was very popular in Denmark down to the Reformation.

The best edition of a Life which may possibly have been written by one of William's canons is M. Cl. Gertz (ed.), *Vitae Sanctorum Danorum* (1908-12), pp. 287-386, which also contains a treatise by William on St Genevieve and an office and hymns in his honour. Over a hundred of his letters survive; for these and other writings attributed to him, see *P.L.*, 209, 655-746. See also *Bibl.SS.*, 7, 464-5. William is not to be confused with another, earlier, English saint who also worked in Denmark, St William of Roskilde (2 Sept.).

St Peter of Verona, *Martyr* (1205-52)

Peter was born in Verona in 1205. His parents were Cathars, members of a heretical dualist sect whose teachings included a denial of the goodness of the material world, the use of sacraments, and the resurrection of the body. For some reason Peter was sent to a Catholic school and grew up fully orthodox in his beliefs. While studying at the university of Bologna he reacted against the licentious behaviour of his companions and decided to become a religious. He joined the recently established Dominicans and received the habit from St Dominic (8 Aug.) himself. After his profession he worked as a preacher through-out Lombardy, gaining a reputation for his learning and effectiveness in win-ning back the lapsed and as a miracle-worker. For a time he was forbidden to preach and had to live in a remote priory because of accusations that he had admitted women to his cell. He was able to prove that the accusations were malicious and returned to his ministry to even greater public acclaim than before. He served as prior in a number of Dominican houses, and in 1234 Pope Gregory IX appointed him inquisitor for Milan; in 1251 his jurisdiction was extended to cover almost all of northern Italy.

His activities were now directed mainly against the Cathars and he soon made enemies among them because of the zeal he brought to denouncing and hounding them. In 1252 he learned that they had put a price on his head, and in his sermon on Palm Sunday he said, "Let them do their worst, I shall be more powerful dead than alive." A fortnight later, on 6 April, he was am-bushed on his way from Como to Milan and murdered along with a compan-ion, Brother Dominic. His killer was one Carino, who later repented of the murder and became a Dominican lay brother, dying many years later with a reputation for holiness that gave rise to a small local cult. He reported that Peter had died with the words of St Stephen (26 Dec.) forgiving his assailants on his lips. The story that as he died he tried to write the words "Credo in Deum" with his finger dipped in his own blood seems to be apocryphal.

A popular cult of Peter started straightaway, and he was canonized the fol-lowing year by Pope Innocent IV. While there can be no doubt about his holiness and his martyrdom, the speed of the canonization was due at least in part to the desire to provide a hero and patron for the crusade against the Cathars, who were severely persecuted. Peter was the first Dominican martyr, and his tomb in Milan became an important place of pilgrimage.

A contemporary Life and the canonization documents are in *AA.SS.*, Apr., 3, pp. 678-719. See also S. Orlandi, *S. Pietro martire da Verona . . .* (1952); A. Dondaine, "Saint Pierre Martyr," in *Archiv. Fratrum Praed.*, 23 (1953), pp. 66-162; *O.D.S.*, pp. 394-5.

Peter's death became a favourite subject for artists, and Fra Angelico painted him with a wound in his head, a dagger in his back, and his finger to his lips. A highly dramatic picture of his murder, painted by Domenichino (1581-1641), is in the municipal art gallery in Bologna. The cult spread to England, and he is featured in the churches at Long Melford (in a stained-glass window) and Thornham Parva (on the altar retable)—both in Suffolk; at Hennock (Devon) he is shown with a sword in his skull, while at East Portlemouth (Devon) he carries a book and a sword.

Bd Catherine of Pallanza, *Abbess* (*c.* 1435-78)

Catherine was born in Pallanza, a small village in the diocese of Novara in northern Italy, about the year 1435. All her family were wiped out in a plague epidemic while she was still young, and she was adopted by a lady who lived in nearby Milan. When she was about fifteen years old she heard a sermon on the sufferings of Our Lord that affected her so deeply that she decided to conse-crate the rest of her life to his service. She withdrew to a wild and lonely mountainous area that had often been used by hermits and where St Ambrose (7 Dec.) was said to have built an altar in honour of Our Lady. She joined a group of women hermits under the direction of the priest in charge of the shrine. The previous edition of this work claimed she was the first woman we know of who lived there as a hermit, but that is clearly not so. Catherine followed this way of life for fifteen years, and even in an area noted for the severe penitential practices of its solitary inhabitants, Catherine's austerities were such as to attract attention. She fasted for ten months in the year and was always dependent on gifts of food brought at irregular intervals by those who sought her prayers and advice. Despite her desire to be left on her own, she was joined by a group of five women disciples, whom she eventually estab-lished as a properly constituted community under a Rule inspired by St Au-gustine (28 Aug.) and St Ambrose (7 Dec.). Their convent was dedicated to Our Lady of the Mountain, and the Sisters were allowed to wear the habit of the Poor Clares. Catherine served as prioress for two years before her death in 1478. During her life Catherine had been credited with the gift of prophecy, and a local cult developed which was approved in 1769. In the 1730s her remains were translated to a special chapel built in her honour and are still venerated there today.

AA.SS., Apr.,1, pp. 643-54, gives a Latin translation of a Life written by her successor, one of the original five disciples. See also *Bibl.SS.*, 3, 992-3.

Bd Michael Rua (1837-1910)

Michael was born in Turin in June 1837, the son of Giovanni Rua and Giovanna Maria Ferrero. His father died in 1845 while Michael was attending the ele-mentary school run by the Brothers of the Christian Schools. At the school he came into contact with the chaplain, St John (Don) Bosco (31 Jan.), who impressed him deeply. At Don Bosco's suggestion he attended the local grammar school for two years, from 1850 to 1852, when he entered the Oratory at Valdocco, Turin, as a boarder and started to wear clerical dress. The Oratory is the name used for the complex of activities that grew up around the original boys' club started by the saint. In Michael's day Don Bosco lived on the premises, which were used for evening classes and which also had a small chapel. The word is used nowadays by Salesians for the youth centres and clubs that are run in conjunction with parishes or schools, often with a resident Salesian community.

In 1854 Michael was one of the first to be associated with Don Bosco in the setting up of the Salesian Congregation. It was dedicated to "a practical charity to our neighbour" and inspired by the gentle kindness of its patron, St Francis de Sales (24 Jan.). In the following year he made his religious vows. During the cholera epidemic of 1855 he nursed the sick in the slums of the city. He worked for a time as a catechist and accompanied the founder on his first visit to Rome. Despite the fact that he was still only a subdeacon, he was appointed first spiritual director of the Salesians. In 1860 he was ordained priest and from then on was always at Don Bosco's side, in 1865 becoming his official vicar in the work of spreading and guiding the new Society.

Meanwhile, in 1863, he had gained a teaching diploma at the university of Turin. Such were his abilities that a learned abbot of the day said, "If I had six men like Don Rua I would open a university." He was so effective in his role as vicar that Don Bosco took the very unusual step of asking the pope in 1884 to declare Michael to be his successor as head of the Society. This was not just because of his abilities as an administrator; on one occasion the saint declared, "If God said to me, 'Imagine a young man with all the virtues and an ability greater than you could even hope for, then ask me and I will give him to you,' I could still never have imagined a Don Rua." On Don Bosco's death in 1888 Michael was confirmed as rector major of the Salesians by the pope.

At that time the Society had sixty-four houses and 768 professed members; when Michael died in 1910 it had 341 houses and just over four thousand members. He was responsible for establishing it in twenty-three countries, from Switzerland to Mexico and from China to South Africa. He was particularly keen to develop the missionary side of the Society's work and was a tireless traveller, not just throughout Europe but also in Egypt, North Africa, and Palestine. After one of these journeys he said, "I have seen poverty everywhere, and yet, thank God, I have also seen thousands of children taken off the streets and changed into honest citizens and good Christians." It was the children of the poor who were his first priority, and to him the way to help them was simple: "If you wish to save a poor neighbourhood, open an Oratory. Even without grounds and buildings, if you are real Salesians, the Oratory will be in you."

His strict fidelity to the Constitution of the Society and to its founder's wishes won him the nickname "the living rule." He spent most of his life as a priest in administration, and sometimes his hesitation and scrupulous anxiety, his perfectionist approach to everything, seemed to prevent him from having a broader vision, and he could be severe with his priests. And yet he was a man of vision and educational innovation. He opened *gymnasia* (high schools) and set up social circles in the Oratories; he developed appropriate curricula for vocational schools, introduced technical and commercial courses, and set up hostels for boarders. He also had a genuine kindness toward those in trouble, whether members of the Society or outsiders.

Don Bosco had said to Michael, "You will have a great amount of work to do, and a great deal to suffer," and during his years in charge of the Society he faced a number of trials. In 1896 its members were driven out of Ecuador by an anticlerical government, and the same fate befell them in France in 1902. In 1907 a violent press campaign against the Salesians broke out in a town in Liguria in Italy. Serious accusations were made against them, and for a time public opinion accepted the truth of the charges. Eventually the case collapsed, and those who had been behind it fled abroad to escape the law. It was believed that Michael's health had been seriously affected by the affair, and in 1908 there was a burden of a different nature to trouble him, when an earthquake in Sicily killed nine Salesian priests and thirty of their pupils. He continued to put his trust in Mary Auxiliatrix, to whom he had a lifelong devotion.

Eventually Michael became seriously ill, in February 1910, with heart disease, and he died on 6 April, at the age of seventy-three. He was buried in Turin by the side of Don Bosco, and on his tomb were inscribed the words, "The Second Father of the Salesian Family." At his beatification on 29 October 1972 Paul VI declared, "The Salesian Family had in Don Bosco its origin, and in Don Rua its continuation. He drew all his teachings from the Saint; he derived an authetic ethos from his Rule, and made the Saint's holiness the model to be followed. Don Rua instituted a genuine tradition."

The basic study is A. Amadei, *Il servo di Dio Don Michele Rua*, 3 vols. (1931). There are a number of English biographies; see especially Angelo Franco, S.D.B., *Venerable Michael Rua* (1954); P. Lappin, *The Wine in the Chalice* (1972); J. Ayers, *Blessed Michael Rua* (1974).

Bd Pierina Morosini, *Martyr* (1931-57)

Pierina was born at Fiobbio, near Bergamo in northern Italy, on 7 January 1931, the eldest of the nine children of Rocco and Sara Morosini. She finished her elementary schooling but had to give up the idea of further studies, for which she showed a natural ability, because the illness of her father meant she had to become the main breadwinner for the family. She trained for a time as a seamstress and then when she was fifteen got a job in a local textile factory. She joined a Catholic Action group and became involved in all the activities of the parish, especially teaching catechism to young children and visiting the sick. She was also keenly interested in fostering vocations to the local seminary and to the foreign missions. A daily communicant, she showed signs of unusual piety, getting up at four o'clock each morning to pray and hear Mass before starting work at six o'clock. She wanted to become a nun so that she could work on the foreign missions but had to keep earning for the sake of her family. She became a member of the Third Order of St Francis and of the Children of Mary. Her colleagues at work spoke highly of her conscientiousness, her general friendliness touched with a certain reserve, and her strong religious faith.

Pierina went on a pilgrimage to Rome in 1947 to attend the canonization of St Maria Goretti (6 July) and was deeply impressed by the example of this young girl who had died in defence of her purity. She is reported to have said on a number of occasions that she would like to die the same death as St Maria. She became a member of a local Purity Crusade and composed a prayer for chastity for its members; part of this runs as follows: "May I never give way to the attractions of the world or of pleasure; may I never allow myself even the smallest compromise with sin, whether in dress, speech, reading, looks, or entertainment. . . . Make me a little apostle of all those girls who are led astray by the world. And if ever I have the misfortune to fall, may your immaculate hand raise me up as soon as possible, O Jesus, and make me find again the intimacy of your heart. . . . If you call me to marriage help me to bring to the altar my baptismal innocence. Raise up from the young women in Catholic Action many holy religious vocations."

In the early afternoon of 4 April 1957 Pierina was making her way home along a lonely path when she was assaulted by a twenty-year old man who tried to force her to have sex with him. When she refused and struggled with him, he hit her repeatedly with a stone and left her in a coma. She died two days later in hospital without recovering consciousness. Apparently the man had been harrassing her for about a year and may have made the assault as the result of a bet with his friends. He was arrested and confessed. It is interesting that the hospital surgeon who tried to save Pierina's life exclaimed when he heard the details of the crime, "We have here a new Maria Goretti!" This idea spread very rapidly and her funeral on 9 April was attended by large crowds. Her grave quickly became a place of pilgrimage, particularly for seminarians and members of Catholic Action, and the first biography of her was published in 1960. In 1983 her remains were moved to a marble shrine in the parish church, and in 1987 she was beatified. It is important for us not to concentrate on her death in isolation from the rest of her life, for it was the logical, if extreme, consequence of a life lived consistently as a Christian.

A.A.S. 79, pt. 2, pp. 1342-6, for the beatification. See also E. Poli, *Pierina Morosini testimone di Cristo* (1985); *Bibl.SS.*, Suppl. 1, 943-4, with photograph; *N.S.B.* 2, pp. 146-9, gives the prayer quoted from above.

7

ST JOHN BAPTIST DE LA SALLE, *Founder* (1651-1719)

Jean-Baptiste de La Salle was born into a wealthy aristocratic family in Reims in northern France in April 1651. He was the eldest of eleven children, three of whom died in childhood; of the surviving eight, three were to become priests and one a nun. It appears to have been a pious and rather strict household, but details of John Baptist's early years are very scarce. His teachers when asked later for their impressions of him could remember very little: we may assume he was little different from other members of his class. When he was nine years old he went to the local Collège des Bons Enfants and remained there for the full eight years of schooling, following the normal curriculum that was based almost entirely on the ancient classics. He received the clerical tonsure when he was eleven, as was customary at the time for those who had some idea they might go on to become priests, and in 1667 he was nominated to succeed a distant cousin as a canon of the cathedral chapter. This custom of making young laymen members of the chapter before they had even started to study for the priesthood was justified by arguing that the income from the canonry should be used to defray the expenses of that study. It was, clearly, open to serious abuses, and John Baptist was hardly in need of any help in paying his fees, but a canon he was, and he carried out the light duties that went with the office. At the end of his schooling he went to Saint-Sulpice in Paris, a seminary opened about thirty years before. It already enjoyed a considerable reputation for the quality of its training and the intense piety fostered by its professors, priests of the Society of Saint-Sulpice.

While he was studying in Paris his parents died, and he had to return to Reims to look after family matters. He completed his studies at the university there and was ordained in 1678. He continued studying and was awarded a doctorate in theology in 1681. To outsiders he must have seemed ideally suited to high office in the Church, destined, no doubt, for a bishopric. He himself had no idea about a particular apostolate or mission at this time, no vision such as other saints have had to inspire them. He had done some catechetical work among the poor as part of his training in Paris and had been involved with a Canon Roland in setting up a Congregation of religious women, the Sisters of the Holy Child Jesus, to provide education for poor girls, but once he had completed this in 1679 he apparently took no further interest in the work. He settled down to the comfortable life of a cathedral canon with private means, attending daily services but without any parochial responsibilities to disturb him.

What happened next changed his whole life. Looking back on it shortly before he died John Baptist wrote that if he had known where it was going to lead he would not have lifted a finger to get involved. But he always encouraged his followers to look for God's purpose in their life by trying to see every event "with the eyes of faith," and that was his own response now. Adrien Nyel, a layman who had opened four free schools for the poor in Rouen, approached him in 1679 for help to open a similar school in Reims. A local parish priest offered part of his presbytery, and a wealthy lady offered money for a second school if John Baptist would take charge of the administration. As pupils flocked to the schools more money was needed to pay for teachers, and the canon put up the funds. By the end of the year the parish priest decided he could no longer offer accommodation to the teachers, and so John Baptist rented a house near his own for their use. Immediately Adrien Nyel opened another school, even though some of the ones in Rouen were running into trouble because of the poor quality of the teachers—he was better at starting schools than at training his teachers. John Baptist took advice from a holy priest in Paris who had tried unsuccessfully to set up an Order of teaching Brothers and was told that he should take the teachers into his own house, live with them, and train them properly. He was horrified; as he wrote much later, "Those whom at first I was obliged to employ as teachers I ranked below my own servants, and the very thought of living with them was unbearable." Prayer convinced him, however, that it was God's will, and so he took six of the teachers into his house and treated them as equals. Given the rigid social structures of the time, it is not surprising that his family were shocked and took away his two young brothers who had been living there. In the end there was so much criticism that he rented a house in the Rue Neuve and moved in with the teachers, leaving his own large and comfortable house to the family. The date was 24 June 1682, the feast of the birthday of St John the Baptist. The episode shows again his desire to do God's will, whatever the cost in worldly terms, and his ability to look on what happened to him with eyes of faith.

By 1684 he had resigned from his canonry and given away his fortune (it went mainly on famine relief) in order to put himself on the same footing as the other teachers. In May of that year he and twelve others formed themselves into a community by taking a simple vow of obedience and adopting the name "Brothers of the Christian Schools." New schools were opened, and their reputation spread quickly. Requests came in from parish priests for teachers to go and open village schools, but John Baptist did not want the Brothers to live singly and so opened a training college for young men in 1686. He also set up a junior novitiate for pupils at the schools who felt they had a vocation to join the Brothers. There were, of course, problems: the continuing opposition of his family, the unwillingness of some of the early Brothers to remain in community, and the jealousy aroused by their success. This last was particularly important when John Baptist opened two schools in Paris where there were already a number of small, fee-paying schools, usually run by a single master. These saw the Brothers as a threat and had their schools closed by a church official; John Baptist had to go to court to have them reopened. In Reims, meanwhile, further trouble had broken out because the Brother left in charge did not know how to handle the community, and eight members left. There had also been a relatively large number of deaths among the Brothers, due at least in part to the deplorable conditions in which they worked, and vocations were drying up. In spite of these problems John Baptist pushed ahead; he opened a novitiate, and in 1694 twelve of the Brothers and himself took perpetual vows, promising lifelong commitment to the Congregation and to the ideal of providing free education for the poor. They still had no official standing in the Church, and in order to gain this it was necessary to have an approved Rule.

There were no precedents for the type of Congregation John Baptist had founded: a body of men wholly devoted to teaching and with no ordained members. His Rule borrowed from existing monastic ones but also had much that was original in it. The apostolate of teaching had to be "a means of holiness for themselves, a service to the poor and to the gospel, and a way of defending and extending the kingdom of Christ" (O'Toole). The Rule contained a chapter on the spirit of faith: "The Brothers . . . will animate all their actions with attitudes of faith and in doing them will always have in view the orders and will of God which they will adore in all things and by which they will be careful to regulate their conduct. . . . The first effect of faith is to attach us strongly to the knowledge, the love and the imitation of Jesus Christ and to union with him." They should not perform a single action "through merely natural impulse or from any simply human motive, but perform them all for the glory of God, with the intention of pleasing him, and through the movement of the Holy Spirit." The Brothers' mission was to be "ambassadors of Christ to the young; since it was their duty to pass on the faith, they must themselves be steeped in it. They must, in St Paul's phrase, 'put on Christ' so that they could radiate him more effectively." The spirituality he laid out for the Brothers was christocentric and marked by the intense piety he had learned at Saint-Sulpice. To get closer to Christ the Brothers must have a "very profound respect for Holy Scripture, and in evidence they will always carry about them the New Testament and pass no day without making some reading in it with an attitude of faith, respect and veneration for the divine words it contains." He laid great stress on meditation and wrote a manual on the different methods of mental prayer. He forbade the use of bodily mortifications beyond the normal fasting rules of the Church: he believed teaching was wearing enough in itself and, if done conscientiously, would develop sufficient self-discipline in the Brothers. The first version of the Rule was written in 1694; it was reworked in 1705 and revised in 1717, and a final version was approved by papal authority in 1726 after the saint's death.

The years 1691 to 1699 were prolific for writing. In addition to the Rule, John Baptist produced his *Conduct of Schools, The Rules of Christian Politeness and Civility* (initially called *The Rules of Good Behaviour*), *The Duties of a Christian*, a *Manual of Piety for Schools*, and other works. Not all of these were printed straightaway, as they were produced originally for the use of the Brothers, and he would frequently revise his texts after consultation. The most popular of these works was that on good manners. It was one of many books on polite behaviour written in the seventeenth century, but John Baptist was unusual in translating such a code from polite society to the rough and tumble of a poor school. In explaining the aim of his work he wrote: "It is a surprising thing that the majority of Christians look upon decorum and civility as a purely human and worldly quality. . . . This well shows how little Christianity there is in the world, and how few people live and act according to the spirit of Jesus Christ." Children should be taught good manners out of respect for the presence of God in other people and courtesy to those who are "members of Jesus Christ and living temples, guided by his Spirit." The book deals with every aspect of daily life, including getting up in the morning, dressing, personal hygiene, eating, forms of address, and so on. To modern eyes the ideal behind the work is marred in practice by basing what was to be taught as manners on the highly artificial and status-ridden French upper-class polite behaviour of the day, "more calculated to create a static and exclusive clique . . . than a method of rendering human intercourse more agreeable and easy" (Battersby). As with so many other reformers who set out to improve the manners of the poor, there was a complete lack of feeling for the positive side of lower-class culture—it was to be an imposition of an alien way of life and not a reformation. But at least in John Baptist's case there was a solidly Christian motive, and he would never have been content with merely external good manners. As he wrote in the preface, if Christians followed his guidelines, "they would sanctify all their actions and allow people to distinguish Christian politeness and civility from that which is purely worldly and almost pagan, and so live as perfect Christians."

This ideal of trying to get people to live as "perfect Christians" was the motivating principle of his educational work. It comes across clearly in another of his books published in 1695, *The Duties of a Christian*. He starts by saying it is not enough to be baptized and make a profession of faith to be a Christian and goes on, "One must, in addition, live by the spirit of Our Lord Jesus Christ, and live a life in conformity with him and with his maxims which are stated for us in the Holy Gospel and in all the New Testament." He stresses the importance of a living, practical faith and the place to be played by prayer and the sacraments—in this context it is interesting that he seems to favour frequent and even daily Communion against the prevailing rigorism of the day. On prayer he suggests a way of praying "by silence, simply being in the presence of God in an attitude of respect and adoration, without saying anything or asking God for anything . . . by thought, without using any words; . . . by affections, when we ask God for something with the sole movement of the heart." Not all the book is as positive as this, and there are long passages on the commandments, sin, and penance that are rather cold and negative. It was written in a hurry, and perhaps he took too much from the catechisms currently in use without adapting it. It was, overall, a very successful exposition of the Church's doctrine and went through more than 250 editions.

The years after 1695 were years of both expansion and crisis. A new novitiate and three further schools were opened in Paris, along with a Sunday school in which young men in work were taught reading and writing, technical subjects, and, of course, religious instruction. Three schools were opened in Chartres (where five Brothers died in an outbreak of plague in 1705) and one in Calais. Then the Brothers were approached to provide education for the children of the Irish followers of the exiled King James II of England who had fled with him to France. A school for fifty Irish boys was set up (the girls were placed in a convent), and it seems this provided John Baptist, who undertook their education himself, with his first excursion into secondary education. The school was successful, but no details of its curriculum or how it was run have survived. At the same time, in 1701, John Baptist sent two Brothers to Rome to open a school there. The move was not a success: the French were very unpopular in Italy, the Roman authorities could not understand why the Brothers were not priests, and schools for the poor were already provided by another Order. One of the Brothers returned to France; the other, Gabriel Drolin, remained in Rome for twenty years, opened a school in 1710, and eventually gained some recognition.

The crisis the new Congregation faced was a twofold one. There were moves to put the Brothers under the authority of the parish priest of the area where a school was located, and in 1702 an attempt was made to depose John Baptist himself in favour of a new superior nominated by the archbishop of Paris. These attacks show the still unapproved status of the new Congregation and the suspicion its novelty could arouse. John Baptist made no attempt to fight his deposition and urged obedience on the Brothers, but they threatened to withdraw from Paris altogether if it went ahead. A compromise was reached that allowed for the appointment of an "ecclesiastical superior" from outside the Congregation. An unfortunate result of this quarrel with the church authorities was that when the Paris lay schoolmasters renewed their attempts to close the Brothers' schools no ecclesiastical support was forthcoming to defend them. Some of the schools and the training college were closed, others were constantly harassed and even sacked, and the courts found against the Brothers in the lawsuits that followed. In the end the situation became so difficult that John Baptist moved the centre of his operations and the novitiate to Rouen.

As some compensation, schools were being opened in several other towns, and a new novitiate was established at Saint-Yon on the outskirts of Rouen. A new training college was opened at Saint-Denis to the north of the capital. Two other developments at this time were particularly important for the future: the Brothers opened a boarding school at Saint-Yon for the sons of the wealthier merchants and manufacturers of the city and began teaching a modern curriculum more suited to commerce and business than the traditional classical one. They also opened a type of reformatory school for difficult and delinquent children, an area in which they were to specialize in later years. As these and other institutions grew, the Brothers developed and refined their teaching methods and their way of organizing the schools.

It is not possible here to describe in detail the extent to which John Baptist was an innovator, but a few points from his major work, *The Conduct of Christian Schools,* will give an indication of his contribution. Most of those who wrote about education in the seventeenth century did so from a theoretical standpoint and were concerned with the education of children of the upper classes. John Baptist's only theory came from his belief in the Christian ideal; for the rest, he knew what the inside of a Paris slum school was like, and everything he wrote about school practice was based on his own and the Brothers' experience. In the preface to *The Conduct of Christian Schools* he wrote, "Nothing has been set down that has not been well agreed upon and well tried out and of which the advantages and drawbacks have not been weighed, and of which the blunders and bad consequences have not been foreseen as far as has been possible." The book gives detailed rules for whole-class teaching to replace the individual tuition common at the time, with regulations about silence and good order in the classroom; lays out the steps for teaching reading (twenty pages are devoted to this); insists the children should learn reading French to begin with and not Latin as was usual; and has a long and sensitive section on punishment. The school is to be a community, with the children taking in their breakfast to eat in common, saying prayers at set times, and attending daily Mass at the local church. The progress of the pupils is to be checked regularly against the following principles: in all areas of the curriculum there is a planned sequence of skills, and a child may not pass to a higher level until proficient in the lower one; children do not all learn at the same rate, and adjustments must be made to allow for individual differences; the class teacher must take into account the age of the child at entry and the likely length of time to be spent at school when planning how much ground the pupil should cover, and great care is needed so that pupils who are not promoted do not feel discouraged. While it was surprisingly modern in some respects, the *Conduct* was a product of the circumstances surrounding its composition and was bound to become out of date. It is clear, however, from reading it that the Brothers "were inspired by both a consciously pursued Christian realism and a pedagogical realism to prepare the children for their future." All his writings taken together show that "De La Salle understood the vocation of the Christian teacher as a basic ministry in the Church" (Calcutt).

John Baptist spent most of the period from 1711 to 1714 visiting houses in the south of France, apart from a short stay in Paris to deal with a lawsuit over the training college property. In this he was let down by people he had trusted, the case went against him, and he had to pay heavy legal costs as well as losing the training college. Some of the Brothers were upset by his long absence at a difficult time. Illness was part of the reason, but it is also clear that John Baptist wished to give up running the Congregation and even to retire as much as possible from its day-to-day activities. The work of setting up the Congregation was now done, and it was up to others to take it forward. It had survived many vicissitudes, and he was sure that it would last. In 1714, however, he was called back under his vow of obedience to become superior general.

By 1717, when the general assembly of the Congregation that elected his successor took place, there were twenty-two communities in France with a hundred Brothers and eighteen novices, and Brother Drolin was still on his own in Rome. The assembly relieved John Baptist of all administrative responsibility, though he was asked to help in revising the Rule. This he did over the next year, and "the final outcome was the product of much thought and study, prolonged prayer and years of experience. Every sentence had been weighed, every prescription subjected to trial over a long period." He was indebted to various sources, but the work was still original, "the product of a mind that had made its own all that was good in the past, and used it to create something which fits a given case and will profit future generations" (Battersby). He retired to Saint-Yon and devoted himself to writing, prayer, teaching the novices, and as much solitude as he could find. He was approached frequently for advice and counsel from inside and outside the Congregation. He had a reputation for dealing successfully with hardened sinners and other difficult cases brought to him by local priests. During this final phase of his life he was also an example of perfect obedience to his successor, sometimes to the point of embarrassment, so that Brother Barthélemy joked that the founder would not even die without his permission.

In addition to revising the Rule he wrote over two hundred Meditations for the use of the Brothers. Again, he borrowed widely in composing these, but they have definite signs of his own approach to mental prayer and spirituality and are closely linked to the everyday work of teaching and living in community. His own spiritual life was one of intense prayer and bodily mortification, especially fasting, use of the discipline, and wearing a hair shirt. He accepted the bouts of hard physical poverty that occurred frequently during the early years and that were in such contrast to his former life of comfort. Above all else, however, his holiness was manifested in his total submission to the will of God, witnessed most strongly by his lifelong acceptance of a vocation for which he felt no natural attraction. He could truly say of his Congregation, "This community is founded only on Providence," and of himself, "I will often consider myself as an instrument which is of no use except in the hands of the workman. Hence I must await the orders of Providence before acting, and be careful to accomplish them when known." He stressed the necessity of prayer and submission to a spiritual director to discover as clearly as possible the divine will and the mortification to achieve the self-control required to follow it when known. His last words as he lay dying were: "I adore in all things the holy will of God in my regard."

He died on Good Friday, 7 April 1719. The cause of his canonization was introduced in 1840, and he was beatified in 1888 and canonized in 1900. In 1950 he was declared to be the principal patron of all teachers of the young. The Congregation was approved in 1725, and by 1789 there were 121 communities in France and six in other countries, with about a thousand Brothers in all. Despite its temporary suppression at the time of the French Revolution and the execution of some of its members, the Congregation flourished during the nineteenth century, with a thousand new foundations (276 of them outside France) and more than 11,500 Brothers. Numbers peaked at over sixteen thousand in the 1950s and are currently just under eight thousand (Calcutt).

There is a wealth of published material, and considerable research is in progress. For the saint's writings see *Oeuvres complètes* (1993); A. Loes, F.S.C., and F. Huether, F.S.C., (eds.), *Meditations by St John Baptist de La Salle* (1994); C. Molloy and C. Loes (eds.), *The Letters of John Baptist de La Salle* (1988), vol. 1 of a planned 13 vols. of complete works. For English works see W. J. Battersby, F.S.C., *St John Baptist De La Salle* (1957); L. O'Toole, *St John Baptist De La Salle, The Teachers' Saint* (pamphlet, n.d.); E. Bannon, F.S.C., *De La Salle: A Founder as Pilgrim* (1988); L. Salm, F.S.C., *The Work Is Yours: The Life of St John Baptist De La Salle* (1989). A. Calcutt, F.S.C., *De La Salle, A City Saint and the Liberation of the Poor through Education* (1993), is a very good introduction to recent research and also worth reading in its own right. See also *Dict.Sp.*, 7 (1974), 802-22; this article was translated and published as *Announcing the Gospel to the Poor. The Spiritual Experience and Spiritual Teaching of St John Baptist de La Salle*, by M. Sauvage and M. Campos (1981).

A portrait by Pierre Léger (d. 1733) is in the generalate in Rome; it was the basis of later official portraits. A bronze group in Rouen by Falguière (1875) shows the saint with two children, while a modern statue by Le Jeûne in Reims Cathedral was erected to mark the third centenary of his birth. There are a number of twentieth-century stylized paintings of scenes from the saint's life by Giovanni Gagliardi and Cesare Mariani; some of these are in the generalate, others in the Vatican galleries, and they tend to be reproduced in popular Lives.

St Hegesippus (*c.* 180)

Hegesippus was a converted Jew who probably lived in Palestine. He is said to have travelled to Corinth and Rome to find out what true Christian doctrine was and to have lived in Rome for twenty years, from about 157 to 177. He then returned to the East, where he died at an advanced age, probably in Jerusalem, though the Roman Martyrology, following Baronius, used to claim that he died in Rome. But biographical details about him are scarce and not wholly trustworthy. His fame rested on his "Memoirs," or writings on early

Church history, especially of the Church in Jerusalem, intended to show "the tradition, without error, of the apostolic preaching" (Eusebius). These were in five books, written in a simple style as a polemic against the errors of the Gnostic heretics. Unfortunately they survive only in fragments, principally in the writings of Eusebius, who thought highly of Hegesippus as a historian and tells us he drew up a list of the early popes while in Rome. This may be the important list given by St Epiphanius (12 May)—which would make it the oldest witness to the names and order of the early popes. There is some indication, however, that what Eusebius is referring to is Hegesippus' work in Rome to verify the apostolic tradition of his writings.

AA.SS., Apr., 1, pp. 656-7, collects the references in Eusebius and St Jerome. It is strange that his complete works seem to have survived down to the sixteenth or seventeenth century in some libraries but have been lost since. See also *Bibl.SS.*, 4, 956; *O.D.C.C.*, p. 628; *E.E.C.*, 1, p. 371.

St Herman Joseph (*c*. 1150-1241)

Herman was born to poor parents in Cologne about the year 1150. When he was twelve he applied to join the Premonstratensian monastery in Steinfeld but was rejected on account of his youth. The monks, however, did see to his education and sent him to one of their houses in Friesland, where he received a sound general schooling, despite his reputed impatience with subjects that did not lead him to a greater knowledge of God. He returned to Steinfeld and was allowed to become a monk. Initially he was given the task of serving in the refectory, which allowed him little time for prayer; later on he was appointed to be sacristan, an office he found much more to his liking, since it allowed him to spend most of the day in church. After his ordination as a priest his religious fervour became even more intense, so much so that it was difficult to find anyone to serve his Masses because he was often in ecstasy and took so long to finish saying them. He was given the nickname Joseph on account of his blameless life and total innocence. He was renowned for his kindness to other people and had a practical side to his character as well, being a skilled mechanic and much in demand for servicing and repairing monastic clocks.

Herman suffered from bad health for much of his life, and this was made worse by his fasting and other penitential practices. He experienced severe headaches, and his digestion eventually became so bad that apparently he stopped eating altogether. Fortunately these distressing symptoms eased during the last nine years of his life. In 1241 he was sent to celebrate the passiontide and Easter offices at the convent of the Cistercian nuns at Hoven, but he fell ill with a fever while he was there and died shortly afterwards. There was an early cult, and the cause of his canonization was begun in 1628 but never completed. His cult was officially approved in 1958, and in 1960 he was allowed the title of saint.

He has been credited with numerous writings including prayers, hymns, and mystical treatises: one of these was on the Song of Solomon, which was much admired at the time. Along with most of the other works attributed to him this is now lost. He had a tender devotion to the Child Jesus and to Our Lady and was also active in spreading devotion to St Ursula (formerly 11 Oct.), whose relics were supposed to be housed in Cologne. He composed an office in her honour, but the books of fantastic revelations about her and her maiden companions are probably not his work, and may even have been written as a joke.

Herman's fame rests mainly on the visions and mystical experiences attributed to him in a contemporary Life, written possibly by the prior of Steinfeld, and on his undoubted holiness and faithfulness to the monastic life. The Life was later considerably adapted and circulated in condensed versions similar to the *Little Flowers of St Francis*. One of the stories told of him was that as a young child he used to talk familiarly to statues of Our Lady and the Holy Child. On one occasion she held out her hand to accept an apple he offered her; on another occasion a statue of Our Lady, Mother of Mercy, told him where he could find money to buy shoes. The most famous of these stories tells how Herman was embarrassed by his nickname Joseph until Our Lady reassured him by placing a wedding ring on his finger. This last story was chosen by Van Dyck as the subject of a painting now in Vienna.

AA.SS., Apr., 1, pp. 687-714, gives the contemporary Life. A popular account in French was written by Petit (1929). See also R. van Waefelgham, *Repertoire de l'Ordre de Prémontré* (1930); *Bibl.SS.*, 5, 25-8.

Bd Alexander Rawlins, *Martyr* (1560-95)

Alexander Rawlins was born in Oxford in 1560 and educated at Winchester before studying at Stable and Hart Halls, Oxford. As a young man he worked as an apothecary at Denham in Buckinghamshire. In June 1586 he was arrested with Fr Christopher Dryland, a seminary priest, and St Swithin Wells (10 Dec.) and imprisoned in Newgate in London. He was released and then reimprisoned in the same year, and in November 1586 was in the Fleet prison awaiting banishment for the offence of being a Catholic recusant. While abroad he entered Douai College (temporarily located in Reims) to study for the priesthood, was ordained at Soissons in March 1590, and sent to England in April of the same year. He worked as a priest for about four years, mainly in Yorkshire and Durham, until Christmas Day 1594, when the house of Bd Thomas Warcop (4 July), where he was staying, was searched and he was arrested, along with Thomas Warcop and other members of the household.

Alexander was charged with having been ordained abroad during Elizabeth's reign and being in England as a priest, a capital offence under the Act of 1585. He was tried and condemned at York and executed by being hanged, drawn, and quartered on 7 April 1595. St Henry Walpole, whose feast is also celebrated today, was executed at the same time. There is an eyewitness account of how he and Henry Walpole were drawn together on a hurdle to the place of execution outside the city walls and how Alexander kissed the gallows and the rope and died repeating the name of Jesus. Some of his letters and his will are preserved in the English College in Rome; they were written in prison, which he described as "castle of comfort and palace of pleasure." He sometimes used the aliases Alexander Neal (his mother's maiden name) and Francis Feriman. He was beatified in 1929.

M.M.P., pp. 217-8; Challoner is mistaken about the martyr's birthplace. Anstruther, 1, pp. 285-6. See also "The Forty Martyrs of England and Wales," 25 October.

St Henry Walpole, *Martyr* (1558-95)

Henry Walpole was born at Docking in Norfolk in 1558. He was educated at Norwich Grammar School and studied at Peterhouse, Cambridge, before entering Gray's Inn, London, to study law. Challoner says that his parents were Catholic and does not mention anything about a conversion; other sources say Henry became a Catholic because of the execution of St Edmund Campion (1 Dec.) in 1581, about which he wrote a long narrative poem. It may be that the execution re-awakened or confirmed his Catholic faith, and in 1582 he went abroad to study for the priesthood, first at Reims and then in Rome, where he became a Jesuit in 1584. Ordained priest in Paris in 1588, he worked for a time in Italy and was then sent to Flanders, where he acted as occasional chaplain to the English Catholic soldiers serving in the Spanish army under Sir William Stanley. He was taken prisoner by some anti-Spanish rebels and spent four or five months in prison. On his release he went to France to complete his training and returned to Brussels as librarian and confessor. His wish was to go to England to work as a missioner, but his health was not good and his superiors sent him instead to Spain. He worked in the English Colleges in Seville and Valladolid before returning to Flanders with a warrant from the king to open a new college for the education of English priests and laypeople at Saint-Omer.

Eventually he got his wish and was sent to England in 1593, landing at Bridlington in Yorkshire on 6 December. Unfortunately he was arrested the following day and taken to York on suspicion of being a priest. He admitted the charge and was sent to London to be imprisoned in the Tower, where he spent about a year and was tortured on fourteen occasions. While in prison he wrote to a fellow-Jesuit: "I trust that God will be glorified in me, whether in life or death. . . . Some come to dispute with me, but with clamours and empty words more than with solid arguments." We have his written confessions, which are fuller than those of any of the other martyrs, and "though they begin admirably, they end sadly, . . . Their conclusion is somewhat mysterious, both as to the extent of [his] waverings, and also as to the reason for his instability" (Pollen). He was "affectionate, effusive, facile of speech, and weak in constitution," ill-adapted for the rigours of prison and torture, and the chief cause for his change of mind and his ample confessions was "probably moral pressure—dread of future torments, weakness, depression, helplessness, confusion" (Pollen). After the tortures he was left with crippled hands and in considerable pain; despite the human weakness that may have led him to confess too much, he did not at any stage think of giving up his priesthood, still less of abandoning his faith.

His trial was eventually held back in York. During it he said to the jury, "I confess most willingly that I am a priest, and that I am of the Company of Jesus, and that I came over in order to convert my country to the Catholic faith and to invite sinners to repentance. All this I will never deny; this is the duty of my calling. If you find anything else in me that is not agreeable to my profession, show me no favour. In the meantime, act according to your consciences, and remember you must give an acount to God." He was found guilty according to the Act of 1585, which made it a capital offence to be in England after having been ordained a priest abroad. On the scaffold almost his last words were a denial of the queen's supremacy in religious matters. He was hanged, drawn, and quartered outside the city on 7 April 1595, along with Bd Alexander Rawlins, whose feast-day is also kept today. He was canonized in 1970 as one of the Forty Martyrs of England and Wales.

M.M.P., pp. 218-27; J. H. Pollen (ed.), *Documents relating to the English Martyrs*, C.R.S., 5 (1908), pp. 234-5, 244-68. See also "The Forty Martyrs of England and Wales," 25 October.

BB Edward Oldcorne and Ralph Ashley, *Martyrs* (1606)

Edward Oldcorne (or Oldcorn, alias Hall) was born in York in 1561, the son of a bricklayer, John Oldcorne, and his wife, Elizabeth, who spent some time in prison for her faith. Edward went to school at St Peter's, York, and then studied medicine before going abroad. He studied for the priesthood at the English Colleges in Reims and Rome, was ordained in 1587, and became a Jesuit the following year. He worked as a priest in Worcestershire for about seventeen years, sometimes using the house of a Mr Habington at Hindlip, near Worcester, as his base. Habington's wife, Mary, was the sister of Lord Monteagle, who was to play such a pivotal role in the Gunpowder Plot of 1605. In 1601 Edward went on a pilgrimage to St Winifred's (3 Nov.) shrine at Holywell in north Wales to obtain a cure from a cancer. When this cleared up, he returned to the shrine in 1605 in thanksgiving. Given how dangerous it was for Catholics to practise their religion at that time, it is remarkable that more than thirty people took part in this second pilgrimage, including the Jesuit superior Fr Henry Garnet; two other Jesuits, Fr John Gerard and Fr Oswald Tesimond; a Jesuit lay brother, Bd Ralph Ashley; a secular priest, Fr John Percy; another lay brother, St Nicholas Owen (22 Mar.), and a number of leading laypeople, including Sir Everard Digby and his wife, Mary, whose chaplain Edward was at the time. The timing was unfortunate: the government was able to use the fact of the pilgrimage in its attempts to implicate a number of the participants in the Gunpowder Plot.

In November 1605, when the plot was uncovered, Edward was at Hindlip. He was joined there in December by Fr Garnet, Ralph Ashley, and Nicholas Owen, who were on the run because of their alleged involvement. The house was considered to be very safe because of the large number of hiding places it contained, and Edward and Fr Garnet hid in one of these while the two lay brothers hid in another. When it was searched in January 1606 the fugitives were not found, but they had to give themselves up after eight days because of the insufferable conditions they were having to endure. They were arrested and eventually taken to London, where Edward and Fr Garnet were kept in the Gatehouse prison before being transferred to the Tower. There they were both tortured, along with Ralph Ashley and Nicholas Owen. There was no evidence to connect Edward with the plot, but his friendship with Garnet (quite wrongly in government eyes the chief of the plotters) and the desire of the government to implicate as many priests, especially Jesuits, as possible, meant that he had little chance of avoiding execution. His trial took place at Redhill in Worcestershire. He was charged with being a Jesuit, giving shelter to the traitor Fr Garnet at Hindlip, and approving the plot at least after its discovery. He was found guilty on all counts, and the sentence of hanging, drawing, and quartering was carried out at Redhill on 7 April 1606. On the scaffold he prayed for the king and the royal family, forgave the judges and jury who had found him guilty, and died with the name of St Winifred on his lips. He was beatified in 1929.

Ralph Ashley was executed on the same day, also at Redhill, for the crime of aiding and abetting Fr Oldcorne in his treason. He too was beatified in 1929.

M.M.P., pp. 289-91; Foley, 4, p. 202; A. Fraser, *The Gunpowder Plot, Terror and Faith in 1605* (1996), especially pp. 213-8, 245-8. See also "The Forty Martyrs of England and Wales," 25 October.

Bd Dominic Iturrate Zubero (1901-27)

Domenico was born on 11 May 1901 at Dina in the Basque region of northern Spain. His parents were Simón Iturrate and María Zubero. He joined the Trinitarians when he was sixteen and made his religious profession a year later, taking the name Dominic of the Blessed Sacrament in religion. He then went to Rome, where he studied at the Gregorian University from 1919 to 1926 and gained a brilliant degree in philosophy and theology. He was ordained priest but fell seriously ill shortly afterwards and died on 7 April 1927 at Belmonte in Spain.

From when he was a novice he led a life of prayer and penance and as a student was known for the fervour of his piety. In 1922 he wrote in his spiritual diary, "Our conformity to the will of God must be total, constant and without reservation." In this spirit he took a vow always to do what he thought was more perfect in God's eyes; he proposed never to refuse anything to God but "to follow his holy inspiration in everything generously and joyfully." He understood the vocation of a priest to be that of an intermediary between God and human beings, and for the short time he was a priest himself regarded each Mass he said as an act of personal sacrifice in union with Christ for the good of the world. He also had a strong devotion to Mary and believed the sure way was to "go to the Son through the Mother."

The cause of his canonization was introduced in 1958 and he was beatified on 30 October 1983.

Bibl.SS., 4, 735-6; *N.S.B.* 1, pp. 216-7; Holböck 1, pp. 156-8.

8

ST JULIE BILLIART, *Foundress* (1751-1816)

Marie Rose Julie Billiart was born at Cuvilly in Picardy in 1751, the daughter of fairly prosperous parents who ran a small shop and farmed some land. Unfortunately in 1767 the family lost its money, and Julie had to take on heavy manual work to help them survive. She had already impressed the parish priest by her piety, and he had allowed her to make her First Communion at the early age of nine and to take a private vow of chastity when she was fourteen. She had started to teach catechism to the younger children and farm labourers of the parish and to visit the sick and did what she could to keep up these activities when she was working. When she was in her early twenties her life was suddenly changed when an attempt was made to wound or even kill her father: they were sitting together at home when a shot was fired through the window, and Julie was so frightened she developed a nervous paralysis that gradually prevented her from walking and caused her severe pain. The attentions of a new doctor only made her worse, and from the age of about thirty she was a complete invalid, unable even to stand. Her parish priest continued to be her spiritual director and encouraged her to carry on her catechism lessons from her bed. She developed her own apostolate, giving spiritual advice to an increasing number of people and urging frequent reception of Communion whenever possible. Some wealthy ladies began to visit her, impressed by what they had heard of her patience, holiness, and good humour. Later on she suffered such convulsions that people believed she was possessed by the devil. She ate very little and on several occasions seemed to be about to die—she was anointed five times.

When the Revolution broke out in 1789, Julie was accused of sheltering priests, of being a loyal supporter of the old Church, and of being a friend of aristocrats. Her friends smuggled her out of Cuvilly in a haycart, and she spent the next three years in hiding in Compiègne, being moved from house to house and suffering increased pain; her illness worsened to the extent that she lost the power of speech for several months. During this time she had a puzzling vision in which she saw Calvary surrounded by religious in unusual habits and heard a voice saying to her, "Behold these spiritual daughters whom I give you in an Institute marked by the cross." When the worst of the Reign of Terror was over Julie moved to Amiens, where for the first time she met a devout and well-educated aristocratic lady, Françoise Blin de Bourdon, viscountess de Gézaincourt, who was to be her companion from then on, the co-foundress of the new Institute, and her first biographer. A renewal of persecution made them move to Bettencourt, where they were able to resume teaching catechism to the villagers and where they met Fr Joseph Varin. He became a committed supporter and was convinced that Julie was being called by God to do something great for the Church. It was under his direction that, on their return to Amiens, the foundations of the Institute of Notre Dame were laid in 1803, dedicated to Christian education, the instruction of the poor, and the training of teachers. Julie and Françoise Blin were joined by two or three others, Fr Varin provided a provisional Rule and the first Sisters made their vows as religious in 1804. That was also the year of Julie's recovery from the illness that had kept her an invalid for so many years. It happened after a parish mission in the city during which the new Sisters had been preparing women to receive the sacraments. One of the priests organized a novena to the Sacred Heart to pray for Julie's recovery; during it he spoke privately to her, saying, "If you have faith, Mother, take a step in honour of the Sacred Heart." Julie found she was able to walk, something she had not done for twenty-two years.

So many new Institutes and Congregations for women were founded in the nineteenth century that it is easy to lose sight of the pioneering element in Julie's work. She did away with the traditional division between choir and lay sisters, and the Sisters would have to be free to leave their convents to work in the schools, so there could not be any enclosure. The main form of self-discipline would lie in the conscientious preparation of lessons and hard work in the classroom. Julie was aware of the problem of combining the contemplative and the active life; she wrote, "Ours is one of the most difficult of vocations because we must live an interior life in the midst of external work. But if the interior life were lost, our congregation would not last, or if it did live on it would only be an outward life by uniformity of customs. . . . If in the midst of their occupations they do not keep their hearts united to our Lord, all [the Sisters] will do will come to nothing." A young Sister reported that Julie showed them "how we might live alone with God, even in the midst of a large class of children."

After her recovery Julie spent some months helping the Fathers of the Faith in their mission work, instructing those who because of the disruptions of the Revolution had had no religious teaching. She was worried by an apparent de-Christianization of the country, and this was a principal motive for her educational work. It also explains the range of that work, for while her first interest had always been the poor, she realized that other classes in society were likewise in need of sound Christian education and that her Sisters could never hope to meet the needs by themselves. From 1804 until her death in 1816 she was constantly on the road and was responsible for a rapid expansion of the new Institute. She opened schools in nineteen centres in France and Belgium and laid down the pattern of its future work: poor schools, select day and boarding schools, vocational groups, and teacher-training centres. She and Françoise

Blin de Bourdon brought together into a fruitful merger the two traditions of French education up to that time: the insistence on basic schools for the poor and trained teachers to staff them on the one hand, and, on the other, the appreciation of a broader, more individual-centred education, found, for example, in the upper-class Ursuline schools (Linscott). The education of the poor was her first concern; she wrote: "The principal end of our Institute is the education of the poor. If we ever cease to help the poor, we shall no longer be fulfilling the work entrusted to us." No convent was to be opened unless it could meet the needs of poor people, whatever else it might be involved in.

Julie's own formal education had been limited, and she constantly referred disparagingly to her ignorance. Her other qualities more than compensated for her poor academic background, and her work endured "because it was the creation of a woman of vision, a born leader who combined the capacity for tremendous undertakings with the tranquillity of inner repose" (Linscott). Her letters show us someone who was "quick, lively and vivacious, her Gallic pungency never far from the surface, brisk in manner and ready of wit. . . . She had the kind of intellect that could grasp a situation and appreciate its implications, giving an opinion that was sound and practical . . . sane, detached and balanced" (*ibid*.).

The expansion of the Institute's work was not without difficulties. Fr Varin was replaced as chaplain by a less sympathetic priest who wanted to interfere with the Rule and who, when opposed by Julie and Françoise, turned the bishop of Amiens against them. In the end the community left the city and moved its motherhouse to Namur—hence the title Sisters of Notre Dame of Namur. Attempts were made to alienate some of the Sisters from Julie, and sometimes priests caused problems because they believed they should have more control over the convents set up in their parishes. Various circumstances led to the closing of all the convents and schools in France, and in 1815 a number of the Belgian convents were ransacked by soldiers before and after the battle of Waterloo. Julie coped with the difficulties with commonsense and a complete trust in God's providence, keeping the young Institute together by seemingly endless journeys from convent to convent, encouraging, supporting, and helping out with the teaching or the washing as the need arose. "I remember her kindness and her laughter," wrote one of the early Sisters at Namur. "She was happy and liked to see us happy too, so she used to make us laugh." For her part, Françoise dealt with officious authorities, ecclesiastical and civil, with an aristocratic sureness of touch, quiet firmness, and a conviction that Julie was doing God's work.

The foundress of one of the great teaching Congregations in the Church, Julie did not write a treatise on education or the running of schools. Her ideas have to be gathered from her letters and the conferences and instructions she gave to the Sisters, as well as from the way Françoise put those ideas into practice after her death. Basic, of course, to her views of both education and the person to be educated was Christianity. She wrote: "You are not here just to train children in science, in literature, in handwork. These things are not the essential of our work. What matters is the care of souls . . . putting children in the way of salvation," and again: "Our aim in teaching is to form good Christians who know how to manage their household, their family, their affairs." At the same time she was not content with a mere instilling of doctrine and routine practice of devotions, for she wanted to educate "the whole child: heart, hands and head" and to develop each person's natural gifts. Part of that development lay in teaching pupils how to think things out for themselves; she opposed learning by rote: "You must teach them to think. If they simply memorize and repeat, they will never understand what they are doing." It is important not to interpret these ideas in too modern a way. She was quite clear what young children should be taught: religious instruction, the three Rs, singing and needlework, a simple form of physical education, and, as a hobby, gardening. Once they had grasped the essentials they could go on to other subjects, though she was determined that "dancing and drawing, elocution and deportment masters" should never set foot in the schools: they smacked of artificiality and were in her eyes a waste of time, and for the same reasons she opposed the reading of novels. When asked to say what older children should be taught, her reply was, "Teach them whatever is necessary to equip them for life." The individual was important in her thinking and had to be allowed to develop through education, but that education was to be practical and rooted in reality: in a literal sense it had to be "education for life," as she put it. We must remember that Julie was a foundress, starting out to do what had not been done before. To this task she brought her own conviction, her ability to inspire others, and a deep spirituality. Fortunately she was also willing to experiment and shied away from being over-prescriptive: she would lay down basic principles but not dictate the detail. She wrote to one superior, "I simply will not lay down the law about such things. No, no, no, no! I will go on saying 'no' till tomorrow if you like!" On another occasion she wrote, "Go on, go on, make up your own mind this time. Better mistakes than paralysis." It is not surprising, then, that the Rule was not finalized during her lifetime. This was left to Françoise Blin, who in 1818 published it in three parts, the *Rule and Constitutions*, the *Rules of the Mistresses*, and the *Directory*. This Rule "contained nothing new for the Sisters. It had long been developing in practice and was what Mère Julie called 'the living Rule' before it reached paper. It came from the heart of the Congregation itself as an expression of its way of life and its approach to its work."

For an understanding of Julie's spirituality we are largely dependent on what others wrote about her, for she wrote nothing about it directly herself. Françoise Blin probably knew her better than anyone else, and her summary of Julie is interesting: "By hard experience, she learned detachment from created things and the truth that God alone is unchangeable. Perhaps this lesson was a necessary one, for she was sensitive and warm-hearted, and she might have tended to rely overmuch on those who met her with kindness. But her difficulties impressed on her the frailty of human help, and she leaned her full weight on God, her faithful guide and support." Julie herself, when asked to tell the Sisters what she meant by the simplicity she was always urging on them, answered: "The simple take care to look only to God and his good pleasure; they seek God in humility, confidence, and abandonment to his will; they live in joy and peace." This reliance on God and abandonment to the divine will comes out in one of her favourite prayers: "May Jesus Christ live within us, and as for me may I no longer live but for his pure and holy love. May this love consume me every instant of my life so that I may become a victim of love. Praised be Jesus Christ, praised be Mary!" The richness of her interior life is witnessed by the fact that her spiritual advice was highly valued. A local parish priest said he listened to her with "admiration and edification. This woman, who had received no education beyond that of the village school, spoke about spiritual things as a doctor or director of souls, versed in the highest spiritual wisdom . . . and with fluency and abundance." Another priest, who was her confessor for a time, wrote, "Julie's great love for poverty, her detachment from self, her submission to the divine will, her intimate union with Our Lord, who directed her every action, made her for her daughters an example of every virtue. . . . It was enough to see her, to speak with her, to be convinced that the Spirit of God directed her thoughts, her sentiments, and her whole life."

When Françoise Blin died in 1838, the new Congregation was firmly established, its philosophy and work clear, and its presence accepted and valued. It was innovative in providing education for girls from all social classes and in its stress on the need to educate the poor. It had its system of schools, both primary and secondary, and its new approach to teacher training. Julie had lived through the French Revolution and clearly hankered after much that that Revolution had destroyed. Her outstanding achievement, however, was to create something out of that past that would be flexible enough not just to endure but to develop and be able to meet the demands of the future. By the end of the nineteenth century the Sisters of Notre Dame had spread to the United States, Great Britain, Guatemala, the Congo (Democratic Republic of Congo), and Rhodesia (Zimbabwe). In the twentieth century they have spread to Japan, China, Brazil, Peru, Nigeria, and Kenya. They have lived through another revolution, one that has affected the religious life even more deeply than the one in Julie's lifetime; in this context her own words are most apposite: "There must be no looking back upon the past, no anxieties about the future—I repeat, about the future."

Julie fell ill in January 1816 and died on 8 April. Her remains were translated in 1882, and she was beatified in 1906 and canonized in 1969.

The first biography of Julie was written by Françoise Blin de Bourdon under the title, *The Memoirs of Mother Frances Blin de Bourdon*. This may have included some material written by Julie herself under obedience to Fr Varin. The *Memoirs* were circulated in MS form and only published fully in the 1970s; the English trans. was edited by Sr Mary Godfrey, Sr Julie McDonough, Sr Thérèse of the B.S., in 1975. See also Frances de Chantal, S.N.D., *Julie Billiart and her Institute* (1938); Malachy Gerard Carroll, *The Charred Wood* (1950); Sr Mary Linscott, *Quiet Revolution* (1966); Roseanne Murphy, S.N.D., *Julie Billiart, Woman of Courage* (1995); Jennifer Worrall, S.N.D., *Jubilee: the Sisters of N.D. de Namur celebrate 150 years in Britain* (1996).

The usual portrait of St Julie shows her seated before a crucifix, wearing the habit and holding a manuscript, with rays of light surrounding her head. It was probably painted after her death by one of the Sisters. Another portrait is almost identical but is without the crucifix and the rays of light; this may have been painted during her life and touched up afterwards.

St Dionysius of Corinth, *Bishop* (*c.* 170)

Dionysius was bishop of Corinth during the reign of the emperor Marcus Aurelius (121-80). He wrote a series of letters to the Churches in Athens, Nicomedia, Rome, and elsewhere, and to groups of Christians and individuals. The only fragments of these letters that have come down to us are in the *Ecclesiastical History* of Eusebius. One of these comes from a letter to the Church in Rome, at that time under the rule of St Soter (formerly 22 Apr.), pope from 166 to 175. The letter is interesting for the light it throws on the relationship between the Churches: "From the earliest times you have made it your practice to give all the brethren various kinds of gifts and to provide for the necessities of as many Churches as possible, especially those set up in individual towns. In this way you remove the want of the needy and send relief especially to those who labour in the mines. . . . Your blessed Bishop Soter is so far from falling behind his predecessors in this respect that he actually outstrips them—to say nothing of the advice and consolation which, with fatherly affection, he tenders to all who come to him. On this morning we celebrated together the Lord's Day and read your letter, even as we read the one formerly written by Clement" (presumably St Clement I, 23 Nov.). Dionysius was also concerned with the heresies dividing the Church at the time and laid the blame for these mainly on the mistaken principles of pagan philosophy. Eusebius possessed eight letters written by Dionysius and one addressed to him. These show that the bishop was consulted by his fellow-bishops in Pontus about whether they should receive into the Church all those who were converted, whatever their previous sins. Dionysius told them they should but was apparently reproached by Soter for this laxity; Dionysius replied to the pope explaining and defending his position.

There are no biographical details about him, and almost all that is known comes from Eusebius and St Jerome (30 Sept.). The Greek Church venerates him as a martyr on the grounds that he suffered a great deal for the Faith, but there is no evidence that he was martyred. His body was later translated to Rome and given to the abbey of St Denis near Paris by Pope Innocent III (1198-1216).

D.H.G.E., 14, 261-2; *D.A.C.L.*, 8, 2745-7; *Bibl.SS.*, 4, 638-9; *E.E.C.*, 1, p. 238.

St Walter of Pontoise, *Abbot* (*c.* 1030-95)

Gautier, or Walter, was born at Andainville in Picardy, in northern France, about the year 1030. He was educated in a number of places and went on to become a teacher of rhetoric and philosophy. He became a monk in the abbey of Rebais-en-Brie and was then appointed first abbot of the new monastery at Pontoise. As was customary at the time, he received his office from the king and had to do homage to him in return. It is said that Walter refused to put his hand under that of the king, placing it instead on the top and saying, "It is from God, not from your majesty, that I accept the charge of this church." Whether true or not, the story illustrates the attempts of reformers at the time to break the custom of bishops and abbots receiving their investiture from the king or lay lord. Walter was not happy as abbot, and there is some evidence that he was not suited temperamentally to rule others. He tried to escape the cares of office by leaving Pontoise secretly and taking refuge in the great abbey of Cluny, then under the rule of St Hugh (29 Apr.). His former monks discovered where he was and took him back to his abbey. He used to retire from time to time to a cell in the grounds to try to find the solitude he craved and eventually fled a second time and took up residence on an island in the river Loire near Tours; again he was forced to return. He was still detemined to get away from the cares of office if he possibly could, and on a visit to Rome asked the pope, St Gregory VII, to be relieved of his position as abbot. Gregory refused his request and ordered him to return to his abbey, where he could use the talents God had given him to best effect. Walter finally accepted this as God's will and went back to Pontoise.

He was an outspoken opponent of clerical abuses and faced opposition and violence from supporters of the secular clergy when he denounced their lack of discipline and the simony many of them had used to obtain their positions. At a council in Paris in 1092 he defended the decree of the Roman authorities that forbade people to hear Mass said by a priest living in concubinage, a decree most felt was too harsh. On one occasion he was mobbed and thrown into prison as a result of his preaching. As he grew older he increased rather than reduced his austerities and often spent whole nights in prayer in the abbey church. Almost his last act was to build a convent for a community of holy women dedicated to Our Lady at Bertaucourt. He died on Good Friday, 8 April 1095. His tomb in the abbey was claimed to be the scene of cures and other miracles, but his remains disappeared at the time of the French Revolution. He had spent much of his adult life trying to find solitude in which to concentrate on getting closer to God and had only reluctantly accepted the responsibilities that went with public office. In the end he proved to be an able administrator and outspoken reformer, both of which talents were needed by the Church of his day.

There are two early Lives: see *AA.SS.*, Apr., 1, pp. 749-64; *Bibl.SS.*, 7, 427-9. The new R.M. proposes a date of 23 March for his commemoration, but in the absence of hard evidence to justify this, his entry is left here in this edition.

Bd Julian of St Augustine (*c.* 1550-1606)

Julian Martinet was born in the Spanish town of Medinaceli. His family had fled from France to escape persecution by the Calvinists; they were descended from a long line of French knights but had fallen into poverty, and so Julian was apprenticed to a tailor. He entered a local Franciscan house to try his vocation, but the harsh austerities and unusual devotions he practised persuaded the superiors that he was mentally unstable, and so they dismissed him. He returned to his trade until he met a Franciscan priest, Fr Francis de Torrez, who was giving a parish mission in a neighbouring town. The priest was moved by Julian's devoutness and enlisted him to help with the mission. Afterwards he spoke on Julian's behalf to the superior of another Franciscan house, who agreed to take him as a novice. The result was the same: Julian's extreme religiosity caused him to be dismissed as too unstable for the religious life. Julian built himself a cell nearby and lived the life of a hermit for some years. His reputation for holiness began to spread throughout the locality and the superiors took him in again as a novice. This time he was successful and after a year was professed as a lay brother, taking as his name in religion Julian of St Augustine. He continued his extreme austerities and bodily penances, lacerating his body with various instruments and refusing to sleep in a bed, preferring to sleep leaning against a wall or in the open air. From time to time Fr Francis de Torrez called on his help during missions, and Julian was found to be remarkably eloquent and to have the gift of prophecy. When news of this reached the court he was invited to preach before the king and queen but was so tongue-tied through nervousness when he arrived that he was unable to say a word. He died in 1606. He was immediately venerated as a saint by the people, and there were reports of many miracles, but his beatification did not take place until 1825.

A popular Life by J. Vidal y Galiena was compiled in 1825 from the beatification documents. See *Vies des Saints*, 6, pp. 196-9; *Bibl.SS.*, 6, 1213-5.

9

St Waldetrude (*c.* 688)

Waldetrude (in French Waltrude, or Waudru) belonged to a family remarkable for its holiness. Her parents were St Waldebert (2 May) and St Bertilla, and her sister was St Aldegund; she married St Vincent Madelgarius (20 Sept.), and their four children were all venerated as saints: St Landericus, who became bishop of Paris; St Dentelin, who died very young; St Aldetrude, abbess of Maubeuge; and St Madelberta, also abbess of the same monastery. After the birth of their last child her husband withdrew to the abbey he had founded at Haumont and took the name of Vincent. Two years later Waldetrude also withdrew from the world and went to live in a small house in semi-solitude. Her sister invited her to join the community at Maubeuge, but Waldetrude believed she could lead a life of greater austerity outside the abbey. In the event, she was so disturbed by visitors seeking her advice that she founded her own convent at Chateaulieu in the centre of what is today the town of Mons in Belgium. She was noted for her works of mercy, and healing miracles were attributed to her before and after her death. She died about the year 688. Her cult dates from at least the ninth century, and her relics were authenticated in 1250. Her name was added to the Roman Martyrology in 1679. She is the patron of Mons, where her relics are kept in a fine fifteenth-century church built close to the original Chateaulieu.

There is a ninth-century Latin Life written by a monk of Mons in *AA.SS.*, Apr., 1, pp. 826-33. See also *Bibl.SS.*, 12, 881-2.

St Casilda (? Eleventh Century)

Casilda (or Casilla) was the daughter of al-Mamun, the emir of Toledo. She was brought up a Muslim but was known to have showed kindness to Christian prisoners. She fell ill and either did not trust the Arab doctors or failed to find a cure and so went on pilgrimage to the shrine of San Vicenzo de Briviesca in the diocese of Burgos. The shrine was famous for its healing waters, especially for those suffering from haemorrhages, and Casilda was cured. She became a Christian and led a life of solitude and penance in a cell near the miraculous spring. Eventually her name was added to that of San Vicenzo in the title of the shrine. She was said to be a hundred years old when she died, but we do not know the date of her death. Her cult was popular, and in 1750 her remains were translated to a new shrine.

The first documents we have about Casilda date from the fifteenth century. See *AA.SS.*, Apr., 1, pp. 838-41; *Bibl.SS.*, 3, 894.

St Gaucherius, *Abbot* (*c.* 1060-1140)

Gaucherius was born about the year 1060 at Meulan-sur-Seine to the north-west of Paris. He was well educated in the liberal arts and at the age of eighteen decided to devote himself to the life of a hermit. He was advised to go to the country around Limoges because it was thought that he would be more likely to find solitude there than in his native region. He and a friend named Germond found a suitably remote place and lived as hermits for several years, apparently unknown and forgotten. Gradually, however, their way of life became known, and disciples built other cells to be near them. Eventually he built a small monastery at Aureil for the community and insisted they follow the Rule of the Canons Regular of St Augustine. When he established a convent of women in the same place he also put the nuns under the Rule of the Canonesses Regular of St Augustine. Among those trained at the monastery were St Lambert of Angoulême and St Faucherus, while St Stephen of Muret, the founder of the monastery at Grandmont (8 Feb.), had also been one of Gaucherius' disciples. Gaucherius died in 1140 and was canonized in 1194, when his remains were re-buried.

Bibl.SS., 6, 45-6; *Vies des Saints*, 4, pp. 218-9.

Bd Ubald (*c.* 1245-1315)

Ubald Adimari was born in Florence of a well-to-do family. As a young man he led a rather dissolute life, enjoying his wealth and taking a leading role in the turbulent politics of the day on the side of the emperor against the pope. When he was about thirty years old he heard a sermon by St Philip Benizi (23 Aug.), who was in Florence on a peace mission, and was so moved that he gave up his military pursuits and vowed to spend the rest of his life doing penance for his past. St Philip admitted him to the Servite Order, and he was ordained priest. He became noted for his gentleness, and it was said that when he went into the monastery garden birds would perch on his head and shoulders. Miracles were attributed to him, and St Philip was so impressed by his holiness that he made him his confessor and took him on his preaching campaigns. Ubald lived most of his religious life in the Servite monastery at Monte Senario and died there on 9 April 1315. There is a sixteenth-century painting of him in the Santa Annunziata in Florence in which he is shown as an emaciated visionary. His cult was approved in 1821.

Most of what is known about Ubald comes from Lives of St Philip Benizi. See *Bibl.SS.*, 1, 252.

Bd Thomas of Tolentino, *Martyr* (*c.* 1260-1321)

Thomas of Tolentino joined the Order of Friars Minor as a young man. He was one of the followers of Angelo Clareno and the Spiritual Franciscans, whose views on absolute poverty were condemned; as a result, Thomas spent some time in prison. On his release in 1289 he was inspired by the same missionary ardour that drove the early Franciscans to spread the gospel as widely as possible. His first mission was to Armenia, where with four other Franciscans he worked successfully to strengthen the Church and convert many who had fallen into schism. At the time the country was being threatened by the Muslim Turks, and Thomas returned to Europe to raise support for a crusade against them. He was unsuccessful and so returned to Armenia to continue his preaching, this time with a group of twelve companions. He then moved farther east into Persia and planned an expedition to India and China. He was back in Europe during the reign of Pope Clement V (1305-14) and met the pope in France. As a result of his missionary reports, the pope appointed an archbishop and papal legate for the East with seven Franciscan suffragan bishops. There is a gap in the records for the years 1308 to 1320, and it is possible that Thomas was in India or China for some of this time. We know that he set out for India and China from Ormuz on the Persian Gulf in 1320 with three companions, James of Padua, Peter of Siena, and Demetrius of Tiflis, a lay brother who was their interpreter. Their ship was blown ashore near Bombay, and they were sheltered in the town of Tana by some Nestorian Christians before being arrested by the ruling Muslims. When he was brought to trial Thomas defended his Christian beliefs but also attacked Islam and Mohammed, and it was for this that he was condemned. The four were scourged and tortured and eventually beheaded. Bd Odoric of Pordenone (14 Jan.) called at Tana on his way back from China in 1326, recovered the martyr's body and later transferred it to Xaitou in China; the head was eventually taken back to Tolentino. His cult was approved in 1894; the decree mentioned only Thomas, even though all four were venerated and mentioned in early Franciscan martyrologies.

There is no early Life of Bd Thomas, but see *AA.SS.*, Apr., 1, pp. 51-6, for letters of Jordan de Severac that have details about him. See also *Anal. Franc.*, 3, pp. 474-9, 597-613, and 4, pp. 332-4; *Bibl. SS.*, 12, 587-9.

Bd Antony Pavoni, *Martyr* (*c.* 1325-74)

Antonio Pavoni was born at Savigliano in Piedmont, in northern Italy. He entered the Dominican priory there and gained such a reputation for learning, fervour, and obedience to the Church that he was appointed inquisitor general for Piedmont and Liguria in 1365. He served two terms as prior of Savigliano. The geographical position of the priory brought him into contact with the Waldensians (or Vaudois), a puritanical reformist sect that had been excommunicated. He was involved in a number of disputes with them and was responsible for some of the persecution directed against them. As a result he made many enemies. In 1374 he was invited by the bishop of Turin to preach the Lenten sermons in the area around the Val Pellice and was successful in getting some of the Waldensians to give up their errors. He was preaching in the town of Bricherasio on Low Sunday, and after Mass some armed men, believed to be Waldensians, attacked and killed him. He had apparently foretold his death the day before. His relics were translated in 1468 and since 1832 have been venerated in the Dominican church at Racconigi, where they were re-authenticated in 1965. His cult was approved in 1856.

I. Venchi, *Il beato Antonio Pavoni* (1965); Procter, pp. 85-7; *Bibl.SS.*, 10, 421-2. On the Waldensians, see *O.D.C.C.*, pp. 1714-5.

10

St Fulbert, *Bishop* (*c.* 960-1029)

Very little is known about the early life of Fulbert. He was born in Italy, apparently of poor parents, and studied at Reims in northern France, where he made a considerable impression as a distinguished scholar. When one of his teachers, Gerbert of Aurillac, became Pope Sylvester II (999-1003), he summoned Fulbert to Rome as an adviser. On Sylvester's death Fulbert returned to France and became a canon of Chartres Cathedral and chancellor of the diocese. He also took charge of the cathedral school and built up its reputation so that it became one of the most famous in Europe, developing a wide literary and philosophical programme of studies. Because of the extent of his learning he was described as a reincarnation of Socrates and Plato, and it came as no surprise when he was appointed, much against his will, to be bishop of Chartres in 1007. He used to describe himself as "the very little bishop of a very great church."

Fulbert could not avoid being involved in politics and was the counsellor of a number of leaders, including the king of France and the duke of Aquitaine. He did not, however, neglect his duties as bishop. He preached regularly and visited his diocese to try to ensure the proper instruction of the people. When his cathedral was destroyed by fire his reputation was such that he was able to gather funds from several countries, including a donation from the king of England, to rebuild it on a grander scale; the crypt of the present cathedral remains from his building. He wrote a large number of poems and hymns, including some in honour of Our Lady, to whom he had a great devotion—when his new cathedral was opened he celebrated the feast of Our Lady's birthday (8 Sept.) in it and ordered it to be celebrated from then on throughout the diocese. He preached against clerical abuses and particularly simony. He died on 10 April 1029, noted for his humility, pastoral concern, and practical charity. He was long venerated popularly as a saint, but his cult was approved officially for Chartres only in 1861. He has, perhaps, been better known for his contributions to scholarship than his sanctity.

His extant writings include poems and hymns, sermons, letters, a short penitential, and scriptural extracts about the Trinity, the Incarnation, and the Eucharist. He had learned from his teacher Gerbert how to use reasoning and dialectical argument in the study of philosophy and theology but was always careful not to allow reason too much influence in matters of faith, for the scriptures and traditions of the Fathers were also important: "He never tired of asserting that the human mind . . . should close its eyes in reverence before what it could not understand and should abandon all attempts at argument" (Knowles). His own writings were not especially original, but he was sensitive to the ways of thought that were developing at the time. He seems to have been able to attract and encourage pupils by the force of his personality, and one of these wrote a poem in his honour that likened him to "a spring dividing into many streams, or a fire throwing off many sparks, [and] so he propagated himself through his pupils in many different sciences." His direct influence on the world of learning lasted for about a century.

There is no early Life of Fulbert. His writings can be found in *P.L.*, 141, pp. 163-74; and see F. Behrends (ed. and trans.), *Letters and Poems* (1976). His Easter hymn, "Ye choirs of new Jerusalem," was included in the *Westminster Hymnal*. See also *D.T.C.*, 6, 964-7; *N.C.E.*, 6, pp. 216-7; *Bibl.SS.*, 5, 1299-1300. For background, see D. Knowles, *The Evolution of Medieval Thought* (1962).

Bd Archangelo of Calatafimi (*c.* 1390-1460)

Archangelo Placenza (or Piacentini) was born at Calatafimi in Sicily about the year 1390. As a child he was said to have been religious and retiring, and so it was not surprising that he decided to become a hermit as a young man. He quickly developed a reputation as a spiritual adviser and miracle-worker, and when crowds began to visit his cell he moved to Alcamo to live in greater solitude. He was not left in peace, however, and was asked to restore and re-organize a hospice for the poor that had decayed. When he returned to his hermitage he was soon on the move again, because the pope, Martin V, in an attempt to restore papal authority after the Great Schism, ordered all the Sicilian hermits (of whom there were a large number) to return to the world or join an approved Order.

Archangelo decided to join the Franciscan Friars Minor of the Observance and received the habit from Bd Matthew of Girgenti (21 Oct.) in their house at Palermo. He was sent to set up a new house of the Order at Alcamo, using the hospice he had restored. He lived there in great austerity according to the primitive Franciscan Rule, carrying out a very fruitful and popular preaching apostolate. He became minister provincial for Sicily and helped Bd Matthew when he was not allowed into the house at Alcamo after resigning his bishopric. Archangelo died on 10 April 1460, and his cult was approved in 1836.

A. Gioia, *Il beato Arcangelo Placenza da Calatafimi* (1926), draws on the materials collected for the confirmation of the cult. See also *Bibl.SS.*, 2, 373.

Bd Antony Neyrot, *Martyr* (*c.* 1423-60)

Antonio Neyrot was born in Rivoli in northern Italy and joined the Dominican convent of San Marco in Florence, at that time under the direction of St Antoninus (2 May). After some years Antony was sent to one of the Order's houses in Sicily. Accounts of him as a friar are not wholly complimentary: they mention that he was obedient and pious but also say that he was somewhat unsettled and fond of his pleasures. After only a year in Sicily he received permission to go to Naples and Rome, but on the way his ship was captured by pirates and he was taken prisoner to Tunis. Here he was kept in prison for a time but then released. He seems to have found the privations and difficulties of living as a Christian under Muslim rule hard to bear and after studying the Koran became a Muslim and married. He practised his new religion for several months but then decided that he had done wrong to change, sent his wife away, and resumed saying the divine office—it is said that his change of heart was due to a vision of St Antoninus. He later appeared before the ruler of Tunis in his friar's habit and proclaimed his belief that Christianity was the only true religion. Eventually he was condemned to death and executed by stoning as he prayed on his knees. Part of his remains was taken back to Italy by Genoese merchants. His cult was approved in 1767.

A reliable account of Antony's martyrdom is in a letter of 1461 to Pope Pius II from the Dominican provincial in Sicily, who had received it from an eyewitness; see *Anal. Boll.* 24 (1905), pp. 357-74, for the full text and commentary.

Bd Mark Fantuzzi (1405-79)

Pace (or Pasotto) Fantuzzi was born in Bologna of a wealthy family. He was a brilliant student and seemed cut out for a successful university career. At the age of twenty-six, however, he gave up his fortune and joined the Observant Franciscans, taking the name of Mark in religion. He became a priest and was appointed guardian of the friary at Monte Colombo. He was a successful preacher and was allowed to preach throughout Italy by St John Capistrano (23 Oct.), the vicar general of the Observants. He served two terms as minister provincial and then succeeded St John as vicar general. He was keen to enforce strict observance of the primitive Franciscan Rule and introduced a number of reforms. When the Turks captured Constantinople in 1453 Mark was asked for guidance by the Franciscans who had come under Turkish rule. He urged them to remain in their place and face whatever might happen with courage and faith. He established a convent of Poor Clares in Bologna with the help of St Catherine of Bologna (9 Mar.), who found him to be an excellent guide and confessor. Mark visited officially all the Franciscan houses in Candia, Rhodes, and Palestine and undertook long journeys to Bosnia, Dalmatia, Austria, and Poland as part of his duties. His reputation was so great that he was elected vicar general on three occasions, and Pope Paul II (1464-71) wished to make him a cardinal, but Mark fled to Sicily to avoid this. Mark was concerned throughout his life about the poor and was one of the founders of the Italian system of pawnshops (*monti di pietà*) to help them avoid exorbitant moneylenders.

The next pope, Sixtus IV (1471-84), drew up a plan to unite all the branches of the Franciscans into a single body. This would mean the strict Observants having to join with the unreformed Conventuals, and Mark was strongly opposed to a move that would undo all he had worked for. He spoke out against the scheme at the meeting called to decide the issue and, when he seemed to be losing the argument, threw down a copy of the primitive Rule and appealed to St Francis with the words, "O my seraphic father, defend your own Rule since I, miserable man that I am, cannot defend it." He then left the meeting in tears; the assembly, moved by his outburst, broke up without taking a decision and the scheme came to nothing. Mark died in 1479 while giving a Lenten mission in Piacenza. His relics were translated in 1527 and 1626, and his cult was approved in 1868.

G. Ferrini, *B. Marco Fantuzzi atleta dell'ideale francescano* (1964); C. Piana, "Documenti intorno al B. Marco Fantuzzi da Bologna," in *Studi francescani* 1 (1953), pp. 224-35. See also *Bibl.SS.*, 8, 707-8

St Michael de Sanctis (1591-1625)

Miguel Argemir was born at Vich in Catalonia in 1591. While still young he was inspired by the stories of St Francis told by his mother and wanted to become a Franciscan, but when his parents died he was apprenticed to a merchant and had to be content with whatever devotions he could fit into a busy working life. He attended the divine office whenever he could and recited the Little Office of Our Lady daily. Eventually his master allowed him to join the Trinitarian friars in Barcelona in 1603, and he made his vows at the monastery of Saint Lambert at Zaragoza in 1607, taking the name Michael de Sanctis in religion.

About this time Bd John Baptist of the Conception (14 Feb.) was leading a reform movement among the Trinitarians and set up a new discalced Congregation devoted to a stricter observance of the Rule. Michael was attracted by the possibilities it offered for greater austerities; he joined the novitiate in Madrid and was professed in 1609. Later on he studied at Seville and Salamanca and was ordained priest. Despite his youth he was twice elected superior of the Trinitarian house in Valladolid, setting a high standard of religious observance and stressing in particular devotion to the Blessed Sacrament. He had a strong sense of the supernatural, and this governed all his actions as a priest. He experienced ecstasies while saying Mass and was reported to have worked a number of miracles. Outside the monastery his preaching and pastoral work gained him a reputation for holiness, and he was highly regarded by Philip III and his court. He died on 10 April 1625 and was canonized in 1862. He wrote a short devotional treatise entitled *The Peace of the Soul*, which was published after his death. We also have a poem of his on the spiritual life, a few letters, and some other short writings. Compared to the writings of the great Spanish mystics St Teresa of Avila (15 Oct.) and St John of the Cross (24

Nov.), these writings have little that is original to say about prayer and the spiritual life, but they reveal Michael's own deep mysticism based on his intimate and practical love of God.

A Romano, *Vita di S. Michele dei Santi* (1925); A. de la Asunción, *Opúsculos de S. Miguel de los Santos* (1915); *Bibl.SS.*, 9, 449-50; *Vies des Saints*, 4, 236-8; *Dict.Sp.*, 10 (1980), 1192-3.

St Magdalen of Canossa, *Foundress* (1774-1835)

Maddalena Gabriella di Canossa was born of a wealthy family in Verona, northern Italy, in 1774. Her father died five years later, and Magdalen and her four brothers were abandoned by their mother when she married again. The young girl had an unhappy childhood, as she was brought up by a French governess who did not understand her. When she was fifteen she survived a very serious illness and soon afterwards declared her intention of becoming a nun, much to the horror of her family, who were hoping for an advantageous marriage for the beautiful and attractive Magdalen.

In 1791 she tried her vocation with the Carmelites but left after a short time because she felt the strict rules of enclosure would prevent her assisting and instructing those in need. For a number of years she administered the family estates while at the same time giving what time she could to the care of poor girls in the city who were in danger. Her relatives thought such work was beneath her and tried to stop her doing it, but her usual reply was, "Should the fact I was born a marquess prevent me serving Jesus Christ in his poor?" She was concerned to do away with every kind of poverty, economic as well as moral. As this apostolate developed, she worked with the sick in hospitals and in their homes, bought copies of the catechism for use in the local churches, organized retreats, helped delinquent and abandoned girls, gave alms and food to those who called daily at her door, and visited those who lived in dilapidated cottages and hovels. Letters from her spiritual director at this time show that she was seriously troubled by scruples and a fear of damnation for not following God's will. In the end, her spiritual director advised her to devote herself wholly to the practical apostolate she had already started.

She began in 1799 by lodging two poor girls in her own house; by 1802 she had a permanent refuge and school near the church of St Zeno in the poorest and most notorious part of the city. She recruited a number of teachers and outlined a form of religious life for them, but very few were willing to stay for long. She was still looking after two elderly uncles at home; when they died she at last felt free to start what she called "a big project: an institution where one could instill a true spirit of union with God and at the same time detachment from everything, while engaging in all those works of charity suitable to the circumstances." In 1808 she obtained permission to take over the buildings of a suppressed Augustinian monastery. This allowed her to follow what she increasingly saw as her true vocation, "to serve Christ in the poor." The school flourished and provided a large number of girls with a practical training in housework and handicrafts as well as basic literacy and numeracy and, of course, religious instruction. This was the beginning of the Congregation of the Daughters of Charity, also known as the Canossian Sisters of Charity. Magdalen opened a second house in Venice at the request of two priests who had started a similar school for boys, and in 1812 she drew up the definitive version of the Rule of the new Congregation. In 1816 she obtained provisional papal approval from PiusVII while he was passing through Piacenza on his way back to Rome after his French exile. In the same year she opened a house in Milan and in 1820 one in Bergamo. Eight years later she was in Rome to obtain final approval for the Congregation from Leo XII. Further houses were opened in Trento, Brescia, and Cremona. For a long time she had wanted to set up a Congregation of priests and lay brothers to share in her work, and she cooperated for a time with Antonio Rosmini, the founder of the Institute of Charity (the Rosminians). Eventually, in 1831, she founded the Institute of the Sons of Charity with the help of a Venetian priest and two laymen. One of her most far-sighted initiatives was to set up a training scheme for rural teachers. Young women from rural areas could obtain a diploma that authorized them to teach in primary schools after a seven-month course spent in one of the Congregation's houses. During the course they learned how to teach and also received a spiritual and apostolic formation along Canossian lines.

Magdalen died on 10 April 1835 in Verona. Her life illustrated perfectly her words to her Sisters: "The Religious Life is only the Gospel translated into practice." Her interior life included mystical experiences that she tried to describe in her *Memoirs*: while at prayer, she wrote, "I felt at a certain point as if enraptured in God. I saw him within me like a luminous sun and was absorbed by the Divine Presence to the point that I was unable to stay on my feet and had to lean against something; the strength of heavenly joy was almost suffocating me." At other times she suffered spiritual dryness and temptations: "During this time, with regard to the spirit, as I was not able to pray, I went through a period of spiritual boredom, weariness and temptation especially against faith. I could not find relief in anything nor did anything interest me, be it temporal or spiritual. In the midst of weariness and boredom I knew I could rise above it only when I found the Lord. After several days I began to find him in Holy Communion." She had a special devotion to Christ crucified and to Our Lady of Sorrows, who she believed had become "Mother of Charity beneath the Cross"; she told her Sisters, "Be happy . . . after having experienced Mary's help on so many occasions, how can you be worried or afraid?" It was the universal love shown by Christ on the cross that inspired her to love and help everyone: "In the poor, the sick and those who suffer she always saw Christ crucified. Her own life could be well summed up in these words: 'God alone and Jesus Crucified'" (Pollonara). Her cause was introduced in 1877; she was beatified in 1941 and canonized in 1988. Her remains are preserved in an urn in the chapel of the convent of San Giuseppe in Verona.

A very large number of her letters have survived and been published, as well as a collection of spiritual writings and drafts of the Rule. Under obedience to her directors she wrote a series of notes on her spiritual life that have been published as memoirs; they chart her spiritual progress and provide an insight into the life and work of a remarkable foundress but are not an autobiography. They were originally written in the third person, but modern editions have altered them to read in the first person.

Her Congregations continue her work. The Sisters are currently active in twenty-one countries, with about four thousand members in four hundred houses. The male Institute did not flourish for many years after the foundress' death and existed only in the house in Venice; it now has about two hundred priests and lay brothers working in Italy, Brazil, and the Philippines.

Her memoirs were edited with a commentary by Elda Pollonara, F.d.C.C., in 1988 and published in English as *St Magdalene of Canossa, Memoirs: A contemplative in action* (1988). For her letters and other writings, see Emilia Dossi (ed.), *Epistolario*, 8 vols. (1977-83), and *Regole e scritti spirituali*, 2 vols. (1984-5). See also T. M. Piccari, *Sola con Dio solo* (1966); Elda Pollonara, F.d.C.C., *The Path of Identification with Christ Crucified* (1982); A. Cattari, *Maddalena Gabriella di Canossa* (1984); D. Barsotti, *Dio solo e Gesù Crocifisso* (1985); Modesto Giacon, *Magdalene of Canossa, Humility in Charity* (1988; Eng. trans. by Irene Steinmetz-Crisanti from original Italian).

There is a striking contemporary portrait of the fifteen-year-old Magdalen as a fashionable society beauty painted by Dalla Rosa of Verona. In the convent of San Giuseppe in Verona there is a fresco in the vault of the chapel showing Magdalen being taken up on clouds to heaven; this was executed by Pegrassi in 1949. Visitors to Venice can see a large commemorative plaque just outside the main railway station marking her foundation of the Institute of the Sons of Charity and her educational initiatives in the city.

11

ST STANISLAUS OF CRACOW, *Bishop and Martyr* (*c.* 1030-79)

Stanislaus was born at Szczepanow in Poland about the year 1030, the son of parents of the knightly class. He was educated at Gnesen and, possibly, Liège before being ordained priest and becoming a canon at Cracow Cathedral. He was appointed bishop of Cracow in 1072 and proved to be a successful reformer of his clergy, keen preacher, and generous patron of the poor in the city. At first he had the full support of the king, Boleslaus II, but later became involved in a quarrel with him that led to his death. The reasons for the dispute, however, are not clear. Some nineteenth-century historians accused the bishop of treason for plotting against the king and argue that his subsequent death was a political execution and not a martyrdom; this seems to be unlikely. The more traditional account is that Stanislaus tried to get the king to reform his immoral behaviour and stop the unjust way he was treating his subjects. In the end Stanislaus excommunicated him when he refused. The king in his anger decided to do away with the awkward bishop and ordered his guards to kill him as he took refuge in the chapel of St Michael outside the city. When the guards refused to enter the chapel the king did so and killed Stanislaus himself. The pope, St Gregory VII (25 May), put the whole country under an interdict until Boleslaus fell from power. The saint's relics were moved in 1088 to the cathedral in Cracow, and his cult was strong in Poland and neighbouring countries; he was canonized in 1253. He is patron of Poland, where a large number of churches were dedicated to him; there are also a substantial number in the United States in places where Polish immigrants settled.

His feast-day used to be 7 May, and early Lives are in *AA.SS.*, May, 2, pp. 200-80. See also *O.D.S.*, pp. 440-1; *Bibl.SS.*, 11, 1362-7, has a discussion of the reasons why the saint was killed.

St Barsanuphius (*c.* 550)

Barsanuphius was an Egyptian by birth who lived in a monastery in Gaza in Palestine that had been founded at the end of the fifth century by a monk named Seridos. Later Barsanuphius retired to live as a hermit but kept in touch with the monastery. He led an austere life and gained a reputation for holiness and wisdom, so that he was consulted by people from every walk of life. He refused to communicate with these visitors directly and dealt with them in writing through Seridos, who acted as his secretary. He rarely left his cell and was reputed not to eat or talk; he became known as the "Grand Old Man." Some of the requests for advice were passed on to another hermit who lived nearby, known as John the Prophet

Very little is known about Barsanuphius' life, and his Acts are completely unreliable, but he was very influential because of his writings and is a key figure in our understanding of the spirituality of the time. There are about 850 letters extant, and while probably only half of these are definitely attributable to Barsanuphius, they can be taken together as a coherent and unique record, for the others were written by John, and the two men differed only marginally from each other. The collection of letters remained popular because they gave concise and yet sensitive answers to precise questions and did not just repeat traditional teaching in broad terms; it has been said that their counsel was excellent for incorporation into monastic Rules for this reason. Both writers relied on the scriptures and the sayings of the Desert Fathers and advised against speculative works on theology or mysticism. They taught that prayer, of course, was most important in making spiritual progress, and stressed the need to develop a constant awareness of God's presence even when occupied in worldly affairs: through prayer union with God was achievable by everyone. A regular daily examination of conscience and an honest discussion of one's recurring thoughts with a director were also considered necessary if humility and abandonment to the divine will were to develop. The most important of the virtues were humility and obedience to God, and "obedience is this: not to be free to decide for oneself. What can be more precious than the soul, which the Saviour has said is worth more than the whole world? If, then, you have put that in the hands of God and your spiritual fathers, why do you hesitate to hand over to them what is less important? . . . He who is a true disciple obeys his abbot even unto death."

The Greek Church held Barsanuphius in such high regard that it placed his icon next to those of St Ephraem (9 Jun.) and St Antony (17 Jan.) in the church of Santa Sophia in Constantinople. He was an important influence on other spiritual writers such as St Dorotheus the Younger (5 Jan.), St Dositheus (23 Feb.), St Theodore the Studite (11 Nov.), and St John Climacus (30 Mar.).

Biographical information is in Evagrius' *Ecclesiastical History*, 4, 33, and the *Life of St Dositheus*. For the letters, see L. Regnault, P. Lemaire, and B. Outtier, *Barsanuphe et Jean de Gaza, Correspondance* (1972), and D. Chitty (ed. and trans.), "Barsanuphius and John, Questions and Answers," in *Patrologia Orientalis*, 31, pt. 3 (1966). See also *Dict. Sp*, 1, 1255-62; *Coptic Encyclopedia*, 2, p. 348; L. Regnault, *Maîtres spirituels au désert de Gaza* (1967).

St Guthlac (c. 674-714)

Guthlac was related by blood to the royal house of Mercia. As a young man he led a band of companions in what is usually referred to as a military career but may be more honestly described as a way of life devoted to robbery with violence. Almost all his fighting took place along the Welsh border, and he gathered "immense booty" from these operations. He obviously gained fame as a leader, for his followers came from far afield. After about nine years of this he changed his ways and became a monk at the monastery of Repton in Derbyshire. His Life tells us he was not popular with his fellow-monks because of his extreme asceticism and his refusal to drink any alcohol. Two years after becoming a monk he felt called to a life of solitude and sought a suitably isolated place to live as a hermit. He was told of a spot in the Fens that was so dismal and haunted by evil spirits and monsters that no one dared to live there. After seeing the place, an island in the undrained marshes called Crowland, he retired there about the year 699 with a few companions and lived out the rest of his life as a hermit. He tried to follow the pattern of life established centuries before by the Desert Fathers, taking St Antony (17 Jan.) as his chief model. As well as suffering interior trials and temptations he was attacked by what he called monsters but were probably descendants of the Britons who had fled to the Fens at the time of the Saxon invasions. Despite the isolation, he became famous for his austerities and gift of prophecy and received increasing numbers of visitors. One of these was Hedda, bishop of Lichfield, who ordained him, and another was Aethelbald, the future king of Mercia. His biographer says no one ever saw him angry, excited, or sad. Guthlac foretold the day of his death and invited his sister, St Pega, who was also living a hermit's life in the Fens, to attend his funeral.

His tomb became a place of pilgrimage, especially after Ceolnoth, archbishop of Canterbury, claimed to have been cured of malaria there in 851. At least nine ancient churches and a priory were dedicated to him. His remains were translated in 1136 to a new shrine in Crowland abbey, built a long time after his death on the site of his cell, and he must be reckoned England's most popular pre-Conquest hermit after St Cuthbert (20 Mar.). It must be admitted, however, that a number of incidents in the Life by Felix are closely modelled on episodes in the life of St Antony the Hermit and on Bede's Life of St Cuthbert.

For the Life written by the monk Felix, between 730 and 740, see B. Colgrave (ed.), *Felix's Life of St Guthlac* (1956). See also J. Roberts, "An Inventory of Early Guthlac Materials," in *Medieval Studies* 32 (1970), pp. 193-233; *O.D.S.*, pp. 220-1; *O.D.C.C.*, pp. 608-9. For the Guthlac Roll, see G. F. Warner's facsimile ed., *The Guthlac Roll* (Roxburghe Club, 1928).

A unique pictorial record of his life exists in the British Museum: called the Guthlac Roll, it is a vellum roll with seventeen and a half pictures or roundels, each about six inches across, showing scenes from his life and dating from the second half of the twelfth century. It was probably made for the abbot of Crowland, and the roundels may have been sketches for stained-glass windows. A sculpture in Crowland Abbey shows the saint holding a whip and with a serpent at his feet.

Bd Lanvinus, *Abbot* (*c.* 1120)

Lanvinus (Lanuin) was born in Normandy. About the year 1090 he entered the Grande Chartreuse under St Bruno (6 Oct.) and accompanied the latter when he moved to Calabria in southern Italy. St Bruno died in 1101, and Lanvinus was elected as his successor to rule the two charterhouses that had been opened in Italy. There had been a disupute about the election, and the pope, Paschal II, had become involved; he congratulated the monks on the peaceful solution of the matter and on their choice of Lanvinus. In 1102 the new superior was summoned to Rome to attend a synod, and this was the beginning of a life divided between the seclusion of the charterhouse and involvement in public affairs of the Church—as St Bruno himself had been involved and as was to become a special Carthusian characteristic. Two years later the pope was praising him for the way he had carried out his injunctions and entrusting to his care delicate negotiations with one of the local bishops. In 1108 the pope appointed Lanvinus visitor of all the monastic houses in Calabria and gave him the task of restoring them to strict observance of their Rules. Finally, Lanvinus was in Rome again in 1113 to obtain from Paschal a papal letter protecting the Carthusian foundations from interference. He was noted for his energy and administrative ability. He put into practice St Bruno's ideals and was an important figure in the establishment of the new Order, winning the favour and patronage of the Normans in southern Italy. He died on 11 April 1120 and was buried in the same tomb as St Bruno. There is some doubt about the year of his death, as the martyrology of the southern Italian charterhouse, our oldest evidence, gives it as 1116. His cult was approved in 1893. The Carthusians keep his feast on 14 April.

Bibl.SS., 7, 1116-7; *Catholicisme*, 6, 1813-4.

St Celsus, *Bishop* (1079-1129)

Celsus (in Gaelic, Ceallach mac Aedha, or Cellach mac Aodh) became archbishop of Armagh in 1105. Nothing about his life before then is known except that he belonged to a family that had held the hereditary right to the archbishopric for eight generations and had been elected to the post while still a layman, as had become customary. He was then aged twenty-six. He was ordained and turned out to be a keen reformer, a "worthy and God-fearing man," in the words of St Bernard (20 Aug.). He carried out a number of visitations, restored clerical discipline, defended the rights of his see, and established its position as the primatial see by his journeys around the country and visits to other dioceses. In 1111 he and the papal legate Gilbert of Limerick presided over a great synod at Rath Bresail, called to impose discipline on the Irish Church. New regulations about the liturgy were laid down, simony was condemned, laypeople were forbidden to control appointments to church posts, and a proper diocesan and metropolitan structure was imposed on the

Irish dioceses to bring them into line with the rest of Europe. These measures were not popular, and Celsus needed all his determination as a committed reformer to carry them through. He also faced opposition from several of the great families who wanted his lands and was often called on to act as peacemaker between the warring clans. He is said to have restored Armagh Cathedral at his own expense, founded schools, and introduced the reformed Augustinian Canons Regular into Ireland.

He had strong support from St Malachy (3 Nov.), whom he appointed as archdeacon of Armagh and later bishop of Connor in 1124. Before Celsus died in 1129 he named Malachy as his successor and so broke the hereditary hold that his own family had had on the archbishopric, although it was not until 1137 that Malachy was recognized throughout Ireland. Malachy continued Celsus' reforming efforts, and together the two archbishops may be regarded as important figures in the Gregorian reform movement, which was altering the Church throughout Europe in that period. Celsus may well have been the greater of the two, but Malachy had the advantage of having his Life written by St Bernard. Celsus died at Ard Patrick in 1129 and was buried at Lismore in present-day County Waterford.

The Lives of St Malachy are our main source for Celsus; St Bernard's Life is in *P.L.*,132, 1086, and see H. S. Lawlor, *St Bernard of Clairvaux's Life of St Malachy* (1920). See also *D.N.B.*, 9, p. 418; *The Irish Saints*, pp. 62-71; *Bibl.SS.*, 3, 1118-9.

Bd George Gervase, *Martyr* (1569-1608)

George Gervase (or Jervis) was born at Bosham in Sussex in 1569. He was apparently brought up a Protestant, though he might have been brought up a Catholic and later left the Church for a time, since his mother came from a recusant family and was related to Bd Edward Shelley of Sussex (30 Aug.), while his brother Henry was also a committed Catholic. Challoner says that George was captured by pirates as a teenager and spent about twelve years in the West Indies. He seems to have served with Sir Francis Drake in his unsuccessful expedition of 1595 to the West Indies, perhaps as a "pressed" man. On his return he served as a soldier in Flanders, this time in the Spanish army (another sign that he was a Catholic at heart), until in 1599 he entered the English College in Douai to study for the priesthood. He was ordained a secular priest at Cambrai in 1603 and the following year was sent to England.

He worked as a priest in various parts of the country for about two years before being arrested in 1606. After a spell in prison he and a number of other priests were banished from England by royal decree. He returned to Douai and from there went on pilgrimage to Rome,, where he decided to become a religious. Challoner says he offered himself to the Jesuits but was turned down, but this seems unlikely in the circumstances. The Benedictines had just opened a new house, St Gregory's, in Douai, and it appears that George became a novice there and received the habit from the prior general, Dom Austin

Bradshaw. In any case, he was back in England in 1607, worked in London, but avoided arrest for only two months. He was imprisoned in the Gatehouse at Westminster and tried at the Old Bailey. He refused to take the Oath of Allegiance that had been drawn up at the request of King James I and accepted by some of the English clergy, because it had been condemned in Rome, but professed his loyalty to the king. When asked whether he believed the pope had the power to depose civil rulers, he replied, "I say that the pope can depose kings and emperors when they deserve it." He freely admitted that he was a priest and was condemned to death on that score and for refusing to take the oath. He probably made his final religious vows shortly before his execution, and this may explain Challoner's statement that he became a Benedictine secretly in England. He was hanged, drawn, and quartered at Tyburn on 11 April 1608. He was the proto-martyr of the Benedictine house of St Gregory's, Douai. Both the Benedictines and the seculars claimed him as their martyr and published woodcuts of him dressed accordingly.

The trial is very well documented; see B. Camm, *Nine Martyr Monks* (1931), for a full account. See also *M.M.P.*, pp. 294-6; Anstruther, 2, pp. 128-9.

St Gemma Galgani (1878-1903)

Gemma Galgani was born in Borgo Nuovo di Camigliano, near Lucca in Tuscany, in 1873. Her mother died when Gemma was eight, and in 1897, when her father died, she went to live with Cecilia Giannini, who looked after her and treated her as an adopted daughter. She wanted desperately to join the Passionist Sisters, but her health was poor and she was unable to do so. Her health had caused problems from childhood; she suffered from a number of illnesses and especially tuberculosis of the spine. For a time she seemed to have been cured after an apparition of St Gabriel Possenti (27 Feb.), a Passionist to whom Gemma had a particular devotion and who had died when only twenty-four from tuberculosis. A different account attributes the cure to the intercession of St Margaret Mary Alacoque (16 Oct.). The disease recurred, however, and she died after a protracted and painful illness on 11 April 1903, aged twenty-five. She was canonized in 1940. Her remains are enshrined in the Passionist church in Lucca.

Those who knew her well had no doubts about her sanctity, and the publication in 1941 of over 230 of her letters to her spiritual director and her confessor show us a candid and pious young woman, generous in her response to God's love, humble and obedient to her directors, and willing to suffer everything in imitation of Christ's passion. There is a remarkable spontaneity about the letters, and there is nothing that could be dismissed as conventional piety. Toward the end of her life she seems to have had a constant awareness of the presence of God. What caused concern at the time and have been a controversial issue ever since were the extreme physical and psychical phenomena she experienced. The events themselves are well documented and their existence is not open to doubt. Regularly between June 1899 and February 1901 her body showed the stigmata, or signs of Christ's wounds, between Thursday evening and Friday afternoon, and sometimes also wounds that seemed to replicate those of Our Lord's scourging; these latter were very similar to those depicted on her crucifix. She had frequent ecstasies, during which she would often be heard talking to people in her visions. On some occasions she sweated blood when she heard blasphemous language. Sometimes, however, she appeared to be possessed by the devil and on one occasion spat on the crucifix and broke a pair of rosary beads. Not surprisingly, some people at the time thought she was suffering from chronic hysteria, but the level-headedness of her letters and her normal state of calm peace seem to argue against such a judgment. Her confessor and her spiritual director were themselves divided on the issue. Neither accepted the phenomena easily or credulously, but Father Germano, her director and first biographer, was more willing to see them as a divine confirmation of her sanctity, while Bishop Volpi, her confessor, remained sceptical and wanted more examination of Gemma by independent witnesses. He made the general point that it was not always clear with the saints when God stopped talking to them and their own imagination took over, and it would be difficult, he believed, to accept that everything in Gemma's experiences came from God. It is recognized today that it would be quite possible to have a mixture of causes of such phenomena, and that some of them might have been the result of Gemma's illnesses, others to have been psychosomatic, and still others to have no natural explanation. It is interesting that the decree declaring her Blessed in 1933 went out of its way to say it was not passing judgment on the strange phenomena and that her virtues were heroic in their own right. What strikes a modern reader of her letters is her good humour and commonsense, along with an intense piety flowing from her love of God and her appreciation of Christ's suffering for us.

For the saint's writings see the volumes published by the Passionists in Rome: *Lettere di S. Gemma Galgani* (1941), and subsequent volumes in 1943 and 1958; an English trans., *Letters of St Gemma Galgani*, was published in 1947. See also P. Germano, *Estasi, diario, autobiografia, scritti vari di S. G. G.* (1943). There are numerous Lives and studies; see G. de Guibert, S.J., "A Proposito delle Lettere di S.G.G.," in *La Civiltà Cattolica*, 92 (Nov. 1941), pp. 199-205; P. Germano, *Santa Gemma Galgani* (10th ed., 1949); L. Proserpio, *Saint Gemma Galgani* (1940); Sister St Michael, *Portrait of St Gemma, a stigmatic* (1950), with plentiful extracts from the letters; E. Zoffoli, *La Povera Gemma, Saggi critici storico-teologici* (1957), and his article in *Bibl.SS.*, 6, 105-8; *N.C.E.*, 6, pp. 248-9. On physical phenomena and the saints, see H. Thurston, S.J., *The Physical Phenomena of Mysticism* (1952).

12

St Julius I, *Pope* (352)

Julius was elected pope in 337. Most of his pontificate was taken up with doctrinal disputes between the Arians, who denied the true divinity of Jesus, and the orthodox. In these disputes Julius was a staunch supporter of orthodoxy and in particular of the decrees of the Council of Nicaea (325), and he upheld the rights of St Athanasius (2 May) and Marcellus of Ancyra when they were ejected from their sees by Arian sympathizers. In 340 he held a synod at Rome that cleared the deposed bishops of any heresy and wrote a masterly letter to the Eastern Churches to tell them of the decision. He also rebuked them for their attempts to condemn bishops without reference to the episcopal body as a whole and for ignoring the accepted right of Rome to be consulted in such matters. When this failed to end the quarrels, Julius asked the two emperors (of Rome and Constantinople) to call a general council at Sardica (Sofia) in 342 or 343. The Arian bishops withdrew from the council, however, when the pope insisted on Athanasius and Marcellus being present and excommunicated the leading Western bishops, including Julius. The council vindicated Athanasius and Marcellus, condemned their Arian opponents, and decreed that deposed bishops had a right of appeal to the pope.

Julius was undoubtedly a person of forceful character, and his two surviving letters show his statesmanship. Not very much is known about his other acts as pope, but he may have been responsible for setting up a papal chancery along imperial lines. He had two new churches built in Rome, Santa Maria in Trastevere and the Julian Basilica (now the church of the Holy Apostles). He died on 12 April 352 and was buried in the cemetery of Calepodius on the Via Aurelia. His name was included in the Roman Calendar of 354.

The two letters are in Athanasius' *Apologia*; see *P.L.*, 8, 857-944. See also H. Hess, *The Canons of the Council of Serdica* (1958); *N.C.E.*, 8, pp. 51-2; *O.D.C.C.*, p. 767, and especially *O.D.P.*, pp. 29-30; E. Duffy, *Saints and Sinners: A History of the Popes* (1997), pp. 23-4.

St Zeno, *Bishop* (c. 371)

There is evidence from his writings that Zeno may have been born in Africa. He received a good classical education and seems to have become bishop of Verona in northern Italy in 362. We learn from a collection of his sermons, or discourses to his people, that he baptized a large number of people every year and was successful in winning back to orthodoxy the Arians in his diocese. He praised his people for their generosity to the poor and strangers, a generosity that was later attributed to Zeno's own good example. He himself lived a life of poverty. He seems to have been active in training priests to work in the diocese and was also responsible for setting up a convent under his own direction for consecrated women. He reformed the abuses that had become a scandal in the celebration of the *agape*, or communal meal held in connection with the Eucharist, and forbade the interruption of funeral Masses by loud groans and wailing. In his writings he refers to other practices such as adult baptism by complete immersion and the giving of special medals to the newly baptized. He built a basilica in Verona, but this was replaced by a larger building erected in the ninth century in his honour to house his relics, which are still preserved there in the crypt. He died about the year 371.

Zeno is given the title "martyr" in some early martyrologies and by St Gregory (3 Sept.) in his *Dialogues*, but St Ambrose (7 Dec.), a contemporary of Zeno, speaks of the bishop's happy death, and early records in Verona name him as a confessor. He may have suffered persecution under the emperors Constantius II (351-61) and Julian (361-3), but there was no active persecution at the time of his death.

There are about ninety of his sermons or discourses extant. Thirty of these are complete, the rest are in summary or draft form. Many of them deal with Old Testament exegesis and have a definite anti-Semitic element in them; others deal with moral issues, while a small number deal with doctrine and show Zeno to have been fully orthodox in his theology.

There is no early Life of Zeno. For his writings see *P.L.*, 11, 10-527, and *Corpus Christianorum, series Latina*, 22 (1971). See also *E.E.C.*, 2, pp. 884-5; *Bibl.SS.*, 12, 1477-9; *Studi Zenoniana in occasione del XVI centenario della morte di San Zeno* (1976).

The famous eleventh-century bronze doors of the church of St Zeno in Verona have a head of the saint wearing a mitre. In art he is usually represented with a fishing-rod, from the end of which hangs a fish, or with fish hanging from his crozier. Local tradition says the bishop was fond of fishing in the nearby river Adige, but it is more likely that originally it was a symbol of his success in bringing people to baptism.

St Sabas the Goth, *Martyr* (372)

In 370 the ruler of the Goths in what is nowadays Romania began a persecution against his Christian subjects. The Greek Church venerates fifty-one Gothic martyrs from this period, the best known of whom are Sabas and St Nicetas (15 Sept.). The Christians were ordered to eat meat that had been offered to idols, and a subterfuge seems to have been agreed between them and some of the authorities to substitute other food for the meat so that they could claim to have obeyed the decree. Sabas refused to take part in the deception and publicly denounced those who had done so. He was exiled but soon allowed to return, only to be involved in further controversy with his fellow-Christians when he refused to agree to a statement sworn by the complacent officials that there were no Christians in the town: "Let no one swear for me," he announced, "I am a Christian!" He seems to have escaped punishment, and the two episodes show how reluctant local officials sometimes were to persecute their fellow-citizens in politically-motivated persecutions. When the persecution was renewed in 372, however, Sabas was arrested by soldiers sent in from another region and eventually executed by drowning. The place of his martyrdom was probably Targoviste, north-west of Bucharest.

The Greek Acts are largely reliable; see H. Delehaye, *Anal.Boll.* 31 (1924), pp. 216-21, 288-91. See also *Bibl.SS.*, 11, 531-3.

Bd Angelo of Chivasso (*c.* 1410-95)

Angelo Carletti was born in Chivasso in Piedmont about the year 1410. Early accounts say that he was educated at the university of Bologna, where he gained a doctorate in civil and canon law, but his name is not in the registers of the time. On his return home he became a senator and lived a life devoted to public duties, prayer, and visiting the sick, until his mother died, when he gave away his wealth and joined the Franciscan Observants in Genoa. After ordination to the priesthood he taught for a time and then was sent to the remote mountain areas of Piedmont to preach to the villagers. He developed a special apostolate to the poor, helping them both spiritually and materially; like his fellow-Franciscan and contemporary, Bd Mark Fantuzzi (10 Apr.), he was involved in setting up the Italian style of pawnshops to help them avoid the moneylenders. His reputation spread, and he was consulted by St Catherine of Genoa (15 Sept.) and chosen as confessor by the duke of Savoy. He wrote a manual of moral theology that became known as the *Summa Angelica*. This became extremely popular and went into at least thirty editions. It was a collection of cases of conscience and was liked because it was concise and clear in its treatment. Luther burned it publicly in 1520 along with St Thomas Aquinas' *Summa* because it was for him a symbol of all that was wrong with late medieval penitential practice. Angelo also wrote a treatise on the duty of restitution and a brief exposition of the papal letters of Sixtus IV, and he may have written or at least inspired some of the works attributed to St Catherine of Genoa. Angelo served four terms as vicar general of the Observants, as well as holding other offices. His concern as superior was to uphold the original Rule of St Francis.

After the capture of Otranto by the Turks in 1480 Pope Sixtus IV appealed for support for another Crusade against them and appointed Angelo legate to lead the preaching and the negotiations with the European rulers. His crusading spirit was evident again some years later when, in 1491, he accepted the post of commissary apostolic to preach to the Waldensians, a puritanical reformist sect that had been condemned as heretical. He showed great zeal and an indifference to physical danger and was successful in winning back many of the heretics as well as in bringing large numbers of lapsed Catholics back to the Faith. As a result, Pope Innocent VIII wished to make him a bishop, but Angelo refused. At last, in 1493, he was able to give up all public duties and retire to a more solitary life, his only outside work being to beg for the poor. His last two years were spent at the convent of Cuneo in Piedmont, where he died on 12 April 1495. His cult was approved in 1753.

C. Pellegrino, *Vita del beato Angelo Carletti* (1888). See also *D.T.C.*, 1, 1271-2, on his *Summa*, and *Bibl.SS.*, 1, 1235-7.

St Joseph Moscati (1880-1927)

Giuseppe Moscati was born into an old aristocratic family in Benevento, east of Naples, on 25 July 1880. His father, Francesco, was a judge and the president of the bench in the town. During Joseph's early childhhood the family moved first to Ancona and then to Naples as Francesco was promoted. Despite these disruptions Joseph did extemely well at school, and in 1897, the year of his father's death, he entered the faculty of medicine in the university of Naples. It was an unsettling place at the time, with disputes between those faculties which had adopted a materialistic, positivist approach and those with a more religious, Thomist approach, but Joseph managed to avoid the pitfalls and kept his religious faith alive. In 1903 he was awarded a congratulatory degree and his thesis was published. As soon as his studies were finished he was taken on at one of the local hospitals, but in 1904 he moved to that of Santa Maria del Popolo, known locally as the *Incurabili*. It was here, as he organized the treatment of rabies sufferers, that he found his mission in life.

Joseph saw medicine as a vocation, a form of priesthood, and he practised a type of holistic medicine before the concept became fashionable. He always took care to assess the state of mind and spirit of his patients along with their physical symptoms before making a diagnosis. He also had a deep sense of responsibility for them. In 1906, when Vesuvius erupted, he rushed to Torre del Greco, a small village on the slopes of the mountain, where the *Incurabili* had a subsidiary hospital. Finding that most of the staff had already left, he gave orders for the removal of the patients and worked tirelessly with the staff that remained to evacuate the hospital—as soon as they got the last patient out safely the roof collapsed under the weight of the ash. He showed the same devotion to his patients during a cholera epidemic in 1911.

In 1908 Joseph was appointed to the chair of clinical chemistry in the Institute of Physiological Chemistry. This involved a certain amount of teaching and research, and he published at least thirty-two papers in the course of his relatively short but outstanding academic career. Then, in the spring of 1911, he was promoted to the post of director of the *Incurabili*, while also remaining in charge directly of certain departments. At the heart of this busy and demanding life style was his relationship with God. He received Communion daily and made his work a form of prayer. He had no desire to amass money for himself and always attended to his poorer patients free of charge, paying out of his own pocket for any medicines they needed.

One episode that sums up his vision of his role occurred at a conference in February 1927. One of the principal speakers was the elderly Professor Bianchi, famous for a distinguished career in medicine and politics and a well-known anti-Christian Freemason. As the audience enthusiastically applauded his speech he collapsed on the platform, and Joseph, who had only attended the conference because he had felt drawn there by some outside force, rushed to help the dying man. Bianchi had known Joseph as a student and was aware of his strong religious beliefs; he allowed him to take his hand and showed his assent to Joseph's words of contrition and confidence in God by pressing it before he died.

Joseph died after a short illness on 27 April 1927, at the early age of forty-seven, having been to Mass and visited his parents as usual. The funeral Mass was attended by a huge congregation of grieving people, and one old man summed up the feelings of many: "We mourn him because the world has lost a saint, Naples has lost an example of every virtue, and the sick poor have lost everything." So intense was the public response to the death of the "good doctor" that on 16 November his remains were moved from the cemetery to the Gesù Nuovo church inside the city boundaries. He was canonized by Pope John Paul II on 25 October 1987.

There are biographies by several authors; see especially those by E. Marini (1929/30); A. di Marsico (1939); F. Bea (1961) and G. Papasogli (1959). See also *Bibl.SS.*, 9, 602-4.

St Teresa of Los Andes (1900-20)

Juana Enriqueta Josefina de los Sagrados Corazones Fernández Solar was born in Santiago, Chile, on 13 July 1900. Her parents were Miguel Fernández Jaraquemada and Lucía Solar Armstrong, a pious and well-to-do couple. Juanita, as she came to be called, had a happy and active childhood, was interested in sport and music, and made friends easily. She was said to have inherited her mother's temperament and was lively and energetic but also impatient and at times given to violent outbursts of temper; some thought she was rather vain and arrogant, and it is interesting that she later identified pride as her besetting fault. Juanita attended Mass daily as a child in the family's oratory and developed a more than usually intense piety, with a strong devotion to Our Lord and to Our Lady; she used "to tell her everything and she used to speak to me clearly and distinctly," as she wrote later. She received Communion daily and in 1914 had a spiritual experience during which Our Lord seemed to be telling her to accept her pain (she was suffering from appendicitis at the time) in memory of his sufferings and so become united closely to him.

At the age of fifteen, with permission from her confessor, she made a private vow of celibacy and, after reading the *Story of a Soul* by St Thérèse of Lisieux (1 Oct.), thought about becoming a Carmelite nun. She wrote in her diary at the time: "I am God's. He created me and is my beginning and my end. If I am to become entirely his, I must do his will. If as my Father he knows the present, the past, and the future, why don't I abandon myself to him with complete confidence? From now on I put myself in your divine hands: do what you like with me." Meanwhile she joined the Children of Mary, helped with catechism-teaching in her local parish, and was involved in works of charity, with a particular interest in helping poor children. For a time she was attracted to the life of the Sisters of the Sacred Heart, who ran schools for the poor and worked as missionaries in various countries. Reading the Lives of St Teresa of Avila (15 Oct.) and of Bd Elizabeth of the Trinity (8 Nov.), however, made her more and more convinced that she should become a Carmelite "to learn how to love and how to suffer," and when she was nineteen she joined the Carmel in the town of Los Andes. This was a very poor and rather run-down house without electric light and with inadequate sanitary facilities, but Juanita was attracted by the nuns' strict observance of the Rule, the simplicity of their lives, and their obvious happiness. She took the name of Teresa of Jesus after the great reformer Teresa of Avila, and in Carmelite fashion offered herself a victim for the sanctification of priests and the repentance of sinners. In a set of autobiographical notes she wrote: "I believe holiness consists in love. I wish to be holy, therefore I will give myself to love. . . . Whoever loves has no will except that of the Beloved. . . . I wish to offer myself constantly as a victim so that I become like the one who suffered for me and loves me." These notes show us someone whose life was centred on the gospel and whose spiritual motto could be summed up as love, suffering, prayer, and service. She wrote, "Jesus is our infinite joy" and on entering Carmel claimed she had already found heaven on earth in being able to devote herself wholly to God. Her interior prayer-life developed still further, and she regularly experienced the highest reaches of contemplative prayer. She began an apostolate of spiritual letter-writing to a large number of people, but in Holy Week 1920 she caught typhus and after a few days of suffering died on 12 April, having made her final vows on her death-bed. Her cause was opened in 1947; she was beatified in 1987 and canonized in 1993. Her cult is very popular, and some 100,000 pilgrims visit her shrine every year. She is sometimes referred to as the "little saint" of America in imitation of the Carmelite saint who pioneered the "little way" of sanctity, St Thérèse of Lisieux.

Teresa kept a spiritual diary for several years; for this and her other writings, including 71 letters written from Carmel, see Marino Purroy Remon, O.D.C. (ed.), *Teresa de Los Andes Diario y Cartas* (1983); Michael D. Griffin, *God, The Joy of My Life, St Teresa of the Andes* (2d ed., 1994), contains a trans. of the diary and a full biography, with some illustrations. There are a number of Lives in Spanish: Marino Purroy Remon, O.D.C., *Teresa de Los*

Andes cuenta su vida (1982); A. M. Risopatron, *Teresa de Los Andes, Teresa de Chile* (1987); E. T. Gil De Muro, *"Cada vez que mire el mar." Teresa de Los Andes* (1992). The Life published by the Centro Interprovinciale Carmelitano, *Teresa Di Los Andes, La "Santina Americana"* (1993), is based on extensive extracts from her diary and letters. See also *N.S.B.* 2, pp. 111-3.

13

ST MARTIN I, *Pope and Martyr* (655)

Martin came from Todi in Umbria. After ordination as a deacon in Rome he served for a time in the imperial service in Constantinople, where he learned about the Monothelite belief that Jesus had only a divine will and so was not truly human. This heresy had the support of the emperor Constans II (641-68), who seems to have used it to rally political support. Martin opposed the emperor and showed his independence after being elected pope in 649 by having himself consecrated without Constans' approval. The emperor in return refused to acknowledge him as pope. One of Martin's first acts was to hold a council in Rome in 649 to condemn both Monothelitism and an imperial decree forbidding discussion of the doctrinal issues involved. He then wrote to Constans asking him to accept the doctrinal decrees of the council. The emperor had already heard about the findings of the council and sent a legate to Italy to arrest Martin and take him to Constantinople for trial for treason. This mission failed, and the legate was won over to Martin's side, but a second mission in 653 was successful and the pope, bedridden through illness at the time, was carried off to Constantinople.

After three months of solitary confinement and ill treatment he was tried for treason on the charge that he had helped a plot against Constans; the court refused to take any notice of the real issue, the doctrinal differences between pope and emperor. Martin was condemned to death and publicly scourged. At the request of the patriarch of Constantinople the death sentence was commuted to one of exile, and after a further three months in prison in terrible conditions he was taken to the Crimea in March 654. Martin wrote a number of letters from prison to the Church in Rome, and it is clear from these that he was very hurt by their total neglect of him once he had been taken prisoner. They also went ahead against his wishes and elected a new pope while he was still alive. The conditions in prison were extremely harsh, and he died there in September 655 from starvation and the ill treatment he had received. He is the last of the popes to be venerated as a martyr, and his feast-day is kept in both the Eastern and the Western Church.

For Martin's seventeen letters and other documents see *P.L.*, 87, 119-212. See also especially *O.D.P.*, pp. 73-5; *D.T.C.*, 10, 182-94; *N.C.E.*, 9, pp. 300-1; *O.D.C.C.*, p. 880.

SS Carpus, Papylus, and Agathonice, *Martyrs* (*c.* 170 or 250)

The *acta* of these martyrs are among the more reliable, but it is not clear whether they suffered during the reign of Marcus Aurelius (121-80) or that of Decius (emperor from 249 to 251). Carpus was a bishop from Gurdos, in Lydia, and Papylus was a deacon from Thyatira in the same province. They were brought before the Roman governor at Pergamos and invited to eat meat that had been offered to the idols. Carpus replied, "I am a Christian. I worship Christ, the Son of God, who came in these later times to save us. . . . I do not sacrifice to idols like these." After further questioning he was ordered to be scourged. Papylus replied in the same way to the governor: "I have served God from my youth and have never sacrificed to idols. I am a Christian and that is the only answer you will get from me—there is nothing greater or nobler I could say." Papylus was tortured, and then he and Carpus were asked a second time to eat the meat. When they refused they were condemned to death by burning. Carpus' dying words were, "Blessed are you, Lord Jesus Christ, Son of God, because you have deigned to give me, a sinner, this part with you."

Agathonice was a mother who suffered about the same time. When bystanders urged her to save herself for the sake of her children, she replied, "My children have God, and he will look after them." She was burned at the stake for refusing to sacrifice to the idols. In some accounts she is said to be the sister of Papylus.

The cult of the three martyrs is mentioned by Eusebius in his *Ecclesiastical History* and in the Syriac breviary. One or two sources add a fourth martyr, Agathodorus, a servant, and the Roman Martyrology accepted this and added "and many others."

Pio Franchi de' Cavalieri in *Studi e Testi* 33 (1920) edited the texts of the *acta*. See also H. Delehaye in *Anal. Boll.* 58 (1940), pp. 142-76; *A.C.M.*, pp. 22-37; *Bibl.SS.*, 3, 878-80.

St Hermenegild, *Martyr* (585)

Hermenegild and his brother Reccared were the sons of Leovigild, the Visigothic king of Spain, and his first wife. The king was an Arian Christian, denying that Christ was truly divine, and his two sons were brought up in the same belief. Hermenegild married Indegundis (or Ingunda), who was staunchly orthodox, and the king made him governor of Seville to move the couple away from the court and to avoid trouble with his second wife, Goswinda, who was keen to convert Indegundis to Arianism. It was Hermenegild who was converted from heresy, partly through his wife's persuasion and partly through the arguments of St Leander (13 Mar.), archbishop of Seville. The king reacted angrily by ordering his son to give up his post and all his property, but Hermenegild refused and started a rebellion against his father in 582, using Seville as his base. He was recognized as king by a number of important cities and sought military assistance from the emperor in Constantinople. When that came to nothing he appealed to the small Roman army that still controlled part of Spain. The generals promised to help but betrayed him to the king, and he was forced to accept an offer of arbitration from his brother Reccared. This led to a genuine reconciliation, and Hermenegild was restored to his former position, only to be estranged again from his father through the plotting of Gosvinda. This time he was imprisoned at Tarragona on a charge of heresy and was offered his liberty only if he adopted Arianism and received Holy Communion from an Arian bishop. When he refused to do so, the king had him killed in prison. According to St Gregory the Great (3 Sept.), the king soon regretted what he had done and on his death-bed urged Reccared to make peace with St Leander and give up Arianism; this led to the important conversion of the Visigothic kingdom of Spain to orthodox Catholicism.

There has been considerable debate about whether Hermenegild should be regarded as a martyr or not. He seems to have died rather than give up his orthodox beliefs, but some writers, then and since, have argued that he was executed for treason because of his rebellion. St Isidore of Seville (see above, 4 Apr.), writing only a few years later, describes the rebellion but makes no mention of its religious element or of Hermenegild's execution—though it must be said that Isidore, normally reliable, is not necessarily being impartial here and might have wished to distance the Catholic Church from any taint of rebellion. The rebellion should, perhaps, be judged separately from the death: political motives and ambition may have influenced the first but not the second.

Until the twelfth century there was no cult in Spain, though there is evidence of one in other countries based on the writings of St Gregory the Great. In 1586 Pope Sixtus V (1585-90), at the request of King Philip II, authorized the feast for the whole of Spain, and in 1636 Pope Urban VIII (1623-44) extended it to the universal Church. Because of uncertainties about the martyrdom, however, Pope Benedict XIV in the eighteenth century recommended that the feast should be removed from the universal Calendar, but it remained, as a "semi-double," until 1969.

The traditional account can be found in St Gregory's *Dialogues*, bk. 3, ch. 31. See *Bibl.SS.*, 5, 33-47, with illustrations and a full account of the historical debate. The early history of Spain is summarized in Jedin-Holland, 1, pp. 412-9; see also R. Menéndez Pidal, trans. W. Starkie, *The Spaniards in their History* (1950), esp. pp. 181-3; *idem* (ed.), *Historia de España*, 3, "España visigoda" (2d ed., 1963).

Hermenegild does not feature very often in art, but there are pictures of him in princely costume holding an axe and the martyr's palm. There is a remarkable seventeenth-century triumphalist depiction of his apotheosis by Francisco Herrera in the Prado, Madrid.

Bd Ida of Boulogne (*c.* 1040-1113)

Ida was the daughter of Duke Godfrey IV of Lorraine and his first wife, Doda. When she was seventeen she was given in marriage to Eustace II, the count of Boulogne. Two of their sons, Godfrey and Baldwin, became crusader rulers of the Latin kingdom of Jerusalem, and their granddaughter Matilda became queen of England. When Eustace died Ida was left with considerable wealth and she used this to help the poor and build or restore monasteries; among the latter were Saint-Wulmer at Boulogne, Vasconvilliers, Our Lady of the Chapel at Calais, and Saint-Bertin. As she grew older Ida retired more and more from the world, but she does not seem to have ever become a religious. She was some sort of "spiritual associate" of Cluny and could be considered, perhaps, a secular oblate of the Benedictine Order. One of her principal advisers was the great St Anselm of Bec (21 Apr.), later archbishop of Canterbury. She died in her seventies and was buried in the monastery of Vast—not Saint-Vaast as often stated. In 1669 her remains were moved to the Benedictine church in Paris; when the community moved to Bayeux in 1808 the remains went with them and are still venerated there.

There are two short Lives, one by a contemporary monk; see *AA.SS.*, Apr., 2, pp. 141-5. See also F. Ducatel, *Vie de Ste Ide de Lorraine* (1900), and *Bibl.SS.*, 7, 636-7.

St Caradoc (1124)

Caradoc was born in Brycheiniog (probably present-day Brecon or Brecknock in south Wales). In his youth he served as a harpist at the court of the king of South Wales, Rhys ap Tewdwr (1077-93). It is said that a dispute with the prince, who threatened to kill him, taught Caradoc the uncertainty of worldly favours and persuaded him to become a cleric to serve only God. He went to Llandaff and received the tonsure before going to minister in the church of Saint Teilo. He later spent some years as a hermit near a ruined church in Gower and was ordained in Menevia before retiring with some companions to a remote island off the coast of Pembrokeshire. Unfortunately their solitude was broken by Norse raiders, and Caradoc moved again, this time to what was called St Ismael's cell (now St Issell's) at Haroldston. Like many other solitaries Caradoc was said to have developed a special relationship with wild animals, and a number of miracles involving them were attributed to him. He died in 1124 and was buried with considerable ceremony in St David's Cathedral, where the remains of his shrine can still be seen. Pope Innocent III wrote to a number of abbots requiring them to make inquiries about Caradoc's life as a hermit and his miracles. His biographer, Gerald of Wales, attributed the failure of his own attempts to have Caradoc canonized to the spitefulness of other people.

Baring-Gould and Fisher, 2, pp. 75-8. A twelfth-century Life by Gerald of Wales is no longer extant except for its preface; there is some information about Caradoc in his *Itinerary of Wales*, bk.1, ch.11. See also *Bibl.SS.*, 3, 776-7; *Anal.Boll.* 71 (1954), pp. 461-2.

Bd Margaret of Metola (*c.* 1286-1320)

Margaret was born blind in Metola, near Città-di-Castello in Umbria, about the year 1286. When she was six or seven her parents took her to a shrine in Città-di-Castello hoping for a cure; when this did not occur, they abandoned her. Some local women found the child and looked after her until a couple named Grigia and Venfarino adopted her. The nuns of a local convent then offered her a home, and Margaret, who seems to have already had the idea of becoming a nun, was delighted with the new arrangement. The nuns' way of life, however, was lax, and Margaret annoyed them by her devotion; after a period marked by increasing harshness and petty persecution she was told to leave. She returned to her adoptive parents and at the age of fifteen became a member of the Third Order of St Dominic in Città-di-Castello. From then on she lived a life wholly dedicated to God. She undertook the care and education of the local children, teaching them the psalms, which she had learned by heart and trying to instill in them something of her own devotion to the Holy Child Jesus. She also visited the sick and those in prison. A number of miracles were attributed to her, including curing another tertiary of an affliction of the eyes, and it was said she experienced ecstasies and levitation while at prayer. She practised severe austerities, including self-flagellation, and often went without sleep so that she could spend the night in prayer. After her death at about the age of thirty-three miracles were reported at her tomb. Her cult was approved in 1609, and a new shrine under the high altar in the Dominican church was built for her remains in 1678.

A short fourteenth-century Life was printed in *Anal.Boll.* 19 (1900), pp. 21-36. Another Life was discovered this century by W. R. Bonniwell and was the basis of his *Story of Margaret of Metola* (1952); see also *Bibl.SS.*, 8, 756-9.

BB John Lockwood and Edmund Catherick, *Martyrs* (1642)

John Lockwood (alias Lassels or Lascelles, his mother's maiden name) was born in Yorkshire in 1561 (some accounts say 1555), the eldest son of Christopher Lockwood of Sowerby. He studied at Douai and Rome, where he was ordained, and worked as a priest in England, where he was arrested and imprisoned twice before his final capture and trial. On the first occasion he was banished from the country in 1610 after having been condemned to death; and on the second, when he had also been condemned to death, the sentence was commuted to imprisonment, and somehow he managed to escape or be freed. In the end he was arrested at the house of a Mrs Catenby, near Thirsk, where he had been living for some years, and taken to York for trial. Because of his advanced age and physical disabilities he could not sit on a horse and had to be held on; the journey was very painful and slow. He was condemned for being a seminary priest ordained abroad and working in England, and he was hanged, drawn, and quartered at York on 13 April 1642, despite the protests of some local people who objected to such a terrible death being inflicted on such an old man.

At the same time Edmund Catherick (alias Huddleston), from Stanwick in Yorkshire, was tried and condemned for the same reason. He had also studied at Douai and had started working in England in 1635, when he was about thirty years of age. He was captured at Thornton Watlass in the North Riding. Some of the evidence against him was supplied by a certain Justice Dodsworth, a relative of his by marriage. It seems that an attempt was made by the king, Charles I, who was in York at the time, to reprieve them or at least change the method of execution, but relations between king and parliament were very difficult and he was unable to insist on leniency. The two priests were led out to the scaffold together, and John Lockwood, thinking he saw signs of faltering in his companion, asked to be allowed to die first to encourage the younger man. According to the account of the execution, he said, "My dear brother in Jesus Christ and fellow-sufferer, take courage. We have almost run our race; shall we faint and be tired when in sight of the prize? Let us run in spirit to our Saviour in the garden and call upon him in his agony and bloody sweat. . . . O Jesus, [let us] lay down our lives in obedience to Thy holy will, and in defence of Thy holy religion, with constancy and perseverance."

Some of the martyrs' relics were secured by Mary Ward's Congregation and transferred to their convent at Augsburg in Germany, where they still remain. Part of John Lockwood's body is at Downside. They were beatified in 1929.

M.M.P., pp. 411-6; Anstruther, 1, pp. 211-2, for Lockwood, and 2, p. 49, for Catherick. See the general entries on the Martyrs of England and Wales under 4 May and 25 October.

14

SS Tiburtius, Valerius, and Maximus, *Martyrs* (date unknown)

These three martyrs were venerated by the Church from an early date, but there are almost no reliable details about them. The martyrology of St Jerome of the fifth century mentions them four times under different dates and with different burial places each time. Some of the confusion arose from the mention of the martyrs in the *acta* of St Cecilia (22 Nov.), where the author decided to make Valerius her husband and Tiburtius her brother-in-law, but as these *acta* are entirely fictitious we cannot take the relationships as historical or the dates given as trustworthy. A second cause of confusion was the existence of another St Tiburtius, also a Roman martyr, whose feast-day is 11 August. It is not clear whether the martyrs died on 14 April and were buried in the cemetery of Praetextatus, with a translation of their relics on 21 April to the cemetery of St Callixtus, or whether they died on 21 April, with the burial and translation happening in reverse order. It could be that the three were executed on different days and buried separately, their remains being brought together in the cemetery of St Callixtus when their names became connected through the legend of St Cecilia (as suggested in *Bibl.SS.*). The details given in some accounts of the death of the three martyrs are highly improbable. Their remains were translated to the church of St Cecilia in Trastevere by Pope Paschal I (817-24). Their feast-day was removed from the universal Calendar in 1969.

Propylaeum, pp. 137-8; *Bibl.SS.*, 12, 466-9.

St Lambert, *Bishop* (688)

In his youth Lambert served at the court of King Clotaire but gave up his position to become a monk in the abbey of Fontenelle. The abbot was St Wandregisilis (22 July), the founder of the abbey, and when he died in 668 Lambert was elected to succeed him. The house had already gained a reputation for sanctity and strict observance throughout western Europe, and the new abbot increased it still further. Among his disciples were St Erembert (14 May), who had resigned as bishop of Toulouse in order to enter Fontenelle, and St Condedus (21 Oct.), an Englishman who later became a famous hermit. About the year 679 Lambert was chosen to be archbishop of Lyons. Unfortunately his episcopal *acta* have not survived, and so we have no details of that period of his life, except he seems to have retired from time to time to the abbey of Donzère in Provence, which he had founded from Fontenelle. He died in 688.

Part of an early Life is extant; see *AA.SS.*, Apr., 2, pp. 215-20. See also *Bibl.SS.*, 7, 1078-9.

St Bernard of Tiron, *Abbot and Founder* (*c*. 1046-1117)

Bernard (sometimes known as Bernard of Abbeville) is first heard of as a monk at Saint-Cyprien near Poitiers. He moved from there after about ten years to Saint-Savin, where he become prior. The discipline in the monastery was lax, and Bernard spent most of his twenty years there working to improve it. He refused to accept the post of abbot and, as he had developed a desire for a more solitary way of life, left the monastery to enter a hermitage in the forest of Craon, on the border between Brittany and Maine. Here a large number of solitaries had gathered, following different leaders and Rules. They met for prayer and conferences, and new recruits were assigned to particular masters. This informal grouping included some of the leading reformers and monastic founders of the period, including Bd Vitalis (16 Sept.) and Bd Robert of Arbrissel (25 Feb.), and Craon has been described as "the second great centre of revival" after Cîteaux (Knowles).

After a time he was persuaded to return to Saint-Cyprien, where he was chosen as abbot. When the abbot of Cluny claimed jurisdiction over his monastery and the right to collect tithes, Bernard resisted strongly, resigned, and retired to Chaussey, on the coast opposite the Channel Islands, where disciples soon gathered around him. He did not live wholly as a hermit, for he accompanied Robert of Arbrissel and others on preaching campaigns. In 1109 he moved again, this time to found a monastery on land near Tiron, where he could ensure that the Benedictine Rule was strictly observed. His ideals were similar to those of St Bernard of Cîteaux (20 Aug.): he had a love of simplicity and also wished to give manual work a leading role in monastic life, even, if necessary, reducing the amount of choir singing to make room for it. This new house was the beginning of the Tironian Congregation of Benedictines. It flourished and founded a number of daughter houses outside France, including a cell on Caldey Island, off the south coast of Wales. In the seventeenth century the Congregation merged with the Maurists. Bernard died in 1117 after what the previous edition of this work called "a troubled and chequered career." His cult was approved in 1861.

The early Life by one of Bernard's monks, Gaufridus Grossus, is not wholly reliable; see *P.L.*, 172, 1367-1446. See also D. Knowles, *The Monastic Order in England* (2d ed., 1963), pp. 200-2, 227; *N.C.E.*, 2, p. 343.

St Bénézet (*c.* 1163-1184)

Bénézet was probably born at Hermillon in Savoy, although there is some evidence that his birthplace was in present-day Belgium. He spent his early years as a shepherd and about the year 1178 went to Avignon. Some accounts say that he had had a vision ordering him to go there to build a bridge over the Rhone; others that he had the vision in Avignon after seeing how difficult it was for people to cross the river. As he had no knowledge of the difficult work of bridge-building he was at first treated with scorn when he suggested the idea to the bishop. He made a start with the help of some volunteers, trusting in God's support, and not long afterwards the bishop accepted the project as his own and provided Bénézet with money and technical assistance. Bénézet died in 1184 before the work had been completed. A number of miracles were said to have accompanied the building, and others were reported at his tomb. Later, a chapel was built on the bridge and Bénézet's body was re-buried there. The bridge lasted until 1669, when part of it was washed away. Bénézet's body was recovered and found to be incorrupt; it was re-buried in Avignon Cathedral and moved in the nineteenth century to the church of St Didier. He is one of the patrons of Avignon, and the Guild of Bridge Brothers, founded in 1189, regarded him as their founder. He was referred to as "Saint" from 1237 onward.

There is a considerable amount of evidence to support the main outline of this unusual story, and the cult and early miracles are well attested. The municipal archives contain an official account, and in 1230 the bishop of Avignon launched an official inquiry in connection with Bénézet's beatification, and a summary of the witnesses' evidence survives. There are also references in contemporary chronicles. See *AA.SS.*, Apr., 2, pp. 255-64; *Bibl.SS.*, 2, 1099-1100; *O.D.S.*, pp. 48-9; *N.C.E.*, 2, p. 310.

Bd Peter González (1246)

Pedro González was Castilian by birth and came from a noble family. One of his uncles was bishop of Astorga, and he educated Pedro and also gained him a canonry at the cathedral even though he was under age for such an appointment. The new canon rode into the city in style but was thrown when his horse stumbled and was covered in mud. It is said that the jeers of the bystanders made him think about the vanity of worldly pomp, and he gave up his position to become a Dominican friar. He was a successful preacher and was appointed royal chaplain by St Ferdinand III (30 May), king of Castile and León. He set about the difficult task of reforming the morals of the courtiers. Most of the king's energies went into the struggle against the Moors, and Pedro preached the Crusade and accompanied the army into battle. After the successful siege of Córdoba he was instrumental in restraining the soldiers from the worst excesses of pillaging and in getting the king to impose less harsh terms on the Moors.

He retired from the court as soon as he was allowed and went to Compostela and then on to Tuy. He devoted the rest of his life to preaching in the rural areas of north-western Spain and along the coast. His favourite saying was: "Better one day in the house of the Lord than a thousand in the pavilions of sinners." He had a special mission to sailors and became one of the favourite patrons of both Spanish and Portuguese seamen; they still invoke him, but under the name St Elmo, through confusing him with St Erasmus (2 June). He died at Tuy on 14 April 1246. A large church was built over his tomb in the sixteenth century, and his cult was encouraged by the grant of papal privileges; it was eventually approved in 1741.

Bibl.SS., 7, 108-9; Procter, pp. 94-6.

Bd Lydwina (1380-1433)

Lydwina was born at Schiedant, near Rotterdam in The Netherlands, in 1380. Her father was a poor labourer, and she was the only girl in a family of nine children. She seems to have taken a private vow of virginity in her early teens, but externally there was nothing to distinguish her from other children in the town. When she was fifteen she had an accident while ice-skating; at first it seemed she had only broken a rib, but complications set in and she began to suffer vomiting attacks and other painful symptoms. She was to spend the rest of her life as an invalid, but it was some time before she accepted her situation. It was mainly through the counselling of a local priest, Fr John Pot, that she saw in it a possible religious vocation of a special type. He recommended her to meditate on the passion of Our Lord and to try to unite her sufferings with his. After about three years she felt called to be a victim for the sins of other people and began to accept her sufferings positively. When she was nineteen these sufferings changed dramatically for the worse. Her face became grossly disfigured and her limbs contorted, while she experienced heart attacks that left her completely prostrate, able only to move her left arm. She lost the sight of one eye, and the other became so sensitive she could hardly stand even the light from a fire.

Her medical condition and her patience during her sufferings brought her visits from doctors and those seeking spiritual advice. Reports began to circulate about her miraculous powers, ecstasies, and other phenomena. For the last nineteen years of her life she seemed to take no nourishment except Holy Communion, and this was solemnly attested by a number of witnesses. About 1407 she started to experience visions. While her body lay in prolonged cataleptic trances, her spirit would visit the Holy Places and Rome and converse with Our Lord and the saints. After these events she would suffer an increase in her sufferings. There were other developments, too. A new parish priest refused to acknowledge her holiness, forbade her Holy Communion, and had the people pray for her release from diabolical possession. She was also accused of being a sham and a hypocrite. When these accusations threatened to divide the community, the authorities ordered a full investigtion of her case and found in favour of her good faith and innocence, and she was allowed to receive Holy Communion fortnightly. She died eventually on 14 April 1433. Her cult had already started and was promoted after her death by Lives written by her cousin, John Gerlac, Thomas à Kempis, and John Brugman, all contemporaries of Lydwina. It was approved in 1890.

The most reliable study is by H. Mueffels, *Sainte Lydwine* (1925). The Life by à Kempis was translated by Dom Vincent Scully in 1912, with a useful introduction. See also *Bibl.SS.*, 8, 45-6; *Vies des Saints*, 4, pp. 343-53. On the links between fasting and anorexia see the bibliography under St Catherine of Siena (30 Apr.).

Lydwina is usually depicted with roses or a rosebush because of the legend that, during her final illness, her guardian angel brought Lydwina a rosebush and warned her that she would die when all its buds had opened.

15

St Paternus of Wales, *Abbot* (Fifth or Sixth Century)

Paternus (Padarn, or Badarn, in Wales) was probably born and educated in south-eastern Wales. His name was a common Roman one of the period, and there are other indications of Roman influences in the location of the Welsh place names relating to him. He was abbot of the important monastery of Llanbadarn Fawr, near Aberystwyth, which he had founded, and he is also described as bishop of the same place. He ranks among the leading early Welsh saints, and his cult was very popular, but it is difficult to be precise about biographical details, as the only Life we possess dates from about the year 1120 and is unreliable. It was written by a monk of Llanbadarn Fawr, who conflated an earlier account of the Welsh Padarn with one about a Breton saint of the same name who was bishop of Vannes. It is not impossible that the two saints were the same person, given the close cultural links between south Wales, Brittany, and south-west England, and there were saints who worked on both sides of the Channel, but it is more likely that they were two different people. The Life relates how the Welsh Padarn went about the country as a missionary, preaching to everyone without pay or reward, and was famous for his charity and mortifications. He features in the Lives of St David (1 Mar.) and St Teilo (9 Feb.), where there is a legendary account of a visit by the three saints to Jerusalem. There has been confusion, too, about the date of the feast-day, since there is yet another St Paternus, bishop of Avranches in Normandy, whose feast is also celebrated on 15 April (see below).

G. H. Doble, *St Patern* (no. 43 in his Cornish Saints series, 1940), is a balanced account of the historical problems. See also *O.D.S.*, p. 379; P. Grosjean, "S. Paterne d'Avranches et S. Paterne de Vannes," in *Anal.Boll.* 67 (1949), pp. 384-400. For a modern approach based on a study of the folklore, see Elissa R. Henken, *Traditions of the Welsh Saints* (1987), pp. 121-7, and *The Welsh Saints, A Study in Patterned Lives* (1991).

St Paternus of Avranches, *Abbot and Bishop* (564)

This Paternus, sometimes confused with both St Paternus of Wales (above) and St Paternus of Vannes, came from Poitiers in France, where his father held an important post. He joined the monastery of Ansion in Poitou but after a time left with another monk, Scubilio (locally venerated as a saint), to lead a more solitary life near Coutances in Normandy. They finally settled at a place named Scissy, near Granville, where they attracted so many disciples that they had to set up a monastery, which became known later as Saint-Pair (a corruption of Paternus). After serving as its abbot for several years and founding other houses in the area, Paternus was appointed bishop of Avranches at the age of seventy and lived for a further thirteen years. He attended a council in Paris. He died on the same day as his former companion, Scubilio, and they were buried together in the church at Scissy. Grosjean argues strongly that the feast-day should be 15 April, and this is followed by the new Roman Martyrology.

Venantius Fortunatus (*c*. 530–610) wrote a Life of Paternus, published in *M.G.H., Auctores Antiquissimi*, 4, pt. 2, pp. 33-7. See also the article by Grosjean under Paternus of Wales, above.

St Ruadhan, *Abbot* (*c.* 584)

Some accounts say Ruadhan, or Ruadan, was the son of Fergus Bern of the royal family of Munster, in Ireland, others that he was born in Leinster. He became one of the disciples of St Finnian of Clonard (12 Dec.) and went on to found the monastery of Lorrha (or Lothra) in what is now County Tipperary, which became one of the most important monasteries in Munster. This eventually held about 150 monks, whose way of life consisted of prayer and manual work. Ruadhan was famous in his day and was counted among the twelve apostles of Ireland. The martyrology of Oengus (eighth or ninth century) praises him with the words, "An excellent flame that does not wane, that vanquishes urgent desires: fair was the gem Ruadhan, lamp of Lothra." Unfortunately, the Latin and Irish Lives are late and unreliable and are mainly concerned with an entirely legendary account of how Ruadhan cursed Tara and caused it to be abandoned, and other magical elements. His hand was preserved in a silver shrine at Lorrha until the sixteenth century, and an ancient oratory next to the parish church there is part of the original Celtic foundation. He is retained here although he is excluded from the new Roman Martyrology on the grounds that his cult is not sufficiently well attested.

V.S.H., 2, pp. 240-52; *O.D.S.*, p. 423; *The Irish Saints*, pp. 280-1.

Bd Caesar de Bus, *Founder* (1544-1607)

Caesar de Bus was born at Cavaillon in France in 1544 of an Italian family that had settled there in the previous century. He was educated at the Jesuit college in Avignon and for a time seems to have been undecided between a military and a literary career. He wrote a number of plays but in the end settled for a life in the army and at court. He led the fairly easygoing life of a well-to-do young man, making an impression in society and enjoying its pleasures. It was the time of the French Wars of Religion, and he took part in the battle of Dreux in 1562 and witnessed the St Bartholomew's Day massacres of French Protestants in 1572. During a bout of serious illness he was persuaded to pay more attention to his spiritual life, decided to become a priest, and was ordained in 1582. He had already started what was to become his main pastoral activity, travelling around to teach the catechism in neglected and backward places. He believed that the religious ignorance of the ordinary people, and especially of those who lived in country areas, was a grave scandal and a serious weakness in the Church. In this he was in tune with the reforming Council of Trent (1545-63) and its decision to publish a new catechism to help in the evangelization of both clergy and laity.

He converted his cousin, Jean-Baptiste Romillon, who had adopted Calvinism because of its strict discipline, and together the two formed a partnership to develop the work of instruction and preaching. Caesar read a Life of St Charles Borromeo (4 Nov.), who had founded the Workers of Christian Doctrine to help with the reform in Milan, and was struck by the saint's saying that a catechist would not have laboured in vain if he had made even a single good Christian. Caesar was not content with catechizing the children, as was usual at the time, but developed a whole family catechesis as the best way of avoiding both negligence and heresy among the people. They were supported by the archbishops of Aix and Avignon, who encouraged young men to follow their example. These formed the basis of a new Congregation, for which Caesar wrote a Constitution and which became known as the Fathers of Christian Doctine. The members lived in community but did not take religious vows. This last point eventually caused a split between the two leaders, with Caesar deciding that it would be better if the members took simple vows. About 1602 the community divided into two groups, one remaining with Caesar in Avignon, the other going with Romillon to a house in Aix. At the same time a group of religious women was formed with the name "Daughters of Christian Doctrine."

Caesar's interior life was dominated by his spirit of penance and a determination to conquer the feelings and emotions he had previously indulged. He wanted to offer himself as a sacrifice to God, abandoning himself in everything to the divine will so that he could devote himself entirely to making known as widely as possible the simple message of God's love and our redemption by Jesus. He died on 15 April 1607, and a popular cult started straightaway. He was beatified in 1975. A manual he had written on the teaching of catechetics, *Instructions for the Family on the Four Parts of the Roman Catechism*, was published about sixty years after his death.

Bibl.SS., 3, 613-4; *N.S.B.* 2, 120-3.

Bd Damien De Veuster (1840-89)

Joseph De Veuster was born on 3 January 1840 in the small village of Tremelo near Malines in Belgium. He was the seventh child of Frans De Veuster and Catherine Wouters, farmers of moderate means. It was a pious family: two of Joseph's sisters became nuns and one of his brothers joined the Fathers of the

Sacred Hearts of Jesus and Mary (or Picpus Fathers) in 1857. The letters Joseph wrote as a young man show an unusual awareness of basic religious values (sometimes expressed, it has to be admitted, in a rather sententious way) and a determination to follow God's will where his own vocation was concerned. His parents at first opposed his decision to become a religious, but he was sure it was a divine call and told them so in a respectful but very firm letter. He had thought first of joining the Trappists, but his brother persuaded him to join the Sacred Hearts Community instead. This he did in 1859 in Louvain, taking the name Damien in religion. At first his superiors would only allow him to be a lay brother, as he seemed to lack sufficient education to be a priest. He was deeply disappointed by their decision, but his brother started to teach him Latin and a few months later Damien got his wish and was allowed to join those who were studying for the priesthood. Instead of carving his name on his desk, as was the custom among the students, he carved three words, "Silence. Recollection. Prayer." He made his vows in Paris in 1860 and also began his philosophical studies there, moving on later to Louvain to begin theology in 1862. His teachers commented that he seemed to have the making of a good teacher. A year later his brother was due to leave for the Congregation's mission in the Hawaiian Islands but was taken ill with typhus shortly before his departure. It looked as though the project would have to be abandoned, but Damien offered to go instead and so found himself sailing for Honolulu in November 1863. He wrote to his parents: "Do not worry in the least about us. We are in the hands of the good God, who has taken us under his protection. All I ask you to do is to pray . . . [that we will be given] the courage always and everywhere to do his holy will, for that is our whole life." He arrived in Honolulu five months later and was ordained priest in May 1864.

For nine years Damien served at two of the mission stations on the islands. In 1873 the bishop asked for volunteers to work on Molokai, an island used as a leper colony. His idea was to have a team of missionaries take turns ministering to the lepers so that no individual priest would have to serve there for more than three weeks at a time. Damien offered to go alone and devote himself to the work entirely, and this was accepted. Some time later he wrote to his brother, "On my arrival on Molokai I entrusted my health to Our Lord, his holy Mother and St Joseph. They have the job of preserving me from this terrible disease." At the time there was no cure for leprosy, and it had long been looked on with particular horror; those who contracted it were isolated from all normal human contact. Molokai was called "the Devil's Island" and "the Devil's paradise," because it was believed that its inhabitants lived a dissolute life with no regard for either human or divine laws. While Damien was motivated by a limitless love for his fellow human beings and a spirit of total sacrifice, not everyone (including some of his superiors) understood his motives. He was to be accused of not keeping his vow of obedience in remaining on Molokai, of being too interested in material things because he raised large sums of money to help the lepers, and, most seriously of all, of not keeping his vow of celibacy. This last accusation arose from the belief of the day that leprosy was most commonly transmitted by sexual contact, and so, when Damien eventually contracted the disease, he was accused of having broken his vows. As a result, on the orders of his superiors, he underwent three humiliating medical examinations aimed at establishing his chastity. He was also forbidden to leave the island and was unable to go to Confession for months at a time; he wrote on one occasion, "If I didn't have the continual presence of the divine Master in my poor chapel I could not persevere in my decision to share the lot of the lepers. . . . I am happy and have nothing to complain about; when I have to wait for a confessor to come I confess my faults before the Blessed Sacrament." His letters reveal an unusually intense interior life and a deep simplicity such as only those continually aware of God's presence possess (Geenen).

There were about eight hundred lepers on Molokai when Damien arrived in May 1873, and new arrivals from the other islands added to that number all the time. They were confined to part of the island where a hospital had been built for them and where they were visited from time to time by a government-appointed doctor. There was nothing for them to do, and they seemed to Damien to spend most of the time playing cards and getting drunk on local beer—the cause, no doubt, of the low opinion of their morals. Living conditions were atrocious, and there were so many deaths that Damien called the place a "living cemetery." Despite the conditions, Damien saw in each of his new parishioners "a soul redeemed by the adorable blood of our divine Saviour. . . . If I cannot cure them as he did, at least I can comfort them and through the holy ministry that he in his kindness has given me, I hope that many of them, cured from leprosy of the soul, will go before his tribunal able to enter the society of the blessed." In an early letter home he wrote, "I make myself a leper with the lepers, to gain all to Jesus Christ." He visited them regularly in their huts and administered the sacraments to as many as possible. He was also concerned about their living conditions and what could be done to reduce the effects of the disease by introducing ordinary rules of hygiene. He returned to Honolulu and begged for clothes, collecting enough for three hundred people, and got the Sisters there to send him regular parcels of warm clothing. When news of his work spread people raised money to help: an Anglican clergyman organized three subscriptions through *The Times* and sent Damien over £2,000 in all. Once his work was known outside the islands (very much against his will) it won immediate recognition around the world. The horror of leprosy was so great that anyone who worked among those stricken with the disease had to be someone of heroic virtue. Damien's reply to a benefactor who praised him was, "I am a simple and poor priest just carrying out the duties of his vocation." He kept open house for the lepers, shared meals with them, and enjoyed playing with the children. He helped repair the houses and even administered simple medicines when no doctor was available—after eight years he claimed he had become more effective than some of the proper doctors who visited the island. His constant begging letters included appeals for medicines and new remedies as much as for money. In an attempt to stop the abuse of young orphan girls he set up an orphanage.

Damien was also involved in schemes to improve the roads and the harbour, made suggestions on ways to improve the water supply, and took in hand the enlarging of the hospital so that a new Japanese treatment involving hot baths could be introduced. The list of his activities seems endless and witnesses to both his complete dedication to the spiritual needs of his people and his practical and entrepreneurial approaches to their material needs. He was willing to help all the lepers in these practical ways, including those who refused his spiritual ministry. His ideal was to create a community where he had found "a human jungle."

At the same time, it has to be admitted that he became autocratic and self-opinionated and was not always popular with those who tried to help him. He thought he knew best for his people but was not always correct and, for example, quarrelled unfairly with some of those whose medical knowledge was better than his. His notions of hygiene, both personal and for the lepers, were rudimentary, and some visitors to the island felt he was coarse and boorish. Some accounts give the impression that he worked alone on Molokai, but this is not true: from 1878 Fr André Nolander (who had studied medicine) worked with him for two years and was then replaced by Fr Albert Montiton, an experienced Pacific missionary. Until he developed leprosy himself he went to Honolulu to make spiritual retreats with his fellow-missionaries. Moreover, by the 1880s the Hawaiian government was doing more for the lepers, meeting most of their material needs and paying for two schoolteachers to work there.

It was in January 1885 that Damien was finally diagnosed as having leprosy. He continued to be as active as ever, while his spiritual life developed and deepened. At first he suffered a period of desolation, when he was afraid in a very human way of what would happen to him and wondered what had happened to the special protection he had always hoped for from God, Our Lady, and St Joseph. In addition, at the very time when he needed some human consolation, he was alone: Fr Montiton left a few months later for another mission, and Damien was forbidden to leave the island for any reason; once news of his illness got abroad visitors stopped going there, and, as has been said, he could not rely on seeing another priest for Confession even once a month. Also at this time his superiors were having doubts about him and complaining about his supposed concentration on material things. Part of their attitude could be explained by fear that the Hawaiian government resented the amount of world attention focused on their leper colony and might turn against Catholic missionaries in general, but some of it was also due to the amount of money Damien was attracting for his relatively small mission while others were unsuccessful in raising funds for what they believed were larger and more important projects.

By about October 1885 Damien seems to have overcome these initial feelings of fear and desolation and could write about his peaceful resignation to God's will: "The good God knows what is best for my sanctification and every day I say an honest 'fiat voluntas tua.'" In 1887 he wrote that he believed he was the "happiest missionary in the world," such were the joy and contentment the sacred hearts of Jesus and Mary lavished on him. The only fear that remained with him was that he would become too disabled to say Mass, a "privilege that is my greatest consolation . . . and that of my numerous companions in misery who every Sunday almost fill my two churches." And suddenly things improved. He was able to spend a week in a hospital in Honolulu, where he was visited by the king, the prime minister, and the bishop. Money and offers of prayers arrived from Europe and the United States. In May 1886 an American layman, Joseph Dutton, joined him as an assistant (he stayed on Molokai for over forty years), and in 1888 Fr Lambert Conrardy also arrived, followed later in the year by three Franciscan nuns who were to look after the orphans.

By March 1889 he knew from the progress of his disease that his death could not be far off; as he said, the work for the lepers was now safe and he was no longer needed. He died on 15 April, aged forty-nine. Controversy about his work and way of life continued, however, and a particularly vicious attack came from a Protestant clergyman in Honolulu. It was in answer to this that Robert Louis Stevenson wrote his famous defence of Damien's life and achievements.

Damien's remains were transferred from Molokai to Louvain in 1936 and buried in the chapel of the Sacred Hearts Congregation; a new tomb was built for them in the crypt of the new church in 1962. He was beatified in 1995. "His trust in God's providence had remained intact: he had accepted his illness as something sent by God to help him increase in holiness. His relationship with Christ was enriched by a new union: through his leprosy Damien joined his master on the route to Calvary" (Brion). His vocation had been truly "an option for the poor."

The principal source is O. Van Gestel, *Père Damien De Veuster, Vie, Documents*, 6 vols. (1936); this was used extensively by R. De Becker for his *De Grote Melaatse. De ziel van Pater Damiaan* (1958). See also Robert Louis Stevenson, *Father Damien; an open letter to the Reverend Dr Hyde of Honolulu* (1890). There are many modern studies; see, for example, S. Debroey, *Father Damien, The Priest of the Lepers* (1966); Gavan Daws, *Holy Man: Fr Damien of Molokai* (1973); G. Geenen in *Bibl.SS.*, 12, 1063-8; E. Brion, *Un étrange bonheur. Lettres du Père Damien lépreux, 1885-1889* (1988), and *Comme un Arbre au Bord des Eaux* (1994). Most modern studies are well illustrated with photographs.

16

St Optatus and Companions, *Martyrs* (304)

In 304, during the persecution under the emperor Diocletian, Optatus and seventeen others suffered martyrdom in Zaragoza in Spain. The poet Prudentius (348-*c.* 410), a native of the same city, wrote a hymn about the martyrs, but this does not give any details of how they died. His list of their names includes four named Saturninus, and two named Caius and Crementius who seem to have died from the tortures they received. They are sometimes referred to as "The Innumerable Martyrs of Zaragoza."

The hymn also deals with a St Encratis or Engrazia as a virgin martyr who suffered terrible tortures, which Prudentius describes in graphic detail, in the same persecution. He calls her a "vehement maiden" for the way she defended the Faith. It seems that she survived the tortures, for Prudentius calls her house the shrine of a "living martyr." It is unlikely that she suffered at the same time as Optatus, and she probably lived at a time much closer to Prudentius' own. Her name is found in a variety of forms, and her cult was very popular in Spain and the Pyrenees. Optatus and his companions were especially venerated in the church dedicated to her. On the occasion of the Synod of Zaragoza in 592 the church was re-consecrated and a special Mass written that became known as the "Mass of St Engrazia or the Eighteen Martyrs." The re-consecration took place on 3 November, and the feast of the martyrs has sometimes been kept on that day, but today's date is more accurate.

Prudentius' hymn is quoted at length in *AA.SS.*, Apr., 2, pp. 506-8. See also *Bibl.SS.*, 11, 649-50.

St Fructuosus, *Bishop* (665)

Fructuosus was the son of a general in the service of the Visigothic kings of Spain. The death of his parents left him with a large fortune, and he used this wealth to help the poor and the family's former slaves and also to found religious houses. He studied for the priesthood in the school that Conancio, bishop of Palencia, had established and then founded a monastery at Compludo on his estates in the mountains near Vierzo. He took charge of the monks himself until they were well established and then left them in order to seek greater solitude. He went on pilgrimage to Seville and Cadiz and is said to have founded monasteries in both places; he seems to have found it impossible to be left alone, and wherever he went he attracted disciples. He built monasteries and a convent for them but was faced with a difficult problem when whole families joined him and asked if they could take vows in religion. It seems that their motivation was not always spiritual, for some wanted to avoid military service, and others to be free from paying the heavy taxes levied by the king. Fructuosus founded a number of double houses for them in which males and females were strictly segregated. According to the Rule he gave them, when the children reached the age of reason they had to transfer to another house as oblates. These family houses proved so popular that the provincial governor persuaded the king to decree that entry to the religious life could be allowed only with royal permission. Fructuosus drew up two monastic Rules, the *Regula Monachorum* and the *Regula Communis*. These were to be very influential in northern Spain and Portugal for about three centuries after his death. The second of them contained his famous "Pact," or legal formula for entry to the religious life and profession.

At one stage Fructuosus wanted to go on pilgrimage to Jersusalem and, possibly, Egypt (perhaps to find the solitude that eluded him at home) but was prevented by the king, who feared he would not return. He was made bishop of Dumio and in 656 archbishop of Braga (in present-day Portugal), in which capacity he attended the Tenth Council of Toledo, held in the same year. He faced opposition in his efforts to reform his diocese but apparently won over his opponents by patience and gentleness. He died in 665. His remains were moved early in the twelfth century to the church of San Jerónimo el Real in Compostela, where they are still venerated. Two of his letters survive, including one to St Braulio (26 Mar.), bishop of Zaragoza.

There is a contemporary Life by an abbot of Alcalá, translated into English and published in 1946 by Sr F. C. Nock. The Rules are in *P.L.*, 87, 1098-1132; one letter is in *M.G.H.*, *Epistolae*, 3, pp. 688-9, the other in J. Madoz, *Epistolario de Braulio de Zaragoza* (1941), pp. 186-9. See also M. Martins, *O monacato de San Frutuoso de Braga* (1950); *Bibl.SS.*, 5, 1295-6.

St Magnus of Orkney (*c.* 1075-1116)

Magnus was the son of Erling, one of the twin Viking earls of the Orkneys in the second half of the eleventh century. He seems to have operated as a pirate before being converted to Christianity. The other twin, Paul, had a son, Haakon, who was sent to the Norwegian court in an attempt to stop his political intrigues at home. The plan misfired, and Haakon persuaded the king of Norway to launch a campaign against the Orkneys. This was successful, and Magnus was forced to join in further raids along the western coast of Scotland and the north of England. The Norwegian fleet sailed as far as Anglesey, where it joined battle with a combined Welsh and English fleet. Magnus refused to fight, saying that he would not injure those who had done him no harm; he was held captive in the hold of one of the ships but managed to escape and make his way to Scotland. He repented of his earlier life and started a new régime of prayer and penance, but when Haakon tried to make himself sole ruler of the Orkneys Magnus was determined to claim his inheritance and led an army against his cousin. For a time the two ruled together in an uneasy truce, but Haakon was determined to get rid of Magnus. He tricked him into attending a peace conference and had him murdered at Egilsay; according to the Saga, Magnus refused to defend himself and died praying for his killers. Traditionally Magnus has been regarded as a martyr, but his murder appears to have been wholly political in intent. He was buried first at Christ Church on Birsay, but his remains were moved to Kirkwall about the year 1136. Bones discovered in the cathedral there in 1919 have been proved to be his.

His cult became popular in the north of Scotland, Iceland, and the Faroes, and a number of miracles were attributed to his intercession. He is said to have appeared to Robert the Bruce before the battle of Bannockburn in 1314 and promised him victory. A large number of churches were dedicated to him, including one in the city of London and the cathedral at Kirkwall in the Orkneys.

Sources for the life of Magnus are good. There is an Icelandic text composed shortly after his death, and this was expanded about 1136 by an Orkney writer named Rodbert. See J. Mooney, *St Magnus, Earl of Orkney* (1935); S. Cruden, "The cathedral and relics of St Magnus, Kirkwall," in M. R. Apted *et al.* (eds.), *Ancient Monuments and their Interpretation* (1977), pp. 85-97; H. Pálsson and P. Edwards (eds.), *Orkneyinga Saga. The History of the Earls of Orkney* (1978); *O.D.S.*, p. 313.

St Drogo (*c.* 1118-89)

Drogo, or Dreux or Druon, came from a noble Flemish family and was born in Epinoy in Artois. His father died before he was born, and his mother died giving birth to him. As he grew up and learned that his mother's life had been sacrificed to save him, Drogo is said to have blamed himself for her death and to have suffered from excessive feelings of guilt and depression. He gradually learned to trust in God's mercy and about the age of eighteen began a life devoted to penitential pilgrimages. These helped to cure him of his earlier introspection, and after a time he settled down at Sebourg, near Valenciennes in north-eastern France, and hired himself out as a shepherd. He gained a reputation for sanctity and for bilocation—people claimed to see him attending Mass while he was out in the fields with the sheep, and this gave rise to a local saying, "Not being St Drogo, I can't be in two places at once." After about six years he resumed his travels and had visited Rome nine times when he was afflicted by a severe hernia that made him look repulsive. He spent the rest of his life in solitude, living in a cell built against the wall of a church in Sebourg and attending Mass by means of a squint. He is said to have lived there for forty years, surviving on bread and water and suffering great pain. According to tradition, on one occasion part of the church and his cell were destroyed by fire, but Drogo refused to move and afterwards was found unharmed kneeling in the ashes. A local cult began as soon as he died, and his tomb in the church of St Martin in Sebourg became a place of pilgrimage. He is one of the patron saints of shepherds.

A brief Life was written in 1320 incorporating many legendary elements; see *AA.SS.*, Apr., 2, pp. 443-5. A number of short popular Lives exist in French and Flemish. See also *Catholicisme*, 3, 1090.

Bd Joachim of Siena (1258-1305)

Chiaramonte was born in Siena in 1258. Later accounts say that he was a member of the famous Piccolomini family, but there is no mention of this in the early Life, which one would expect if he had belonged to so important a family. He is said to have been extremely pious as a child, with a particular devotion to Our Lady, and when he was fourteen he received the Servite habit from St Philip Benizi (23 Aug.), taking the name of Joachim in religion. Out of humility he refused to become a priest, but he loved to serve Mass and would sometimes fall into ecstasy while doing so. The Servite house in Siena was noted for its strict observance and the holiness of its members, and when Joachim's reputation for sanctity spread outside the monastery he asked to be moved to another house to avoid the publicity. He spent about a year in Arezzo, but the people of Siena insisted he be recalled, and he lived the rest of his life in his native city, praying for its citizens and edifying everyone who came into contact with him. Miracles were attributed to him while he was still alive. He was forty-seven when he died in 1305. His cult was approved in 1609 by Pope Paul V (1605-21), himself a native of Siena. His remains are still venerated in Siena, especially as a protection against epilepsy, a condition Joachim is said to have contracted willingly to cure someone suffering from it.

The earliest Life of Joachim is attributed to a contemporary, Christopher of Parma; see *Anal.Boll.* 13 (1894), pp. 383-97. See also *Bibl.SS.*, 6, 476-8.
A fourteenth-century marble predella in the municipal art gallery of Siena shows scenes from his life, including his falling into ecstasy while serving Mass.

St Benedict Joseph Labre (1748-83)

Benoît-Joseph Labre was born in 1748 in the village of Amettes near Boulogne, the eldest of the fifteen children of a local shopkeeper. When he was twelve he went to live with his uncle, who was a parish priest about forty miles away, to continue his education and then enter the seminary to become a priest. Benoît-Joseph became absorbed in reading the scriptures and Lives of the saints and decided to join as strict a religious Order as possible to devote himself to God's service. When he was eighteen his parents reluctantly gave him permission to join the Trappists, but he was turned down on account of his age. He then tried the Carthusians and the Cistercians but neither would accept him: he was obviously devout but also rather eccentric and unsuited to community life.

About the year 1770 he seems to have accepted that he would not be able to become a religious and also to have developed the idea of being a permanent pilgrim: he had travelled on foot to the various monasteries he had tried and now set out for Rome, walking all the way and depending entirely on alms. In that way he believed he could follow the scriptural counsels of perfection: he would be in the world but not of it, would have no belongings except the clothes he walked in, and would have "nowhere to lay his head" in imitation of Our Lord. As he walked he tried to keep in the presence of God by prayer and meditation and so rarely spoke to other travellers. Over the years he visited all the main pilgrim shrines in western Europe, including Loreto and Assisi in Italy, Compostela in Spain, Paray-le Monial in France, and Einsiedeln in Switzerland, which he visited five times. He relied on what people gave him voluntarily and did not beg, often indeed giving away gifts of money to others he felt deserved them more. His neglect of personal hygiene made him an unwelcome figure, and he was turned out of churches and subjected to abuse and occasional beatings. From 1774 onward he lived in Rome, except for an annual pilgrimage to Loreto, sleeping rough in the Colosseum until forced by illness to enter a hospice for the poor. He spent his days visiting churches, especially those where the Forty Hours Devotion was being held, and became known as "the saint of the Forty Hours," often spending hours in contemplation before the Blessed Sacrament. He fell ill during Lent 1783 and finally collapsed after hearing Mass in his favourite church, the Madonna dei Monti, on the Wednesday in Holy Week. He died later that day, 16 April 1783, at the age of thirty-five. A popular cult started immediately, and demands for his canonization were helped by a biography written by his confessor. It is interesting that the first English account of his life was an abridged version of this that appeared as early as 1785. He was canonized in 1883 after a particularly rigorous examination of his way of life and is a "representative example of those who, at all times in Christian history, have refused in the name of Christ to be 'respectable'" (*N.D.S.*). He is the patron saint of tramps and homeless people, and may be considered the unofficial patron of pilgrims, since he made pilgrimage a lifetime profession instead of an occasional exercise, not unlike St Godric of Finchale (21 May), before he finally settled as a hermit.

The British Library has copies of the several volumes of documents prepared for the beatification and printed between 1820 and 1840. There are many Lives, the more popular of which tend to emphasize some of his less-important characteristics (*N.D.S.*). See, for example, F. Gaguère, *Le Saint Pauvre de Jésus-Christ: Benoît-Joseph Labre* (rev. ed., 1954); A. de la Gorce, Eng. trans. by R. Sheed (1952). In a biography published in 1964 P. Doyère, O.S.B., linked him with other Western and Eastern "wandering saints." See also *N.C.E.*, 8, p. 302; *Bibl.SS.*, 2, 1218-20; *O.D.S.*, pp. 286-7.

There is an eighteenth-century portrait by Antonio Cavalluci. Benedict Joseph is usually shown with a pilgrim's staff and with rosary beads in his hand. His death-mask is in the church of the Madonna dei Monti, Rome.

St **Bernadette** (1844–79)

Marie Bernarde Soubirous was born in Lourdes in the Hautes-Pyrénées in 1844, the eldest of the six children of François Soubirous and Louise Castérot. Bernadette, as she was known in the family, was not a healthy child; she suffered from asthma and caught cholera in the epidemic of 1854, which left her even weaker. Her father was a miller but had no business sense, and so the family gradually sank into severe poverty and were reduced to living in the basement of a dilapidated house in the town. Bernadette received little by way of education and was, anyway, regarded as rather dull; she had not made her First Communion by 1858, the year her very ordinary life was transformed by a series of apparitions that made her and the town known throughout the world.

A full account of those apparitions may be found under the feast of Our Lady of Lourdes (11 Feb.). Bernadette insisted that between 11 February and 16 July she experienced a series of visions of a Lady in a cave or grotto in a local rock-face known as Massabielle, and a stream sprang from the ground at a spot indicated by the Lady. After she had reported the first of these visions, Bernadette was accompanied to the cave by increasing numbers of people, but she was the only one to experience anything out of the ordinary. The message of the Lady was one of penance for the conversion of sinners and a request for people to visit the place on pilgrimage. When asked who she was, the Lady replied, "I am the Immaculate Conception." The dogma of the Immaculate Conception of Our Lady had been defined by the Church in 1854—see the entry for the feast on 8 December. At no time did the apparition promise that sick people visiting the place might be healed; indeed, no benefits in this life were promised, but the Lady said that she would make Bernadette happy in the next. A chapel was built by the grotto in 1862, and after the Franco-Prussian War of 1870 Lourdes quickly became the most popular pilgrimage site in Europe.

At first Bernadette faced considerable opposition and open disbelief from both church and civic authorities; she was dismissed as a simple, uneducated girl suffering from hallucinations. What won many of the sceptics round were her obvious sincerity, her disinterestedness, and her commonsense. She hated the publicity her story brought her and refused to accept money or gifts from the many people who went to see her. She never referred to the apparitions unless asked directly about them and refused to believe that she had any special powers; in particular she refused to lay her hands on sick people and while for a time she would touch visitors' rosaries she stopped doing this on the advice of her confessor. From 1861 to 1866 she boarded in a hospice run by the Sisters of Charity. In 1864 she asked if she could enter the convent of the Sisters of Notre Dame at Nevers, but ill health prevented her doing so until 1866, when she was accepted as a novice and took as her name in religion Maria-Bernarda.

She spent the rest of her life in the Order, living the ordinary life of a nun and not leaving the convent even to take part in the celebrations that marked the opening of a new basilica in Lourdes in 1876. Her absence from the celebrations seems to have been her own choice: she was interested but wanted to avoid notice; as she put it, "Oh, if only I could see without being seen!" In the same way, she became reluctant to write letters from the convent when she learned those she had written were being handed around as though special. As Thurston says, perhaps one of her secrets was that she was never of her own free will to do anything that would attract the attention of other people to her. In the convent she was appointed infirmarian and then assistant sacristan. As with everything else, she adopted a straightforward approach to the spiritual life: "I must be holy," she wrote, "my Jesus wants it and I'm obliged to be so by my vocation." The path to that holiness lay in obedience to the Rule and as close a union as possible to the crucified Christ. One of her prayers was: "O Jesus, keep me under the standard of your cross. Let me not just look at you crucified but have you living in my heart." With regard to what had happened before she entered the convent, she likened herself to a broom: "Our Lady used me. They have put me back in my corner. I am happy to stop there." Later on she wrote, "The heart of Jesus, with all its treasures—that is mine, and I will live for it and die peacefully for it amid my sufferings."

Her health continued to cause trouble. She had been anointed only four months after joining the Order and had made her vows early, as she seemed to be dying. From 1875 on she had scarcely any break from illness: her asthma got worse, and she suffered from tuberculosis of the bones and a great amount of pain. She put up with everything with great patience and resignation and died on 16 April 1879. "The only 'extraordinary' months in her life were those of the apparitions; before and after, her life was humdrum in the extreme" (*O.D.S.*). She was canonized in 1933 under the name Maria Bernarda, not for her visions but for her life of prayer, simple devotion, and straightforward obedience both to the Rule and to whatever God required her to undergo. A more balanced and, indeed, ordinary visionary would be difficult to find. Perhaps because she offered so little that was colourful to popular writers, apart from the apparitions themselves, stories were invented about early miracles she was supposed to have worked as a child, including crossing a river dry foot and multiplying food for her family. There is no foundation for these stories nor for those attaching to the time of the apparitions, such as the often repeated story of how a candle-flame played on her fingers for a quarter of an hour without harming her while she was talking to Our Lady.

The basic study is L. J. M. Cros, *Histoire de Notre-Dame de Lourdes*, 3 vols. (1925-7); see also R. Laurentin, *Histoire authentique de Lourdes* , 5 vols. (1966); H. Thurston, "Blessed Bernadette's Path to Holiness," in *The Month* 151 (1928), pp. 147-57. There have been many Lives, not all of them reliable; see H. Petitot, *The True Story of St Bernadette* (1949); F. Trochu, *Sainte Bernadette Soubirous* (1957); A. Ravier, *Bernadette Soubirous* (1979). Franz Werfel's very popular *The Song of Bernadette* (1942) was used as the basis of a film of the same name; it was strongly criticized by Bede Lebbe, *The Soul of Bernadette* (1949). See also *N.C.E.*, 13, pp. 446-7; *O.D.S.*, pp. 50-1; *Bibl.SS.*, 8, 1035-41, with two photographs of the saint.

17

St Simeon Barsabae, *Bishop*, and Companions, *Martyrs* (341)

Simeon, named Bars'abae or "son of the fuller," was appointed bishop of Seleucia-Ctesiphon in Persia as a result of the deposition in 324 of the previous bishop. When the sentence of deposition was not upheld, Simeon was reduced to being an auxiliary; we do not know when he became bishop in his own right. When the king, Sapor II, renewed the persecution of the Christians in the year 340, he ordered them to pay a double tax and decreed the closure of their churches. Since most of his people were poor, Simeon refused to collect the money and so was arrested. When he was brought before the king he refused to prostrate himself before him or to worship the sun and was imprisoned with about one hundred others. He won back to the Faith the king's tutor, Usthazanes, who was then executed, and on the following day all the prisoners including Simeon were executed. The former edition of the Roman Martyrology named three of them: two priests, Abdechala and Hanania, and the superviser of the king's works, Pusayk. It also listed another group of Persian martyrs on the following day, but there seems to be some overlap between the two lists. The persecution under Sapor II seems to have been particularly fierce.

Simeon heads the list of martyrs in the Syriac *Breviarium* of 412. He is probably the same person as the St Barsabas venerated on 11 December as a martyr under Sapor II.

A French translation of the ancient and reliable *passio* is printed in H. Leclercq, *Les Martyrs*, 3, pp. 145-62. See also *Bibl.SS.*, 11, 1097-1100, with a long bibliography.

The Persian Martyrs (344)

Today the Roman Martyrology celebrates the martyrdom of 120 men and women in Persia. The group was made up mainly of priests and monks, with a small number of holy women, and probably suffered at Seleucia-Ctesiphon during the persecution ordered by King Sapor II (309-79). The reason for the persecution was the refusal of the Christians to worship the sun and perhaps also their alleged loyalty to Rome—they were sometimes called the "allies of the Caesars." We do not know any of their names, and the *acta* give far more detail about a holy and wealthy woman from Arbela, by name Yazdandocta, who ministered to the martyrs while they were in prison for about six months and told them the day fixed for their execution. She urged them to seek God's grace so that they would not weaken and would be able to shed their blood for the cause of the Faith they shared. She went on, "As for myself, I ask most earnestly that by your prayers you will obtain for me the happiness of meeting you all again before the heavenly throne." At the place of execution the prisoners were offered their freedom if they would worship the sun, but they refused, saying they regarded the day as a joyful feast-day. They were executed by being beheaded. Yazdandocta was able to remove their bodies and bury them some distance away.

This account is free of the miraculous elements that so often arouse suspicion but is still not wholly trustworthy. There are similarities between it and other accounts, and Yazdandocta appears in the same role in the *passio* of SS Acepsima, Joseph, and Aeitala. The martyrs are listed in a number of Byzantine martyrologies, sometimes mixed up with other saints, and Baronius included them in the Roman Martyrology.

Bibl.SS., 10, 504-5; *Vies des Saints*, 4, pp. 139-40.

St Donnan, *Abbot,* and Companions, *Martyrs* (618)

Donnan, or Donan, was one of the many Irish monks who followed St Columba (9 June) to Iona to evangelize Scotland. That was about the year 580, and some time later he left with fifty-two fellow-monks to found a monastery on the island of Eigg in the Inner Hebrides. As he was celebrating Mass for the community on the Easter Vigil, the island was attacked by a gang of robbers; he and the monks were herded into the refectory and the building set alight; those who tried to escape were killed in cold blood. The traditional account relates how the raid, perhaps carried out by Vikings, had been organized by a local woman who had lost her grazing rights when the monks had taken over the island. There is another account that says the monks were killed by pirates, who were a constant threat among the islands, and were beheaded and not burned. It is not clear why the monks should be regarded as martyrs, but reports that they were would have increased the popularity of their cult since martyrs were rare among the early Irish saints. A cult did grow up quickly, and at least eleven churches were dedicated to Donnan; on Eigg there is Kildonan and a St Donnan's well.

K.S.S., p. 325; *O.D.S.*, p. 135; D. P. Mould, *Scotland of the Saints* (1952), pp. 142-9. C. Mooney, in *D.H.G.E.*, 14 (1960), 662-4, discusses the different sources and the place names.

St Robert of Chaise-Dieu, *Abbot* (*c.* 1000-67)

Robert de Turlande was born about the year 1000 of a noble family in the Auvergne region of central France. His parents placed him with the canons of St Julian's church in Brioude, and in 1026 he joined the community and was ordained priest. He built a hospital for pilgrims and the poor at his own expense but became dissatisfied with the way of life. He thought about entering the monastery of Cluny but was dissuaded by the other canons and so went on a pilgrimage to Rome and the great Benedictine monastery of Monte Cassino. On his return he decided to become a solitary, and taking two lay companions with him, he found a suitable place to settle about five miles from Brioude. They built cells and lived a life of prayer and manual work, providing for their own needs, assisting the poor, and preaching. The settlement flourished in a way similar to that of St Bernard of Tiron (14 Apr.): within three years Robert had attracted so many disciples that it was necessary to establish a monastery for them, and this was the beginning of the great abbey of Chaise-Dieu (or House of God), started in 1043. This later grew to hold a community of about three hundred monks following the Benedictine Rule. Robert established a large number of daughter houses, about fifty in all in the Massif Central alone. His aim was to maintain as simple a way of life as possible, and so the houses were kept small, with between two and six monks in each—they were cells rather than monasteries—and he insisted on manual work being a major part of the monks' day. To some extent the growth of Chaise-Dieu and the organization of the daughter houses meant that his original ideals of poverty and simplicity were lost, but his dying words were, "I have always wished that niggardly thrift and avarice could never find even the smallest place there." He died in 1067. Miracles were attributed to him before and after he died, and he was canonized by Alexander II in 1070. He had been one of the earliest, if not the earliest, of the important eleventh-century monastic reformers in France. His Congregation survived as a separate Benedictine branch until it merged with the Maurists in 1640.

A Life was written by Gerard of Laveine, Robert's chaplain, immediately after his death and taken to the pope as the basis for the canonization; another Life was written about 1100 by Marbod, the bishop of Rennes; both are in *AA.SS.*, Apr. 3, pp. 316-33. See also *Bibl.SS.*, 11, 235-7.

Bd James of Certaldo, *Abbot* (1292)

James was born at Certaldo near Florence and was a member of the ancient Guidi family. Through regularly visiting the church of SS Clement and Justus, run by Camaldolese monks in Volterra, he developed a vocation to the religious life and in 1230 was received into the Order. His devotion and austerity impressed everyone, and when he was given charge of the parish in 1239 he carried out his duties so effectively that he was responsible for bringing many people back to the practice of their religion. His father was moved by his son's way of life to enter the monastery himself as a lay brother. One of his brothers, who had joined the Knights of St John of Jerusalem, left them after a short while and also entered the monastery as a lay brother. James was twice elected abbot but refused the post out of humility. The third time he was elected, in 1268, he accepted but resigned as soon as he could and returned to running the parish. He was noted for his life of prayer and penance. He died in 1292.

AA.SS., Apr., 2, pp. 152-5; *Bibl.SS.*, 6, 352-3.

Bd James of Cerqueto (1367)

Few details are known about the life of Giacomo of Cerqueto (in Umbria). As a young man he joined the Hermits of St Augustine in Perugia, an Order formed in 1256 by amalgamating several Italian communities of hermits under one Rule, and spent the rest of a very long life devoted to prayer. Members of the Order claimed that it was due to his prayers they were allowed on certain occasions to wear a white habit in honour of Our Lady. Stories were told of his power over wild animals and how they kept quiet while he was preaching in the open, but the stories are very similar to those told of many hermits who lived solitary lives in touch with nature. James died in the church of St Augustine in Perugia on 17 April 1367. Because of the large number of miracles reported to have taken place at his tomb, in 1754 the bishop of Perugia had James' body carried through the streets and re-buried in a new shrine. The cult was approved in 1895.

The decree approving the cult has some biographical details; see *Anal.Eccles.*, 1895, pp. 253-4; *Bibl.SS.*, 6, 352.

Bd Clare of Pisa (1362-1419)

Theodora, or Thora, was born either in Venice or Florence in 1362, the daughter of Piero Gambacorta, one of the leading citizens of Pisa. Her older brother was Bd Peter of Pisa (17 June), founder in 1380 of a small Order of hermits. At the age of seven Thora was betrothed to her future husband and at twelve left home to live in his parents' house. There she took a special interest in the poor of the neighbourhood, and when her mother-in-law forbade her to give away any more of the household stores Thora joined a group of pious ladies who ministered to the sick. When she was fifteen she and her husband caught an epidemic disease; she recovered, but he died, and his family immediately began to arrange a second marriage for her. She refused this and decided to become a religious, inspired in part by a letter from St Catherine of Siena (29 Apr.). Thora cut off her hair, gave away her rich clothes to the poor, and made secret arrangements to join the Poor Clares, taking the name Clare in religion. Her relatives, however, would not let her stay in the convent and forced her to return home in disgrace. After failing to get her to change her mind, her father gave in and allowed her to enter the Dominican convent of Holy Cross. This was a lax house, and Clare set out to reform it, but most of the nuns refused to follow her. Then her father built a new convent for her, and she transferred there in 1382 with the nuns who agreed to follow a strict observance of the Rule.

Clare had become friendly with Bd Mary of Pisa, who had been widowed twice by the age of twenty-five. Both women came under the influence of St Catherine of Siena and were especially determined to implement strict rules about poverty and enclosure in the new house. Clare interpreted these so rigorously that she would not even give shelter to her own brother when he was fleeing from the assassin who had killed their father and two of their brothers, although later she forgave the murderer and supported his widow and daughters in the convent. She was first subprioress of the convent, then prioress, and it became a training centre and model in a campaign to restore strict observance throughout the Order's houses in Italy. It was from there that Bd John Dominici (10 June) took the nuns to initiate the reform in the famous Corpus Domini convent in Venice, which he founded in 1394, and some writers have claimed that Clare deserves a place alongside St Bernardino of Siena (20 May) and St Teresa of Avila (15 Oct.) as a reformer of the religious life. The nuns led an enclosed life of prayer, manual work, and study—the importance of this last element was underlined by Clare's director, who told her, "Never forget that in our Order very few have become saints who have not likewise been scholars." Her convent was troubled by financial worries for most of the rest of her life, but she still insisted on using a large legacy to found an orphan hospital rather than spend it on the convent. She died in 1419, and a cult began shortly afterwards; it was approved in 1830.

A few of Clare's letters survive. They reveal a person whose spiritual life was built on deep piety and severe asceticism but who was neither sentimental nor rigorist in her advice to others. The letters were published by C. Guasti in 1871. Sources for her life are plentiful and reliable. A contemporary Italian Life by a nun is in *AA.SS.*, Apr. 2, pp. 503-16. See also M. E. Murphy, *Blessed Clara Gambacorta* (1928); T. McGlynn, *This is Clara of Pisa* (1962); *N.C.E.*, 3, p. 913; *Bibl.SS.*, 6, 23-6.

Bd Henry Heath, *Martyr* (1599-1643)

Henry Heath was born in Peterborough in 1599. He was brought up a Protestant and after graduating from St Benet's College, Cambridge, was appointed librarian at the college. This gave him the opportunity to study the current religious controversies in detail, and he was particularly impressed by the arguments of St Robert Bellarmine (17 Sept.). He became a Catholic and then went to Douai to study for the priesthood; after a while he decided to join the English Franciscans who had recently opened a house there. He took the name Paul of St Magdalen in religion, and after his profession and ordination he spent the next nineteen years as a member of the community in Douai. He led an austere life of fasting and penance and devoted himself to study. He taught theology at the university and held various offices in the Order, including that of guardian of the Douai house and commissary provincial for Flanders. In 1641 he felt called to go to England to work on the mission there. A large number of priests had been condemned to death that year, and when Henry wrote to his superior asking permission to be one of the replacements he argued, "you cannot allow that soldier to be a man of courage who, hearing that the army is drawn up in battle array, the drums and trumpets sounding to the charge, and yet shall indulge himself at home in sloth and cowardice." He had earlier written to the condemned priests asking for their prayers: "Wherefore I humbly beseech you, for the love of God, to pray for me that I may come to you and never be separated from you." It appears that his main motive in going to England was not to minister to the Catholics there but to suffer martyrdom.

His superiors seem to have been rather reluctant to allow him to leave Douai but in the end agreed, and he set out for England in 1643. He was ill-prepared for the journey, walking barefoot from Dover to London disguised as a sailor and with nowhere to stay when he arrived, and was arrested almost immediately. He openly admitted that he was a priest and wanted to convert people to Catholicism, and so was condemned to death. Before the judges had passed sentence on him, he wrote to a fellow-priest: "I beseech the Divine goodness that it may answer my desires, that I may suffer death for my Lord Jesus Christ." He was hanged, drawn, and quartered at Tyburn on 17 April 1643. Authenticated relics consist of two small pieces of bone, a corporal dipped in his blood, and a piece of the rope used to hang him. A work written by him was published in Douai in 1643: *Soliloquia seu Documenta Christianae Perfectionis*; this went through six editions and was then published in English in 1674 as *Soliloquies; or, the Documents of Christian Perfection*; this was reprinted in London in 1844. Gillow says the book "gives a clear insight into his saintly soul, and deserves to be in every Catholic library." He was beatified in 1987.

M.M.P., pp. 439-47, cited above; Gillow, 3, pp. 239-42. See also the general entries on the English and Welsh martyrs for 4 May and 25 October.

Bd Kateri Tekakwitha (*c.* 1656-80)

Tekakwitha was the daughter of a Christian Algonquin and a pagan Mohawk chief. She was born about the year 1656 at Ossernenon (present-day Auriesville, in New York State) and at the age of four was left an orphan through the death of her parents, and a brother, from smallpox. She herself was left disfigured and partially blind from the disease. While living with an uncle, and before she had become a Christian, she seems to have made some sort of vow not to marry. The motives behind her decision are not at all clear but must have been strong, as she came under considerable pressure to marry and faced mockery and ill treatment when she refused to do so, and there was nothing in Mohawk culture to support her decision. In 1667 she met Christian missionaries for the first time when three of them lodged with her uncle, but while apparently impressed by them she did not seek instruction, still less Baptism. About eight years later she met another missionary, Jacques de Lamberville, S.J., and was eventually baptized by him at Easter 1676, taking the Christian name of Kateri (Catherine). Her uncle raised no objections to her conversion, as long as she remained at home; he strongly opposed conversions when they led to the newly baptized leaving the villages and going to live near the mission stations. Before long, however, Kateri found life in the village very stressful: it was difficult to live the life of a Christian, and she was still subject to considerable sexual harassment. Fr Jacques advised her to leave, and so she made a journey on foot of about two hundred miles to settle at Sault St Louis, near Montreal, where there was a Christian village. She arrived there in October 1677 and made her First Holy Communion on Christmas Day the same year—the missionaries insisted on a long period of probation between Baptism and reception of the Sacrament.

For the next three years Kateri led an exemplary life: she heard two Masses every day, fasted on Wednesdays and Saturdays, and, as her director put it later, "In attaching herself to God, she attached herself to continued efforts to remain in communion with him and to preserve throughout the entire day the good sentiments she had experienced in the morning at the foot of the altar." In 1679 she made a private vow of perpetual virginity. She died on 17 April 1680 at Sault St Louis. One of the missionaries who knew her best wrote: "She had an insatiable thirst for spiritual knowledge, and a great zeal to put into practice all she understood. Her soul was well disposed toward perfection." Her cult was strong immediately after her death, and cures and other miracles were reported at her tomb and through her intercession. A number of the miracles, and some of the appearances reported after her death, were well attested by the Jesuit missionaries. She was beatified in 1980, the first native American to be honoured in that way.

R. G. Thwaites (ed.), *Jesuit Relations and Allied Documents* (1896–1901; new ed., 1959); E. Lecompte, *Glory of the Mohawks* (Eng. trans. by F. Ralston Werum, 1944); M. C. Buehrle, *Kateri of the Mohawks* (1954); *N.C.E.*, 13, pp. 978-9.

18

St Alexander of Alexandria, *Patriarch* (*c.* 250-328)

Alexander was born about the year 250 and became patriarch of Alexandria in 312 in succession to Achillas. According to one source, his candidature was opposed by a fellow-priest, Arius, who became his bitter enemy when he was unsuccessful. Another source, however, says that Alexander owed his election to the support given him by Arius, but this account may have been designed to show the patriarch in a bad light for later turning against Arius. At the start of his pontificate Alexander had to deal with an internal controversy about the date of Easter and was faced by the continuing schism of Bishop Melitius of Lycopolis in Egypt. This concerned the re-admission to full communion of those who had fallen away during times of persecution. Melitius took a strict line against the guidelines agreed by a former patriarch, St Peter (26 Nov.), and had begun to ordain his own priests. It was Arius, however, who was to cause Alexander the greatest trouble. It appears that Arius, unable to find any fault in the patriarch's personal life or performance of his duties, began to put forward his own doctrinal beliefs secretly in an attempt to discredit Alexander's teaching on the Trinity. Alexander was in charge of one of the city's most important churches, had a popular reputation because of his ascetic way of life, and was an effective preacher, and so, when he began to expound his views openly, he made a considerable impression. Those views concerned the nature and person of Jesus: was he truly divine, equal to the Father in his Godhead and co-existing with him from all eternity, or was he, as Arius taught, created by the Father and so inferior to him and only "the son of God" because God gave him that title in recognition of his holiness? Here was the basis of a heresy, Arianism, that was to divide the Church and the empire for centuries.

At first Alexander tried to deal with Arius kindly by inviting him to discuss the doctrinal issues involved. When this failed and Arius continued to preach and win over sections of the people and the clergy, Alexander called a local council of around a hundred bishops from Egypt and Libya about the year 320. The council condemned Arius' doctrines as heretical, but he went to Palestine to recruit support and won over two influential bishops, Eusebius of Caesarea and Eusebius of Nicomedia. The latter then wrote to several bishops in Asia Minor and the East to uphold Arius against Alexander, who, after the council, had written about seventy letters to various bishops to defend its decision. A number of Eastern bishops seemed willing to uphold Arius against the patriarch even though they disagreed with his doctrines. At one stage in the controversy Alexander wrote a statement of what he believed to be the orthodox position and sent it to as many bishops as he could, asking for their signatures by way of support; he received 250 signatures, including one hundred from his own diocese. He also sent a copy of the document, known as his "Tome," to Arius, saying he was willing to die for the beliefs it expressed, and a copy to the pope, St Silvester I (31 Dec.). This internationalization of the controversy, as it has been called, meant that Arius' doctrines became known widely very quickly. When the emperor, Constantine, heard how they were dividing the Church and beginning to cause violence, he reproached both Arius and Alexander for pursuing what he considered to be "petty discussions on unintelligible minutiae" (Atiya) and appointed Hosius (or Ossius), the bishop of Córdoba, to arbitrate between them. Arius was still seeking support and composed a number of popular songs or hymns so that the people would pick up his doctrines without realizing they were doing so. Hosius attended a synod at Alexandria in 324 but decided the question could be solved only at a general council and persuaded Constantine to call one at Nicaea, near Constantinople, the following year. Alexander attended, despite his age and ill health, and was accompanied by St Athanasius (2 May), then a deacon, who was to succeed him as patriarch. The council condemned Arius and issued the famous statement of orthodox belief known as the Nicene Creed, in which Christ is said to be "consubstantial with the Father" and "begotten, not created." Alexander had a major hand in drawing up this statement. The council also recognized Alexander and his successors as having authority over Egypt and Libya, and it settled the Melitian schism that had troubled Alexander's early years by accepting a compromise offered by the patriarch in the interests of peace.

Alexander returned home after the council but died about five months later, unable to carry out a planned programme of reconciliation. Traditionally his death has been put in 326, which would support the idea of his dying soon after his return, but some modern sources put it as late as 328, the year Athanasius became patriarch. The month of his death is also disputed. Two of his letters survive, but other writings attributed to him are almost certainly not his. He was a man of great learning, intent on peaceful solutions wherever possible but a stalwart and energetic defender of orthodoxy when required. He reformed his clergy, giving precedence to those who had spent some time as hermits in the desert, and had the great church of St Theonas built in the city. His work has been overshadowed by that of his more famous successor, Athanasius.

See *P.G.*, 18, 571-82, for the letters. See also A. S. Atiya, in *Coptic Encyclopedia*, 1, pp. 81-5; *Bibl.SS.*, 1, 768-70; *E.E.C.*, 1, p. 20, with an excellent up-to-date bibliography of scholarly works. See also *O.D.C.C.*, under Alexander, Arianism, and Arius.

St Laserian, *Abbot* (639)

Laserian, or Laisren, is also known as Molaise, an affectionate form of the name. He was an important Irish saint of the seventh century, but we know little for certain about him. He seems to have been born of a royal Ulster family, and Cairell, king of Ulster, may have been his grandfather. He studied with St Fintan of Taghmon (21 Oct.) and then settled in Leighlin, County Carlow, where there was a monastery of which he later became abbot. He opposed his former teacher, St Fintan, over the dating of Easter and is said to have gone to Rome to look for evidence to settle this controversy and other issues that were dividing the Irish Church. One account says that while in Rome he met Pope Honorius, who consecrated him bishop and made him legate to the whole of Ireland. This is almost certainly not true, though Leighlin did become an important centre for the promotion of Roman usage.

At some stage in his youth Laserian had visited Iona in Scotland; he is the patron saint of Lamlash Bay on the island of Arran off the Scottish coast, where there is a cave of Molaise. Laserian died in 639, and a holy well at Leighlin was for many centuries associated with his cult. This was restored in 1914 after a local farmer claimed to have been cured through the saint's intercession by using water from the well, and an ancient stone cross was re-erected; the site became a place of pilgrimage again. It is sometimes claimed that Laserian founded a monastery on Inishmurray, County Sligo, but this appears to be the result of a confusion with another St Molaise (12 Aug.); the monastery there was founded in the previous century.

The Life of St Laserian is late and of little historical value. See *The Irish Saints*, pp. 203-4, 252; *O.D.S.*, p. 288.

St Ursmar, *Bishop and Abbot* (713)

About the year 689 the great abbey of Lobbes in modern Belgium, founded earlier in the century by St Landelin (15 June), was entrusted to the care of Ursmar, who may already have been a bishop, although it is more likely that he was invested with episcopal jurisdiction as abbot. We know nothing for certain about his early life, despite the existence of a number of Lives written about a century after his death; they consist in the main of conventional statements about his sanctity, austerity, and apostolic zeal. He appears to have been born at Floyon in northern France, perhaps about the year 640, and to have received a monastic education. It is possible he became a monk at Lobbes and was elected abbot in the normal way. He probably introduced the Benedictine Rule and was certainly responsible for extending the abbey's buildings. He consecrated the abbey church of Lobbes and dedicated it to SS Peter and Paul in August 697 and later built a separate church for the use of the local people, dedicated to Our Lady. He is said to have founded a number of other monasteries and appears to have played an important role in evangelizing Flanders.

He died on 18 April 713 and was buried in his church of Our Lady. His relics were subsequently venerated in the abbey church and in the fifteenth century were translated to Binche, east of Mons in modern Belgium, where they remained until they were destroyed in 1794. His cult was popular locally, and he is still prayed to for children who are slow to walk.

Bibl.SS., 11, 866-7. *Anal.Boll.* 23 (1904), pp. 315-9, prints a short acrostic poem written by Ursmar's successor, Ermin, which refers to him as a bishop and a martyr because of the sufferings he had to endure.

Bd Idesbald, *Abbot* (*c.* 1090-1167)

All that is known about Idesbald's background is that he was from the aristocratic Van der Gracht family and became a canon of Saint Walburga's in Furnes in Flanders. He may have been a widower when he became a priest. After some time he left his canonry and applied to join the Cistercian abbey of Dune. He impressed the rest of the community by his integrity and wisdom and was a meticulous cantor; the divine office was his main concern and the centre of his monastic life. Eventually he was elected abbot, and the monastery thrived during his rule, gaining privileges from Pope Alexander III (1159-81). When he died in 1167 he was buried in the monastic church, something the Cistercians allowed only for special reasons, in this case his sanctity. The abbey was destroyed in 1577 during the religious wars, but the monks were able to save his body and eventually took it to Bruges, where it is still venerated. When it was inspected at the beginning of the seventeenth century it was found to be incorrupt. His cult was approved in 1894.

There is no early Life of Idesbald. See J. De Cuyper, *Idesbald van der Gracht* (in Flemish, 1946); *Bibl.SS.*, 7, 642-3.

St Galdinus, *Bishop* (1176)

Galdinus was a member of the famous Della Scala family of Milan. He served under two archbishops as chancellor and archdeacon and became involved in a quarrel between the emperor, Frederick Barbarossa, and Archbishop Hubert of Milan, who supported the genuine pope, Alexander III, against the emperor's antipope. In 1165 Galdinus was created cardinal, and the following year Alexander III appointed him archbishop in succession to Hubert—he was the first archbishop of Milan to be a cardinal. He was an active, pastoral bishop, preaching regularly, reforming clerical discipline, and looking after the poor, whom he often visited in their own homes. His provision of bread to the poor became famous, and after his death such provision was referred to as "St Galdino's bread." In addition, he rebuilt the cathedral and the archbishop's palace. It was a difficult time owing to the divisions in the Church and the political troubles with the forceful emperor, and Galdinus worked to heal the schism caused by the election of the antipope, deposing any bishops who continued to support him. He had also to counter the activities of the Cathar heretics who had established themselves in northern Italy, and he was preaching against the evils of heresy when he collapsed in the pulpit of the cathedral and died. In the litanies of the Milanese rite his name is associated with those of St Ambrose (7 Dec.) and St Charles Borromeo (4 Nov.) as one of the principal patrons of the city. His relics are still venerated in the cathedral.

A short early Life is in *AA.SS.*, Apr., 2, pp. 594-5. See also *Bibl.SS.*, 5, 1359-60.

Bd James of Lodi (1364-1404)

Giacomo, or Iacopo, was a native of Lodi, a small town south-east of Milan, whose parents were Marchese Oldi and Fiordonina. His father died when he was young, leaving him well off, and he married Caterina Bocconi. They had three children and dedicated themselves to the pleasures of the social round until an outbreak of plague drove them into the country, to Lodivecchio. Here James entered a local church that contained a reproduction of the Holy Sepulchre, and this moved him very much. On returning to Lodi they found that their two daughters had died from the plague, and James had a total conversion experience. He gave up his former way of life, spent as much time as possible in church, and did penance for his sins. He also took on the care of a sick priest, who taught him Latin. He and Catherine continued to live together for another seven years, but for the last three of these they lived as brother and sister. Catherine also experienced a conversion, and together they took a vow of perpetual continence and became Franciscan tertiaries.

James was ordained priest in 1397 and turned one of his houses into a chapel where they met with a small group of friends for prayer and mutual encouragement. Their way of life raised suspicions among the local Franciscans that they were trying to set up a new branch of the Order, and they had to leave the town. James was accompanied by the tertiaries who had been meeting together, and they worked in Lodivecchio as a community until they could return to Lodi. Here James devoted himself to looking after the sick and especially prisoners of war, gaining a reputation for his good works and penitential way of life. He died on 18 April 1404 from a disease picked up from one of his patients. He was buried in St Julian's, the church he and his wife had founded. A public cult started immediately, and miracles were reported at his tomb. In 1580 his remains were moved to the neighbouring church of San Egidio and in 1789 to the cathedral. The cult was approved in 1933, but he is not included in the new Roman Martyrology.

A Life of James was written by his confessor; see *AA.SS.*, Apr., 2, pp. 599-609. See also *Bibl.SS.*, 9, 1147-9; C. Salvaderi, *Il b. Giacomo Oldi, sacerdote terziario* (1959).

Bd Andrew Ibernón (*c.* 1534–1602)

Andrés Ibernón came from a poor family living in Alcantarilla, near Murcia in Spain. Because of their poverty Andrew was hired out to an uncle at an early age. It is said that his conversion to a life of religion came about when he was returning home after scraping together enough money to provide a dowry for his sister; he was attacked and robbed on the way, and this taught him the folly of depending on worldly goods for happiness. He joined a house of Conventual Franciscans but after seven years left to become a lay brother in a stricter house of the Alcantarine reform, about 1563. His wish was to lead a life of humility, austerity, and prayer in as much solitude as possible, but his fame as a miracle-worker and the gift of prophecy he was given prevented this, and he was consulted by large numbers of visitors to the monastery, many of whom claimed to have been converted to a holier way of life by his advice and example. St Paschal Baylon (17 May), a fellow lay brother, was particularly impressed by his sanctity. Andrew died at Gandia in 1602. He had been honoured as a saint while still alive, and there was a strong local cult after his death. He was beatified in 1791.

Bibl.SS., 7, 592.

Bd Mary of the Incarnation (Barbe Acarie) (1618)

Barbe Avrillot was the daughter of a high government official in Paris. She was educated at her aunt's convent in Longchamp, where she showed signs of unusual piety and seemed destined to become a nun. Her parents, however, wanted her to marry, since she was their only surviving child. She reluctantly agreed, saying, "If I am unworthy through my sins to be the bride of Christ, I can at least be his servant." At the age of seventeen she married Pierre Acarie, an aristocrat with a post in the treasury. He was pious and charitable and did much to help the exiled English Catholics. She was affable and gracious (hence her nickname "la belle Acarie") and became well known and influential in ecclesiastical and court circles. They had six children; the three daughters became Carmelite nuns and one of the sons a priest. Pierre had spent a great deal of money to support the Catholic League during the civil wars of religion in France. When the Protestant Henri IV became king in 1589 he was exiled from Paris, his property was confiscated by his creditors, and his family left in very difficult circumstances. Barbe Acarie defended him in the courts, recovered part of the confiscated land, and finally obtained permission for him to return to Paris, helped, no doubt, by the conversion of the king to Catholicism in 1593.

Barbe became known throughout Paris for her charitable good works and seems to have been entrusted with the distribution of their alms by other people. She was involved in visiting the sick, feeding the poor, and assisting the dying, as well as instructing converts from Protestantism and helping a number of religious houses. Inspired apparently by two visions of St Teresa of Avila (15 Oct.), she persuaded the king to allow Carmelite nuns to open a convent in the capital and in 1604 welcomed the first group of Spanish Carmelites of the Reform to Paris. Four more convents were opened elsewhere with her help in the next five years, and she worked to train suitable young women for entry to these houses—she set up a small Congregation to help her in this and became an "unofficial married novice-mistress" (*B.T.A.*). Among her spiritual advisers at this time were St Francis de Sales (24 Jan.) and Pierre de Bérulle, the founder of the French Oratorians. While most people knew her as an extremely active person, she had a highly developed interior life and reached the heights of contemplative prayer marked by increasingly frequent ecstasies. These frightened her at first until she was reassured they were sent by God.

When Pierre died in 1613 Barbe entered the Carmelite convent in Amiens as a lay sister, taking the name Mary of the Incarnation in religion. Her three daughters were already Carmelites, and when her eldest was appointed sub-prioress shortly afterwards, Barbe was the first to promise her obedience. Disagreements with Pierre de Bérulle led to her transfer to Pontoise in 1616, where she wished to become "the last and poorest of all." One of her spiritual directors in her last years was the English Capuchin Fr Benet Fitch. In her last illness the prioress asked her to bless the nuns at her bedside; before doing so she prayed, "Lord, forgive me for the bad example I have set," and then added, "If it should please Almighty God to admit me to eternal bliss I will ask that the will of his divine son be accomplished in each one of you." She died on 18 April 1618. Miracles were reported at her tomb, and she was beatified in 1791. Her remains are still venerated in the Carmel at Pontoise. Only a few letters from her large correspondence remain; she had burned a treatise she had written on the spiritual life. A short work, later published under the title *The true exercises of Blessed Mary of the Incarnation . . . suitable for souls that desire a good life,* survives.

There are many biographies, beginning with one by André Duval, written in 1621 and republished in 1893. See also Fr Bruno, *La Belle Acarie* (1942); L. C. Sheppard, *Barbe Acarie* (1953); M. Marduel, *Madame Acarie et le Carmel français* (1963). Her influence was such that she merits a mention in Pastor, vols. 11 and 12, and in H. Bremond's *Histoire littéraire du sentiment religieux en France*, 2, pp. 193-262. See also *Dict.Sp.*, 10 (1980), 486-7.

Bd Savina Petrilli, *Foundress* (1851-1923)

Savina was born in Siena in 1851, the daughter of Celso Petrilli and Matilda Vetturini. During her time at a school run by the Daughters of Charity she developed a great admiration for St Catherine of Siena (29 Apr.) and also became interested in helping the poor and the sick. She joined the Children of Mary, and this led to a new apostolate, teaching cathechism to children she found on the streets and whom she used to gather together in her house.

Gradually she felt called to devote herself entirely to God and the care of abandoned children and the poor. With three friends she took temporary vows in 1868 and perpetual ones the following year, and when she was twenty-two she began the work of founding a new Congregation. She faced the usual obstacles and opposition, but her trust in God's providence was strong and she was able to gain enough supporters and benefactors to keep it going. The Congregation's work expanded to include nursing the sick in their own homes as well as in hospitals and looking after the elderly, but its main apostolate was always to the poor and disadvantaged. For Savina and her Sisters, Christ lived in the poor, and she wrote: "Whoever looks at us must see Jesus in us, for charity is the virtue above all others that makes God present." Impulsive by nature, she struggled to acquire patience and submission, and she gradually came to see that in tempering her zeal for helping others lay her particular way of the cross. She made a special vow never deliberately to refuse God anything.

When Savina died on 18 April 1923 her Congregation of the Sisters of the Poor of St Catherine of Siena had over five hundred Sisters, with houses in Italy, South America, the United States, India, the Philippines, and elsewhere. She was beatified in 1988.

G. Bardi, *Madre Savina Petrilli, fondatrice delle Sorelle dei Poveri di S. C. di S* (1959); R. De Rosa, *Una povertà che si chiama Cristo: Profilo spirituale di Madre Savina Petrilli* (1979); M. Franchi Mussini, *Biografia di Madre Savina Petrilli* (n.d.); *Bibl.SS.*, Suppl. 1, 1036-7; *N.S.B.* 2, p. 171.

19

St Leo IX, *Pope* (1002-54)

Bruno was born in Alsace in 1002, the son of Count Hugh of Egisheim, who was closely related to the imperial family. Bruno was educated at Toul, already a centre of monastic reform, and became a canon of the cathedral there while still a young man. In 1026 he led part of the army of his relative, Emperor Conrad II, on a successful expedition to Italy and distinguished himself as a leader. He was still in Italy when the bishop of Toul died and he was appointed as his successor. He was bishop for twenty years and showed himself to be an energetic reformer, attacking in particular the clerical abuses of simony and failure to observe celibacy and insisting on a thorough reform of the monasteries in his diocese.

When Pope Damasus II died in 1048, the emperor, Henry III, nominated Bruno to succeed him, and he was crowned pope in 1049, entering Rome dressed as a pilgrim and taking the name Leo "to recall the ancient, still pure church" (*O.D.P.*). Leo held his first reforming synod in Rome in August 1049 and then began a series of visits to other important centres throughout Europe: altogether he presided over twelve synods (including three more in Rome) and visited Pavia, Reims, and Mainz in 1049; Siponto, Salerno, and Vercelli in 1050; Mantua and Bari in 1053. The influence of these gatherings spread beyond the local churches where they were held because delegates attended them from other dioceses and countries, and they showed, more than anything else in his reign, how committed Leo was to reform. Most of the business of these synods was to do with clerical abuses, and Leo took a rigorist approach to those who had been appointed to their posts by simony or nepotism—in some cases he deposed bishops or got them to resign and receive their posts afresh from himself. He insisted that bishops should be elected by the clergy and people in an attempt to reduce the influence of lay powers over the Church, despite his own appointment both as bishop and pope by the emperor. He also used the synods to deal with cases of heresy, as with Berengar of Tours and the doctrine of the Eucharist. All this activity, of course, enhanced the position of the papacy, whose claim to universal primacy was upheld forcibly by Leo at the synod at Reims.

Leo chose a body of capable and reform-minded advisers from outside the Roman Curia: Hildebrand, who was to become Pope St Gregory VII (25 May); Frederick of Liège, who was to become Pope Stephen IX (1057-8); and Humbert of Moyenmoutier. He also took advice from reformers such as St Hugh of

Cluny (29 Apr.) and St Peter Damian (21 Feb.). The last year of his reign was, however, marred by failures that must be attributed at least partly to lack of judgment on his part. In May 1053 he personally led an army against the Normans in southern Italy in defence of the Church's territories there, but he was easily defeated at Civitella and held captive for some months. Peter Damian, among others, strongly criticized him for this military involvement. This expedition was the occasion of his second, and much more serious, failure. The Byzantine Church claimed jurisdiction over parts of southern Italy and Sicily, and the patriarch of Constantinople was outraged by Leo's holding a papal synod at Siponto in 1050, by his appointment of Humbert as archbishop of Sicily, and finally by Leo's military interference. The pope wanted help from the East against the Normans and so sent a delegation, unfortunately headed by Humbert, to Constantinople at the beginning of 1054 to try to bring about a reconciliation. Both parties proved too intransigent, however, and when Humbert publicly excommunicated the patriarch and his followers, the patriarch responded by issuing his own excommunications against Humbert and the pope. This was in July 1054 and is usually regarded as the start of the schism between East and West. Although Leo was dead by the time the break came, he must be held responsible for the ill-judged delegation.

In March 1054 Leo was taken back to Rome from Benevento, where he had been held captive. He was already ill and ordered his bed and his coffin to be placed side-by-side in St Peter's so that he could prepare himself properly for death. He died there on 19 April and was immediately hailed as a saint. A large number of miracles were attributed to his intercession, and in 1087 Bd Victor III (16 Sept.) approved the popular cult by solemnly re-burying Leo's remains in St Peter's. Leo is usually regarded as the first pope of the great Gregorian reform, but perhaps it would be fairer to see him as the link between two worlds, with a foot in each: he owed his position to the secular power of the day and was too ready to use secular means to achieve his ends: "He seemed to many unwise in drawing the sword gainst the Normans as he seemed also unwise in sending Humbert to Constantinople" (Knowles). At the same time, a devout and spiritual person himself, through his journeyings he made the Church known as a serious agency of reform and raised the prestige of the papacy after years of neglect and even degradation: "For the first time for almost two centuries a pope of ability, energy and spirituality was in office," and it was "the moment when individual attempts at reform [were] replaced by action from the centre" (*ibid.*).

There is a wealth of material on Leo IX. His own letters and other documents are in *P.L.*, 143, 457-800. See A. Poncelet, "Vie et miracles de S. Léon IX," in *Anal. Boll.* 25 (1906), pp. 258-97; L. Stittler and P. Stintzi, *St Léon IX: le pape alsacien* (1950); *O.D.P.*, pp. 147-8; *O.D.S.*, p. 296; E. Duffy, *Saints and Sinners: A History of the Popes* (1997), pp. 89-91. On the general background, see D. Knowles and D. Obolensky, *The Christian Centuries*, 2: *The Middle Ages* (1969). For a lively contemporary account of the council at Reims, see R. W. Southern, *The Making of the Middle Ages* (1975), pp. 122-5; for the more general problems of the papacy at the time see C. Morris, *The Papal Monarchy: the Western Church from 1050 to 1250* (1989).

The oldest representation of Leo appears to be in an illuminated manuscript of the second half of the eleventh century, where he is shown receiving the model of a monastery. A miniature from the following century shows him giving up his bed to a leper. Later pictures are traditionally papal in their portrayal, such as that in a stained-glass window in Freiburg Cathedral (1512).

St Mappalicus and Companions, *Martyrs (c. 250)*

The persecution under the emperor Decius (249-51) was the most systematic attack yet on Christianity. Decius was determined to wipe out its followers altogether because they obeyed an authority that they claimed to be higher than his own and because he was a firm believer in the old Roman religious values. An imperial edict appointed a day on which all those whose religious allegiance was doubtful had to appear before a commission and offer sacrifice while declaring Christianity to be false; afterwards, all were to share a meal consisting of the sacrificial offerings. Those who refused were not condemned to death but imprisoned and tortured in the hope of converting them. In April 250 a proconsul arrived in Carthage in north Africa to carry out the edict, and many Christians gave up their beliefs and adopted paganism. The first one to die as a result of the persecution was Mappalicus, who died under torture; he was followed by about seventeen others, most of whom died of starvation and the terrible conditions under which they were kept in prison. St Cyprian (16 Sept.), bishop of Carthage at the time, singles out Mappalicus and his companions for special praise in his *Letter to Martyrs and Confessors*, as "firm in their faith, patient under suffering, victorious over torture," and as an example to be followed.

The names of these martyrs appear in the *Calendarium Carthaginense* and the *Hieronymianum*, but all we know about them comes from St Cyprian's *Letter*; see edition by L. Bayard, 2 vols. (2d ed., 1961), 1, pp. 23-7. On Decius' persecution, see P. Hughes, *A History of the Church*, 3 vols. (1948), 1, pp. 164-6.

St Geroldus (978)

Geroldus came from the family of the counts of Sax of Vorarlberg, the west-ern-most province of present-day Austria. We know nothing of his early life, but in middle age he retired from the world to lead a solitary life of prayer and penance. It has been suggested that he was the Adam whose lands were re-stored by Otto I in 949, but this now seems unlikely. Tradition says he had given his own lands to the abbey of Einsiedeln, where his two sons, Kuno and Ulrich, were monks, and so a friend, Count Otto, gave him a plot of land in a forest, but there is no record of the abbey receiving such a gift. He was a hermit in the Walsertal, a valley of Vorarlberg, at a place called Friesen about five miles north of Bludenz; this changed its name in 1340 to Sankt Gerold. He lived there in a cell, and when he died in 978 his sons were allowed to live in it and care for his tomb. In later years, when the forest was cleared, the abbots of Einsiedeln, several of whom were related to Geroldus' family, built a church where his cell had been. This was destroyed during the Reformation, but in 1663 Abbot Placid built a new church with a shrine for Geroldus' relics next to those of his sons. This is now the village church of Sankt Gerold and is still a place of pilgrimage.

No early Life of Geroldus exists, but see *AA.SS.*, Apr., 2, pp. 628-30, for an account based on various sources. See also *D.H.G.E.*, 20 (1984), 999-1000; *N.C.E.*, 6, p. 448.

St Alphege of Canterbury, *Bishop and Martyr* (*c*. 953-1012)

Alphege (more correctly Aelfheah; also Elphege) became a monk at Deerhurst in Gloucestershire but after a time left the monastery to lead a more solitary life in Somerset. St Dunstan (19 May) appointed him abbot of the monastery at Bath, where the community seems to have been made up largely of Alphege's former disciples. The new abbot would not tolerate the slightest relaxation of the Rule and used to say to those who objected to his severity that it was far better for a man to remain in the world than to become an imperfect monk. In 984 he became bishop of Winchester, where he became known for his austere way of life and his generosity to the poor. Finally, in 1005, Alphege was appointed archbishop of Canterbury and went to Rome to receive the *pallium* from the pope.

England at the time was subject to almost continual raids and invasion by the Danes. In 1009 they arrived again with their strongest army so far and within a year had raided and pillaged in fifteen counties. By 1011 they were in Kent and laying siege to Canterbury, which they captured through the treachery of an Anglo-Saxon archdeacon. Alphege was taken prisoner and held to ransom for £3,000. According to Thietmar's usually reliable account, Alphege replied to requests for money by saying: "I am ready at once for anything you now dare to do to me, but, by the love of Christ, that I may become an example to his servants, I am untroubled today. It is not my wish, but dire poverty that makes me seem a liar to you. This my body, which in this exile I have loved immoderately, I offer to you, guilty as it is . . . but as a suppliant I commit my sinful soul to the creator of all, for it does not concern you." When he refused to allow the money to be collected from his tenants a mob of drunken Danes attacked and murdered him while he was being held at Greenwich. The *Anglo-Saxon Chronicle* states: "They led him to their tribunal on Saturday evening, within the octave of Easter . . . and one of them smote him on the head with the iron head of an axe, so that he sank down and his holy blood fell upon the earth, and his holy soul went to God's kingdom." The Danish leaders had not ordered the attack and were aware of the enormity of the crime; they made sure the body of the archbishop was handed over for Christian burial, which took place in St Paul's, London. In 1023 the Danish king Cnut had the body transferred to Canterbury "with great pomp and rejoicing and hymns of praise . . . to the holy salvation of all those who daily resort there to his holy body with devout heart and all humility" (*A.S.C.*).

His death at the hands of the Danes made Alphege into a national hero, and his cult was popular, but a later archbishop, Lanfranc, questioned whether he should be included in the calendar of saints as a martyr. He consulted St Anselm (21 Apr.) about this, and Anselm replied that Alphege deserved the title of martyr because he had been killed in the cause of justice. His body was found to be incorrupt when the shrine was opened in 1105, and this led to an increase in his cult and in pilgrimages to Canterbury in his honour, but it was later overshadowed by the cult of St Thomas à Becket (29 Dec.), who, just before he was murdered, commended himself to God and St Alphege.

A Life of St Alphege was written by Osbern, a monk of Canterbury, about 1087, but it is not wholly reliable; see *AA.SS.*, Apr., 2, pp. 627-41. The murder is described by the contemporary Thietmar of Merseburg in his *Chronicle*; see *E.H.D.*, 1 (2d ed. 1979), pp. 347-50. See also *A.S.C.* for the relevant years; *O.D.S.*, pp. 17-8.

Bd Bernard the Penitent (1182)

Bernard was born of an aristocratic family in the diocese of Maguelone in Provence. He took part in a rising that resulted in the death of an unpopular governor and during this or at some other time committed crimes for which he spent the rest of his life doing penance. It is not known for certain what these crimes were, but the letter from his bishop giving the penances imposed on him has survived, and from its severity the crimes must have been public and indeed "horrible," as the bishop says, and they almost certainly included a murder. Bernard was to go barefoot for seven years, not to wear a shirt for the rest of his life, and to observe the forty days before Christmas as a full Lenten fast. On Wednesdays and Saturdays he should abstain from meat and fat and on Fridays take only a little bread and wine. The bishop then requested those who met Bernard to "give to this very poor penitent the necessary food and clothing and to shorten his penance so far as reason may allow." The letter is dated October 1170 and is "in force for seven years only." There are some difficulties in interpreting the letter. Bernard appears to have followed it strictly and even to have gone beyond its requirements, and this raises the question as to how far the penances were to some extent self-imposed with the bishop's approval: he went on various pilgrimages dressed as a penitent and loaded with iron fetters and seems to have courted hardships. He is reported to have visited Jerusalem three times and to have gone to India to ask St Thomas (3 July) for help, but this is very unlikely. At the end of an unspecified period he was in Saint-Omer in north-eastern France, where it was revealed to him that his travels were over. A benefactor gave him a small house next to the monastery of Saint-Bertin, and he lived out the rest of his life there, attending all the monastic offices and involving himself in works of mercy in the town. He was reputed to have worked several miracles and to have the gift of prophecy, and his biographer testified that he had seen the cures himself. Some time before his death in 1182 he had become a monk in the monastery. The miracles continued at his tomb.

A Life printed in *AA.SS.*, Apr., 2, pp. 674-97, purports to have been written by a monk of Saint-Bertin. See also *Bibl.SS.*, 3, 65-6.

Bd Conrad of Ascoli Piceno (1234-89)

Conrad de' Miliani was born of an aristocratic family in Ascoli Piceno in the Marche region of Italy. He joined the Franciscans as a young man and studied at the university of Perugia, gaining a doctorate in theology. He began his public ministry as a preacher in Rome but then obtained permission to work as a missionary in Libya, where many thousands are reported to have been converted by his preaching and miracles. He is said to have been the first missionary since ancient times to explore the region of Cyrenaica in eastern Libya. He led a very austere life, always going barefoot, wearing a very rough habit and fasting on bread and water four days a week. One of his special devotions was to the Trinity, and he is reported to have worked several healing miracles and even to have raised two people from the dead in its name. He was also devoted to the passion of Our Lord; it was said that he experienced visions of Jesus in his sufferings and even shared in those sufferings himself. He was recalled to Italy, perhaps for health reasons, and appointed to accompany the minister general of the Order, who was going to France as papal legate to try to prevent war between France and Spain. The minister general was Jerome Masci, a lifelong friend of Conrad's, who was to become Pope Nicholas IV (1288-94). After their return from France, Conrad spent two years in Rome and then went to Paris to lecture in theology. In 1289 the pope sent for him to make him a cardinal, but Conrad fell ill on the way and died at Ascoli Piceno in 1289. He was buried in Rome in a tomb specially built for him by Nicholas IV in the church of San Lorenzo alle Piagge. His cult was approved in 1783, but he is not commemorated in the new Roman Martyrology.

The best source of information is Wadding, *Annales Minorum*, 5, pp. 212-5. See also Léon, 2, pp. 83-8; G. Fabiani, *Missionari Ascolani* (1954); *Bibl.SS.*, 4, 198-200.

Bd James Duckett, *Martyr* (1602)

James was the younger son of a Mr Duckett of Skelsmergh in Cumbria. Although he was the godson of James Leyburn, who was hanged, drawn, and quartered for the Faith in 1583, James was brought up a devout Protestant. He was apprenticed to a publisher and bookseller in London and while there was given a book entitled *The Firm Foundation of the Catholic Religion, against the*

Bottomless Pit of Heresies, which made him give up the practice of his religion. When he was examined by a local minister about his reasons for no longer going to church he replied that he did not go because he got no satisfaction from that religion. He spent two short periods in prison for non-attendance at church and was released on both occasions by the efforts of his master. The latter was unwilling to take any further risks on his behalf, however, and James bought out the rest of his apprenticeship and set up in business on his own. This also gave him the freedom to become a Catholic and to marry Anne Hart, a Catholic widow. He spent a considerable part of his twelve years of married life in various prisons because he used his book trade to supply Catholics with books "as well for their own comfort and instruction, as for the assistance of their neighbours' souls" (Challoner). Finally he was arrested on the word of a Catholic bookbinder who had been imprisoned and hoped to save his own life by reporting that James had forbidden books in his possession. At first the jury acquitted him because there was only one witness against him, but the judge ordered them to reconsider their verdict, and he was found guilty and sentenced to be hanged, drawn, and quartered. When his wife visited him in prison he urged her to keep herself as God's servant "and in the unity of God's Church, and I shall be able to do you more good, being now to go to the King of kings." He was executed at Tyburn on 19 April 1602 along with his betrayer, whom he forgave as they stood together by the scaffold. He was beatified in 1929. His son John became prior of the English Carthusians at Nieuport in Flanders and wrote an account of his father's life and martyrdom.

M.M.P., pp. 261-4; J. H. Pollen, *Acts of the English Martyrs* (1891), pp. 238-48; *Bibl.SS.*, 4, 848.

20

St Anicetus, *Pope* (166)

Anicetus was pope from *c.* 155 to *c.* 166. The *Liber Pontificalis* says he was born in Emesa in Syria, but we have few details about him or his pontificate of which we can be certain. He took part in the controversies over Gnosticism and almost certainly met St Hegesippus (7 Apr.), the scholarly author of anti-Gnostic writings. He was also involved in the debates about the date of Easter. He discussed this second issue with St Polycarp (23 Feb.), bishop of Smyrna, who had gone to Rome to settle a number of disputed questions, but they parted amicably without agreement. The *Liber Pontificalis* attributes a number of disciplinary decrees to Anicetus, but it is doubtful if they were his. He was probably responsible for building the shrine to St Peter (29 June) on the Vatican Hill traditionally attributed to Pope Anacletus. He has always been regarded as a martyr and was said to have suffered during the persecution of the emperor Antoninus Pius, but there is no historical evidence to support this. The previous edition of this work held that he "at least purchased the title of martyr by the sufferings and trials he endured."

O.D.P., pp. 10–11; *N.C.E.*, 1, p. 544; *Diz.dei Papi* (1995), p. 18.

St Marcellinus of Embrun, *Bishop* (374)

Marcellinus is venerated as the first bishop of Embrun, a small town in the Hautes Alpes in south-eastern France. He was an African priest who, with two companions, St Vincent and St Domninus (both also venerated today), evangelized a large part of what is now known as the Dauphiné region. Marcellinus made Embrun the base for his missionary labours and built an oratory on a cliff above the town; this was replaced by a large church in the town itself as the number of Christians increased. St Gregory of Tours (17 Nov.), who died in 594, tells us that even in his day the font in the baptistery of this church used to fill to overflowing of its own accord with water that had powerful healing qualities. Marcellinus was made a bishop by Eusebius of Vercelli but suffered persecution at the hands of the Arian heretics and had to go into hiding in the mountains, from where he made occasional visits to encourage his clergy and people. He died in 374 on 13 April but was not buried until the 20th, to allow other bishops to attend his funeral, and his commemoration in the new Roman Martyrology has been kept to the latter date. Much later, his remains were moved to Puy to avoid damage or theft by Saracen raiders but were destroyed in 1792, apart from his head that had been kept at Digne, where St Domninus had set up his missionary base.

The short Life is early and trustworthy; see *AA.SS.*, Apr., 2, p. 749. See also *Bibl.SS.*, 8, 659-60; *Catholicisme*, 8, 410-11.

St Anastasius II of Antioch, *Patriarch and Martyr* (609)

Patriarch Anastasius I of Antioch (21 Apr., below) opposed the emperor Justinian's politico-theological tenets and was exiled from his patriarchate for twenty-three years, returning in 596. Three years later he died, and he was succeeded by Anastasius II, a monk from the monastery on Mount Sinai. The new patriarch was anxious to establish good relations with Rome and at once sent a profession of faith and notice of his election to Pope Gregory the Great (3 Sept.). In his reply Gregory approved the orthodoxy of Anastasius and urged him to purge the churches of Antioch of simony. Anastasius was responsible for the translation into Greek of Gregory's *De cura pastorali*, though some writers have assigned this to his predecessor and mistakenly identified the two patriarchs as one.

In 609 the Syrian Jews, alarmed by the forcible conversions odered by the emperor, Phocas, rioted. The patriarch was one of their victims. He was treated with great indignity and put to death. His body was mutilated before being burned. The riots were put down with a severity and injustice no less criminal. Anastasius is regarded as a martyr, and his name has been inserted in the Roman Martyrology, but he has no cult in the East.

See Theophanes, *Chronographia*, in *P.G.*, 108, 624; *Epistle 49* of St Gregory the Great, in N.P.N.F., 13, pp. 13-14; *D.H.G.E.*, 2, 1460; *N.C.E.*, 1, p. 140.

St Caedwalla (*c.* 658-89)

Caedwalla's name (spelled in various ways) indicates that he had some British blood in his mainly Saxon ancestry. He is described by Bede as "a daring young man of the royal house of the Gewisse or West Saxons"; his military exploits were marked by violence and murder. When he was expelled from Wessex he launched a campaign aginst Sussex and in 685 murdered King Ethelwalh of the South Saxons and "wasted the province with slaughtering and plunder" (Bede). When he became king of the West Saxons by force in 686 he conquered the Isle of Wight and "strove to exterminate all the natives and replace them by settlers from his own province" (*ibid.*). However, he gave about a quarter of it to St Wilfrid (12 Oct.) in fulfillment of a vow, that he would do so if his conquest were successful, and this was the beginning of the conversion of the island to Christianity.

It is not clear from Bede's account why he should have made such a vow, for he was not yet a Christian himself. He was possibly already thinking of becoming one or had even taken the first steps, for after ruling Wessex successfully for two years he gave up the throne to go to Rome: "having learned that the road to heaven lies open to mankind only through baptism, he wished to obtain the particular privilege of receiving the cleansing of baptism at the shrine of the blessed Apostles" (*ibid.*). He was baptized on Holy Saturday 689 and given the name Peter by Pope St Sergius I (8 Sept.), who had a special interest in the English Church. Caedwalla died a few days later on 20 April, still wearing his white baptismal robe and only about thirty years old. He was given the honour of burial in the crypt of St Peter's, and a long epitaph was composed by Crispus, archbishop of Milan. This is printed in Bede; a few lines may be given here:

> High rank and wealth, offspring, and mighty realms,
> Triumphs and spoils, great nobles, cities, halls,
> Won by his forebears' prowess and his own—
> All these great Cadwal left for love of God . . .
> Wise king, his earthly sceptre to resign,
> And win from Christ in heaven His promised crown.

There is no evidence of an early cult: "His reputed sanctity is accounted for partly by Bede's account of him and partly by the belief that the sacrament of Baptism remits all sin and makes the recipient, if he commits no subsequent sin, worthy of immediate heavenly reward" (*O.D.S.*). The epitaph may still be seen in St Peter's crypt, but this is not considered of sufficient weight for him to be included in the new Roman Martyrology.

Bede, *H.E.*, bk. 4, chs. 15, 16; bk.5, ch. 7; *O.D.S.*, p. 78.

Bd Hugh of Anzy (*c.* 930)

Hugh was born in Poitiers and educated at the abbey of Saint-Savin in Poitou, where he received the religious habit and was ordained priest. He then became a monk in the monastery of Saint-Pierre in Autun, gained a reputation as an able administrator and reformer, and was appointed to assist Abbot Arnulf in reforming the monastery of Saint-Martin, also in Autun. After this he went with Bd Berno (13 Jan.) to reform the monastery at Baume-les-Messieurs, near Besançon, and then accompanied him to Cluny to help organize the new monastery there. Hugh's last appointment was as prior of Anzy-le-Duc, where he gained a reputation for wisdom and as a miracle-worker and built a hospital and other houses. He was concerned to stamp out the last traces of paganism among the local people and was particularly severe in condemning anything idolatrous and the excesses of the pagan feasts still celebrated there. He is said to have spent his last three years in retirement preparing for his death, but we have very few details of this period and do not know the year when he died, reputedly at a very advanced age. He was an important if minor figure in the monastic reform movement of the tenth century. During the Council of Anse in 1021 his relics were transferred to the Romanesque church at Anzy built for the purpose and which is still there. Unfortunately the relics were destroyed in the French Wars of Religion in 1562.

An eleventh-century Life of St Hugh is unreliable both with regard to the foundation of the monastery at Anzy and its account of Hugh's sanctity and miracles. See *Bibl.SS.*, 12, 748-9; *Vies des Saints*, 4, pp. 503-6. On Anzy-le-Duc, see *D.H.G.E.*, 3, 911-2.

St Hildegund of Schönau (1188)

The cult of St Hildegund was very popular in the Middle Ages but has never been approved by the Church, and she is not included in the new Roman Martyrology. At first sight the story of her adventures, ending as it does with her living disguised as a man in a monastery, is so full of incredible wonders that it might seem better to label it apocryphal and move on. There seems, however, to be more than a vestige of truth in it, and it has some importance for those interested in medieval hagiography.

The basic story is easily told. Hildegund was the daughter of a German knight who decided, when his wife died, to go on pilgrimage to Jerusalem. He took Hildegund with him but, for safety reasons, dressed her as a boy and called her Joseph. He died on their way home, and the servant to whom he had entrusted his money and his daughter absconded and left her penniless in Tyre. After several adventures she made it back to Europe, still pretending to be a boy. More adventures awaited her there: she was hanged as a robber but survived through angelic intervention and underwent the ordeal of red-hot iron successfully. At length she was advised by a saintly recluse to try the monastic life and offered herself as a novice to the Cistercian abbey at Schönau, near Heidelberg in Germany. She was accepted with the name Joseph, but died shortly afterwards still a novice, and was only found out to be a woman after her death. Her tomb was visited by pilgrims and her name entered in a number of martyrologies, and she was honoured in the Cistercian menology.

In a critical examination of a Life written the year she died, Herbert Thurston concluded that the basic story was true but there was no evidence for the miraculous events; she was certainly received as a novice at Schönau, but "that Hildegund was divinely guided in the course she followed or that she was in any proper sense a saint seems . . . to be a conclusion supported by no serious argument." It was, of course, to the advantage of the monks in avoiding possible scandal to say they had been divinely chosen to harbour a saint. Thurston also argues that the whole account was important because it gave added credence to later stories concerning the existence of Pope Joan, accounts of whose existence first appear about 1240. Stories of women disguising themselves as men in order to become monks, and being recognized as female only after their deaths, had a long tradition. There were examples as early as the times of the Desert Fathers, for example, St Pelagia of Antioch.

H. Thurston, "St Hildegund, Maiden and Monk," in *The Month*, Feb. 1916, pp. 145-55; *Catholicisme*, 5, 741-2.

St Agnes of Montepulciano (*c.* 1270-1317)

Agnes was born to well-to-do parents in the Tuscan village of Gracchiano-Vecchio, a few miles from Montepulciano. There are some doubts about the date of her birth; this is usually given as 1268, but her first biographer, Bd Raymond of Capua (5 Oct.), gives it as 1274. She was only a young girl when she entered a local convent of the Sisters of the Sack (so called because of their rough clothes), who followed an austere way of life. After a time the Sisters opened a new house at Proceno, a small village near Viterbo, and Agnes joined the new community, later becoming bursar and superior—a special dispensation had to be obtained from the pope because she was still only fifteen. Her austerities were extreme: for fifteen years she lived on bread and water and slept on the ground with a stone for her pillow; she modified these penances only after a severe illness. It is reported that she experienced visions and ecstasies and worked miracles to feed the Sisters when food ran short.

As her fame spread, the people of Montepulciano decided they wanted her back among them. She returned and was able to open a new convent, which she put under the care of the local Dominicans, since her experience in her former communities had convinced her of the benefits to be gained from association with a large, recognized Order. She became prioress, and the new house flourished under her rule. Toward the end of her life she suffered from a painful illness and was persuaded to take the waters of a local spa as a remedy. When her health did not improve she said to the Sisters, "If you loved me, you would be glad because I am about to enter the glory of my spouse. Do not grieve over much at my departure: I shall not lose sight of you. You will find I have not abandoned you and you will possess me for ever." While she was famous for her miracles, her sanctity was grounded in a basic simplicity and an intense piety toward Our Lord and Our Lady. She died on 20 April 1317. Her tomb became a popular place of pilgrimage and was visited by the emperor Charles IV and St Catherine of Siena (29 Apr.). She was canonized in 1726. There is a painting of her by Tiepolo in the Jesuit church in Venice, and another, earlier one in the public gallery of Siena in which she is shown holding a model of the city of which she is the patron.

Her biography was written fifty years after her death by Bd Raymund of Capua (5 Oct.), confessor to the convent; he also wrote the Life of St Catherine of Siena, and this might account for some of the similarities between the two saints' Lives—see under the entry for Catherine for theories about "holy anorexia," for example. His Life is in *AA.SS.*, Apr., 2, pp. 791-817. See also *O.D.S.*, p. 8. *Bibl.SS.*, 1, 375-81, reproduces the two paintings.

Bd Simon of Todi (1322)

Simon Rinalducci was a native of Todi in Umbria. In 1280 he joined the Hermits of St Augustine and became famous as a preacher. He served as prior of various houses of the Order and provincial of Umbria but then fell under suspicion and had to give up his posts. The basis of the suspicion was some serious accusations brought against him in a general chapter when he was not present. Instead of trying to clear his name he apparently decided to suffer in silence, because an official inquiry would have caused scandal and might have split the Order. He died in Bologna in 1322, and his tomb became famous for the many cures reported to have occurred through his intercession. His cult was approved in 1833.

Simon is known from accounts written by two of his contemporaries, Henry of Friemar the Elder and Giordano di Quedlinburg; see *AA.SS.*, Apr., 2, pp. 818-31. See also *Vies des Saints*, 4, p. 497.

BB James Bell and John Finch, *Martyrs* (1584)

James Bell was born about the year 1525 in Warrington in Lancashire and educated at Oxford University. He was ordained priest during the reign of Queen Mary (1553-8), but when Queen Elizabeth changed the religion of the country, James conformed and worked as a Protestant minister in various parishes. In 1581 he was reconciled to the Catholic Church and began working again as a priest, only to be arrested in January 1584, probably while saying Mass, and imprisoned at Manchester. From there he was taken to Lancaster and tried on a charge of denying the Queen's supremacy. He admitted in court that he was a priest and had been reconciled to the Church (itself a treasonable offence under the 1581 Act) and denied the Queen's supremacy in religious matters. He was hanged, drawn, and quartered at Lancaster on 20 April 1584.

John Finch was born in Eccleston, in Lancashire. He was a yeoman farmer who at first adopted the new religion under Queen Elizabeth but then was reconciled to the Catholic Church. He spoke openly about his beliefs in an attempt to convert other people, and he offered support and shelter to missionary priests working in the area, sometimes accompanying them to other safe houses. Eventually he was betrayed by one of his brothers and arrested along with two seminary priests named George Ostcliffe and Laurence Johnson. He was kept in awful conditions in prison on and off for two years, until he was tried at Lancaster on a charge of upholding the pope's jurisdiction over the Church in England. He was sentenced to death and was hanged, drawn, and quartered at Lancaster on the same day as Fr James Bell.

Both martyrs were beatified in 1929.

M.M.P., pp. 100-2; Gillow, 1, pp. 173-4, for Bell, and 2, pp. 257-9, for Finch; *L.E.M.*, 1, pp. 107-26; C.R.S., 5, pp. 74-81. See also the general entries on the English and Welsh martyrs for 4 May and 25 October.

BB Richard Sergeant and William Thompson, *Martyrs* (1586)

Richard Sergeant (he used the aliases Lee and Long) was born in Gloucester-shire and educated at Oxford University. He went to the English College in Reims to study for the priesthood, was ordained at Laon (not Lyons, as Challoner states) in 1583, and returned to England the same year. He worked there for about two and a half years before he was arrested and tried at the Old Bailey in London in 1586. He was condemned to death for treason because he had been ordained abroad and then returned to England, contrary to the severe legislation passed by Parliament the previous year. He was hanged, drawn, and quartered at Tyburn on 20 April 1586.

William Thompson (alias Blackburn) was born in Blackburn in Lancashire. Like Richard Sergeant, he studied for the priesthood at Reims and was ordained in 1584. On his return to England he served as chaplain to St Anne Line (27 Feb.) but was arrested in 1586 in the house of Robert Bellamy in Holborn, tried on the same charge as Richard Sergeant, and condemned to death. He was hanged, drawn, and quartered at Tyburn on 20 April 1586, aged about twenty-six.

Both martyrs were beatified in 1987.

M.M.P., pp. 113-4; Anstruther, 1, pp. 305, 351; C.R.S., 5, p. 129, for trial of Richard Sergeant. See also the general entries on the English and Welsh martyrs for 4 May and 25 October.

Bd Antony Page, *Martyr* (*c.* 1563-93)

Antony Page was born at Harrow-on-the-Hill, Middlesex, about the year 1563. He was educated at Christ Church, Oxford, before going to study for the priesthood at Reims, where he was ordained in 1591. He left for the English mission in January 1592. He worked for a time in Yorkshire, staying, perhaps, at the house of a Mr John Hodgson on the coast, but was soon arrested and imprisoned. Challoner tells us he suffered a great deal in prison but held his own in various disputations with Protestant ministers. He was condemned for treason, on the grounds that he was a seminary priest ordained abroad and living in England, and was hanged, drawn, and quartered at York on 20 April 1593. He was beatified in 1987.

M.M.P., p. 189; Anstruther, 1, p. 264. See also the general entries on the English and Welsh martyrs for 4 May and 25 October.

BB Robert Watkinson and Francis Page, *Martyrs* (1602)

Robert Watkinson (alias John Wilson) was born to Catholic parents at Hemingborough in Yorkshire about the year 1579. After attending school in Castleford and Richmond he studied for the priesthood at Douai and Rome. He suffered from ill health and had to leave Rome to return to Douai; he was ordained priest in 1602 at Arras in north-eastern France and on 3 April left for England to seek medical help. While he was receiving treatment in London he was betrayed by a certain John Fairweather, a government spy who had been allowed to study at Douai for five months and who had left the college just a few days before Robert to give the bishop of London a list of the newly-ordained priests. Robert was charged with being a Catholic priest in England who had been ordained abroad since the start of the queen's reign. He was condemned to death and hanged, drawn, and quartered at Tyburn in London on 20 April 1602, less than a month after his ordination and, as far as we know, without ever having served as a priest in England.

Francis Page was born at Antwerp but at his trial was said to be from Harrow-on-the-Hill in Middlesex and so was probably related to Bd Antony Page (above). He was brought up a Protestant and worked as a lawyer's clerk in London, where he fell in love with his employer's daughter, a Catholic. She introduced him to Fr John Gerard, S.J., who was in jail at the time, and the two became friends. Moved by Fr John's teaching and example, Francis decided to become a Catholic and a priest. His visits to the Tower to see Fr John, however, led to his arrest, but he was able to purchase his release and go to Douai, using the alias John Hickman. After ordination at Arras in April 1600 he was sent to England, where he was caught some months later saying Mass in the house of St Anne Line (27 Feb.), a house she looked after for the use of John Gerard and other priests. Francis escaped but was betrayed the following year by an apostate Catholic woman who had taken to denouncing priests for the sake of the reward. He was charged with being a seminary priest and saying Mass in England, was condemned to death, and hanged, drawn, and quartered at Tyburn on 20 April 1602, along with Robert Watkinson and Thomas Tichburn. On the scaffold he declared he was very willing to die for a good cause, "*viz.*, for his faith and priesthood, and for aiding and assisting by his priestly functions the souls of his neighbours" (Challoner). He had been received into the Jesuits while a prisoner in Newgate prison.

Robert Watkinson and Francis Page were both beatified in 1929.

M.M.P., pp. 264-8; Anstruther, 1, pp. 265 (Page), 372 (Watkinson). There are several references to Francis Page in P. Caraman, S.J. (ed.), *John Gerard, The Autobiography of a Hunted Priest* (1952). See also the general entries on the English and Welsh martyrs for 4 May and 25 October.

ST ANSELM (over page)
The ship symbolizes his defence of the independence of the Church. Gold ship with silver sails and white pennants with red crosses, white waves on blue field.

21

ST ANSELM, *Bishop and Doctor* (*c.* 1033-1109)

Anselm was born about the year 1033 in Aosta, a town on the border of Lombardy and Burgundy. His father, Gundulf, was an important man in the town and was said by Anselm's biographer to have been "regarded not only as generous and good-hearted, but even as prodigal and spendthrift." His mother was Ermenberga, conscientious and much more religious in outlook. Anselm was an outstanding pupil and by the time he was fifteen had decided to become a monk, but the local abbot to whom he applied for admission refused to accept him, fearing his father's opposition. Perhaps under Gundulf's influence Anselm gave up any thought of a religious vocation and became engrossed in secular affairs and what he was in later life to condemn as dissipation.

After his mother's death relations with his father deteriorated to the point where Anselm decided to leave home to pursue his studies in Burgundy with his mother's family. Three years later he moved to the abbey of Bec in Normandy, attracted by the reputation of its prior, Lanfranc, as one of the greatest teachers in Europe; he spent some time there as a secular student before deciding to become a monk of Bec in 1060. It was not a decision he made easily: he was attracted to the monastic life of Cluny, in Burgundy, but wondered whether the style of life there would allow him to develop his great interest in study; at the same time, if he joined the community at Bec he would be overshadowed by Lanfranc, and this did not appeal to him, for he had ambitions to make a name for himself—he was "not yet tamed," as he put it later. Perhaps he should return to Aosta and take up his inheritance, as his father had died, or perhaps he might even become a hermit. In the end he took the advice of the local bishop and put himself under Lanfranc's spiritual rule. Three years later Lanfranc was made abbot of Caen, and Anselm was appointed prior of Bec in his place, despite the opposition of some of the senior monks there who objected both to his youth and to the short time he had been a monk. But he proved himself to be an able administrator and loving father, paying particular attention to the training of the younger monks and creating a body of monks who were to fill important posts in various places while remaining devoted to him.

In 1078 Anselm was unanimously elected abbot of Bec. It was a position that necessarily involved him fully in the affairs, secular and ecclesiastical, of Normandy and Anglo-Norman England, for abbots of important houses were great lords with substantial estates, wide influence, and considerable patronage. He had to defend and, if possible, expand those estates and the privileges of his abbey, attend the ducal court, act as political adviser, be present at synods and councils. "The abbot's responsibility was to serve God by striving for the prosperity, well-being, and visual splendour of God's special communities of servants on earth—the abbeys" (Vaughn). Anselm was successful in all these areas, and his period as abbot added a great deal to Bec's standing. He made several visits to England, where the abbey owned estates and where Lanfranc had become archbishop of Canterbury, and obtained from the king, William the Conqueror, a charter confirming all the abbey's English lands and rights. He was there again in the autumn of 1092, when the see of Canterbury had been vacant for three years after Lanfranc's death because the new king, William Rufus, wished to enjoy its revenues and did not want another strong archbishop interfering in his running of the Church. The king was taken seriously ill early in 1093, however, and, thinking he was about to die, promised to treat the Church better and appoint an archbishop if he recovered, naming Anselm as archbishop-elect.

It is clear that Anselm had been the front-runner for the post ever since Lanfranc's death, and many of the king's advisers had been urging his appointment for some time. Anselm must have known this when he went to England in September 1092, and some writers have suggested that he had already become convinced it was God's will that he should be the next archbishop and was therefore willing to be elected, not out of personal ambition but in obedience to that will, which he sought to follow in all his actions. Others take his expressions of reluctance to accept the office—he had to be physically forced by the other bishops to hold the crozier—at their face value and deny he ever had any thought of being archbishop until forced by others to accept election. The debate is important for the interpretation of Anselm's troubled years as archbishop: was he "essentially a monastic contemplative man, with his eyes wholly directed towards God, and with his energies mainly absorbed in the task of calling others to the monastic life" (Southern), a reluctant and not very effective administrator who always wanted to return to the cloister he loved and had never wanted to leave? Or should we admire instead "Anselm's political awareness, his conviction (at some point prior to . . . consecration) that God had destined him for Canterbury, and his sense that as God's steward of the mother church of Britain, he must take effective action in the world of high politics" (Vaughn), which he did skillfully and successfully? Whatever the truth of the matter, Anselm was soon to find himself in a crisis he could not solve.

William Rufus' change of heart did not last, and he soon returned to his former attacks on the Church. He continued to draw the revenues of Canterbury, appointed simoniacal bishops and clergy, forbade Anselm to hold a reforming synod, and even tried to have him deposed by the pope. In the end Anselm felt that he had to leave the country, even though the king threatened never to allow him to return. "I saw in England," the archbishop wrote, "many evils whose correction belonged to me and which I could neither remedy nor, without personal guilt, allow to exist." He left England in 1097 and spent some time with St Hugh, abbot of Cluny (29 Apr.), and at Lyons. He wrote to the pope asking to be allowed to resign from his archbishopric and then went to Rome to consult the pope in person. The pope wrote to the English king ordering him to allow Anselm to return and exercise his office freely, threatening excommunication if he did not comply. Anselm returned to Lyons and waited, but nothing happened until the king's sudden death in 1100, when his successor, Henry I, invited him to return to England as archbishop. The new king gave back his lands and allowed him to call a reforming synod, and it seemed the two could work together fruitfully. The troubles that ensued, leading to Anselm's second period in exile, arose because the new pope, Paschal II (1099-1118), insisted on enforcing decrees against lay investiture—decrees passed at a Roman synod that Anselm had attended while in Rome and that he had given his assent to.

The investiture controversies of the Middle Ages were complex; basically they concerned the granting of the symbols of ecclesiastical office, such as the crozier and ring, by laypeople to clerics. In the feudal system of the day, the paying of homage to the layperson by the cleric usually followed. In the interest of reforming the Church and freeing its bishops from lay control, reforming popes wanted to stop the practice altogether, and Paschal II was adamant that no exceptions to the general prohibition could be allowed. For their part, kings and princes argued that bishops and abbots were often great landowners and little different in practice from lay magnates in the power they exercised; it was essential for a ruler to be sure of their fidelity and to have at least some control over their appointment. Anselm does not seem to have objected to lay investiture in principle and had not objected to the practice under William Rufus. He even tried to persuade the new pope to make an exception for England, but if the pope insisted on enforcing the decrees he had no choice but to do the same, since he had personally given his assent to them; not to do so would have been a cause of great scandal. Anselm was not being stiff-necked or inflexible in supporting the pope against the king; he sincerely believed his conscience allowed him no alternative.

For his part, Henry believed he could not give up ancestral customs without lessening his authority; moreover, those customs had been allowed by Anselm under William Rufus and by Anselm's great teacher and predecessor at Canterbury, Lanfranc, under William the Conqueror. He could not, he said, allow any one in his kingdom who was "not my man." Henry withdrew his initial demand that Anselm himself should do homage, and Anselm supported the king by personally leading troops to Pevensey to face a possible Norman invasion. But when Anselm's mission to Rome failed to persuade the pope to compromise, Henry refused to allow him back into the country, and so Anselm started his second period of exile, lasting from December 1103 to August 1106.

Both king and archbishop used this period to publicize their cases, and Anselm's skillful use of propaganda hardly fits in with the image of him as a retiring monk and ineffective administrator. By 1106 an agreement was reached by which Henry gave up his right of investiture and promised not to interfere in episcopal elections; important clerics would continue to pay him homage as a sign of their loyalty. Anselm had gained more than the king, and his return to England was a triumphal one. He also gained from both pope and king a confirmation of Canterbury's power and privileges as the primatial see, and by the end of his period in office its prestige had reached a peak unknown in previous years, including a recognition of its jurisdiction over the Church in Wales. Until his death in April 1109 Anselm enjoyed the king's "unmitigated favour and confidence" (Vaughn), proved above all in 1108 when Henry made the archbishop guardian of his son and viceroy of the whole kingdom while he himself was away in Normandy. Also in 1108 Anselm held a second reforming synod in London, and its decrees against clerical incontinence were fully backed by Henry's royal authority. Anselm may not have enjoyed being an administrator, but once he was convinced that it was God's will for him he accepted the role, whether as abbot of Bec or archbishop of Canterbury, and performed it very effectively for the good of the Church.

While it would clearly be a mistake to regard Anselm as a contemplative out of his depth among the worldly-wise, there is no doubt that the main principle that guided his life was devotion to the Rule of St Benedict, and it can be assumed that he would want to be judged as monk, prior, and abbot rather than as archbishop. He was quite clear what becoming a monk meant: "When I professed myself a monk I surrendered myself in such a way that thereafter I could not be my own man . . . that is, I could not live according to my own will, but only in accordance with obedience either to God or to the Church of God." But if obedience was the foundation, the building above it was held together and illuminated by love. The warmth of his letters to his monks destroys any thought of a formal monastic obedience being sufficient and also makes him one of the most attractive personalities of the Middle Ages. Even his opponents acknowledged his genuine charm and were often won over by it (though not William Rufus), and his circle of friends was very large.

The letters he wrote between 1071 and 1093, while he was at Bec, are the most revealing of his personality. Their extremely emotional language can be embarrassing for the modern reader and has even led to suggestions that Anselm was a repressed homosexual, such is the force of the images they evoke. How should we interpret a passage such as this: "My eyes eagerly long to see your face, most beloved; my arms stretch out to your embraces. My lips long for your kisses; whatever remains of my life desires your company, so that my soul's joy may be full in time to come"? The words were written to two young relatives who were thinking of becoming monks and whom Anselm had almost certainly never seen. Again, he wrote to a monk of Bec who left the monastery to join Lanfranc in Canterbury: "Sweet to me are the gifts of your sweetness, sweetest friend, but they cannot possibly console my desolate heart for its want of your love. . . . The anguish of my heart when thinking of this bears witness, and so do the tears dimming my eyes and moistening my face and the fingers that write this."

These extracts, typical of many of his letters, show "the emotionally charged affection that bound Anselm to his monks and friends . . . a reflection of his heartfelt devotion to his comrades in God's service, lamenting their absence and rejoicing in their presence" (Vaughn). The letters were not private letters in our sense: he directed them to be shared among the brethren and even read out in public in the monastery. From that point of view they were part of a long tradition of abbots writing to their monks, but there was nothing traditional about the language he used, which is more like the language of the later medieval literature of romantic love. Again, however, there was a major difference: romantic love was essentially individualistic and possessive, but Anselm's letters were not intended to convey private emotional attachments: they were public statements about the rewards of the monastic life dedicated entirely to God. "All his warmest expressions of friendship were reserved for those who either were sharers in his religious life or were about (as he hoped) to share it" (Southern). For Anselm, the friendship between those who had devoted themselves to God's service should create stronger ties than existed in a family that was united only by human and physical love; his language might be sensual and reminiscent of the Song of Songs, but the friendship was essentially intellectual and spiritual, and "the unity of souls in friendship was a dramatic realization of that unity in which all men are one" (*ibid.*). Given the warmth of these letters, however, it is easier to understand the human bitterness of the monks of Bec when he left them to become archbishop of Canterbury.

Some of the characteristics of his early letters can be found in his devotional works, most of which were written in the 1070s while he was at Bec. Such was his reputation even then that collections of his prayers and meditations were circulating in Normandy almost as soon as they were written, and for a hundred years after his death they were more popular than any of his other writings. He had many imitators, and by the later Middle Ages the collections contained more spurious than genuine works; it is now accepted that we have only nineteen prayers and three meditations written by Anselm. These pieces were not written for his own use, although they grew out of his own deep spiritual experiences; they were designed for his fellow-monks or for aristocratic ladies. Before Anselm, schemes of private prayer had been imitations of the monastic divine office, with selections from the psalms interspersed with short prayers to Our Lord, Our Lady, and a small number of saints. These prayers, especially those to Our Lady, were already becoming longer and more emotional in their language by the time Anselm began to compose his early ones. With him, the prayers became longer and more important than the extracts from the psalms and lost all connection with liturgical prayer: they were for private meditation, and so, as he wrote to Countess Matilda, "the reader ought not to be concerned to read the whole, but only so much as he feels sufficient to arouse in himself the impulse to pray. He can begin and end where he chooses, lest superfluity or the frequent repetition of the same place cause boredom." While the prayers and meditations seem to be "poignant personal effusions" (Southern), full of emotion and with a heavy stress on self-abasement, they are at the same time carefully constructed, with an eye to rhyme and rhythm and an often complex development of biblical imagery. "They are certainly the work of a man with great literary gifts, great originality in transforming traditional models, great sensibility, and an overwhelming sense of the grievousnes of sin. . . . [They] opened the way which led to the *Dies Irae*, the *Imitatio Christi*, and the masterpieces of later medieval piety" (*ibid.*).

A successful abbot, spiritual guide, and father to two communities of monks, archbishop of Canterbury, statesman (willingly or unwillingly), with an attractive and saintly personality: there is sufficient here to make sure that Anselm's name would not be forgotten. Yet there is more: he is "one of the rare significant figures who belong to all time, one to whom philosophers and historians and innumerable readers will turn for enlightenment and counsel" (Knowles). He produced what was, in effect, a systematic study of the principal beliefs of Christianity, guided throughout by his famous motto, *Fides quaerens intellectum* ("Faith seeking understanding"). He took it for granted that those who would read his works were believers, and he was not saying their belief was dependent on reason; what he wanted to do for them was to examine, using only his reason, what they believed. He explained this in the opening to the first of his treatises, the *Monologion*: "Some of my brethren have persistently asked me to write down some of the things I have proposed to them in speech for meditation . . . on condition I should persuade them of nothing on the authority of scripture, but plainly and simply put down whatever the argument might require, without overlooking any objections." He deliberately moved away from the quoting of authorities, scriptural and otherwise, that was the commonest form of argument at the time, and launched out into a philosophical inquiry, not to prove the truth of particular doctrines but to understand them as deeply as possible and show their consistency and inevitability, given God's plan for our salvation. For Anselm this was what "meditating" on the truths of the Faith meant, and it is not surprising that some of his treatises are rather like extended prayers.

Anslem wrote eleven major treatises, starting with the *Monologion* in 1077. This dealt with the existence of God and his attributes, as knowable from the natural world, and was followed in 1078 by the *Proslogion,* in which Anselm put forward his famous "ontological argument" for the existence of God. He wanted to see if a single argument could be found to show God exists and is the "Supreme Good, needing no one else yet needed by all else." The short passage in which the argument is stated "has been pored over and commented upon more than any other text of equal brevity in medieval philosophy" (Knowles) and is the only philosophical discovery of the early Middle Ages to excite the interest of modern philosophers (Southern). He argued that if we mean by God "that than which nothing greater can be conceived," then that entity must exist, otherwise we could conceive of something greater, that is, an actually existing entity. The argument was attacked in Anselm's own day, and he defended it in one of his rare excursions into literary controversy. Many later philosophers have questioned its validity, but often for different reasons, and have not always agreed about what Anselm had in mind: the rest of his thinking is so acute that one hesitates to accuse him of a simple error of logic.

The other work for which he is most often remembered is his *Cur Deus Homo?* ("Why did God become man?"). Most of this was written in England in 1097, then finished in exile in Italy the following year, and was directed mainly against the teaching of a certain Roscelin, who had claimed Anselm's support for his views on the Incarnation. In reply, Anselm set out his thinking on the redemption and established a theory of atonement that was to dominate Christian thinking for many centuries. According to Southern it was Anselm's greatest intellectual achievement, with an "unrivalled combination of sustained argument, intense moral force, and originality in general conception and in detail." In Anselm's view, satisfaction was owed to God because of the human race's initial disobedience; the dignity of God, however, demanded a satisfaction greater than any mere human could make, and God became incarnate so that the Son could make it on our behalf. This contradicted the view that had been accepted since the early Fathers, that the devil had acquired rights over the world and the human race through our original sin that only Jesus on the Cross could "buy back" or redeem. Anselm's work was not regarded highly in the years after his death, perhaps because it seemed too subtle, and the traditional view of the devil's rights continued, along with a pessimistic view about the possibility of salvation for more than a few (and those mainly in monasteries and convents). But at least the potential for a wholly different approach is hinted at when Anselm allows his opposite number in the dialogue to say, "It seems to me that God will reject no man who comes to him under this name [*i.e.*, of Christ]."

Whatever the logical strengths and weaknesses of Anselm's carefully constructed arguments, it would be a mistake to concentrate on them and so miss the spirit of his inquiring mind. At the beginning of his *Proslogion* he wrote, addressing himself: "Come now, little man, put aside your business for a while, take refuge for a little from your tumultuous thoughts; cast off your cares, and let your burdensome distractions wait. Take some leisure for God; rest awhile in him . . . put out everything [from your mind] except God and whatever helps you to seek him. . . . Say now to God with all your heart, 'I seek thy face, O Lord, thy face do I seek.'" Reason may have been his guide, but faith was his life.

In 1163 St Thomas Becket (29 Dec.) tried to have his illustrious predecessor canonized, but the pope referred the cause to a provincial council, and no record survives of what, if anything, was decided. Anselm was listed in a Canterbury calendar of about the same time, but his cult there was soon eclipsed by that of Becket himself. Other attempts to have him canonized all seem to have failed, but a cult continued, especially in Flanders. In 1720 he was declared a Doctor of the Church.

Eadmer of Canterbury was a monk of Canterbury and Anselm's constant companion as archbishop, so his *Vita Anselmi* is the major source; see the ed. by R. W. Southern, *The Life of St Anselm* (1972). Eadmer also wrote the important *Historia Novorum in Anglia*, ed. and trans. by G. Bosanquet (1964). Another major source are the many letters of Anselm; see F. S. Schmitt, O.S.B. (ed.), *Sancti Anselmi Cantuariensis archiepiscopi opera omnia* , 6 vols. (1946-68), and his article in *N.C.E.*, 1, pp. 581-3. The major treatises and a selection of the letters were ed. and trans. by J. Hopkins and H. Richardson, 4 vols. (1974-6). For important modern studies of the life, see R. W. Southern, *St Anselm and His Biographer* (1963), and *St Anselm: A Portrait in a Landscape* (1990); Sally Vaughn, *Anselm of Bec and Robert of Meulan, the Innocence of the Dove and the Wisdom of the Serpent* (1987). For an interesting debate between Southern and Vaughn about Anselm as statesman, see *Albion* 20 (1988), pp. 181-220. See also J. Hopkins, *A Companion to the Study of St Anselm* (1972); G. R. Evans, *Anselm and a New Generation* (1980); D. Knowles, *The Evolution of Medieval Thought* (1962), esp. pp. 97-106; C. Warren Hollister, "St Anselm on Lay Investiture," in *Anglo-Norman Studies* 10 (1988), pp. 145-58; *O.D.S.*, pp. 23-4; Martin Brett, *The English Church uder Henry I* (1975). *O.D.C.C.*, p. 60-1, has a useful bibliography of modern eds. of Anselm's individual works.

In art Anselm is depicted variously as archbishop, abbot, and monk, and is sometimes shown holding a book or a pen, sometimes with a ship by his side. He features in a number of illuminated manuscripts in the Bodleian, Oxford, and there are two reliquary busts of him in Aosta, one fifteenth-century, the other nineteenth; the British Museum has his seal, which shows him in full episcopal dress. There are relatively few paintings of him, but some show him as a supporter of the Immaculate Conception of Our Lady, as, for example, that by Luca Signorelli in Santa Maria Novella in Florence.

St Apollonius, *Martyr* (185)

Apollonius was probably born in Greece or Asia Minor. Both Eusebius, in his *Ecclesiastical History*, and St Jerome (30 Sept.), in his *On Famous Men*, tell us about him and how he came to be martyred. St Jerome says he was a Roman senator, and although it is strange that Eusebius does not mention this, it fits in with the rest of what is known. Apollonius was denounced as a Christian by his servant and was interrogated by the prefect and a tribunal. He was then ordered to defend himself before the senate. He was heard with great respect, perhaps because of his reputation for learning but more likely because he was a senator himself. As part of his defence he attacked paganism and declared its idols to be worthless: "I serve my God, not idols made with human hands. I will never worship gold, silver, bronze, iron or supposed deities of wood and stone, which are blind and deaf, the works of craftsmen, jewellers, and sculptors, fashioned by carnal hands and with no life of their own. It is the God of heaven whom I serve, and him alone do I worship." He went on to argue that Christianity was superior by its concepts of death and life: death was a natural necessity that had nothing frightening about it, while the true life was the life of the soul. Above all, Christianity surpassed paganism through the work of Christ, the revealing Word of God: "This Word is our saviour Jesus Christ. He was made man in Judaea. He was just in everything and filled with divine wisdom. For love of men he has shown us who is the God of the universe and what rule of life our soul must adopt. . . . By his passion he has ruined the empire of sin." In arguing in this way Apollonius was using the tactics of the early apologists, who rarely argued about theological issues but tried to show Christianity to be morally superior to paganism. His statement gives an attractive picture of early Christian faith and morality. St Jerome gives the impression of a formal document read out before the senate, but it is more likely that Apollonius just gave a well-prepared speech.

There are two accounts of the trial and *passio*, one Greek and the other Armenian—the latter was discovered only in 1874. They agree on the great courtesy accorded Apollonius by both the judge and the senators but differ on details of the interrogations and the execution. The Greek text says he died after severe and prolonged torture, while the Armenian says he was beheaded— more in keeping, certainly, with the tone of the rest of the account. There is no evidence of an early cult, and in the Middle Ages the martyr was confused with the St Apollonius who died with St Philemon (8 Mar.) and with the Apollos mentioned in connection with St Paul (see Acts 18:24; 1 Cor. 3:4). This confusion led to his feast-day being kept on 18 April, when the day of his death can be fixed accurately for 21 April. His *apologia* for Christianity is among the best of the period, and his *acta* are refreshingly free of the usual stereotyped features.

Eusebius, *H.E.*, 5, 21; *D.H.G.E.*, 3, 1012-3; *O.D.S.*, p. 28; *Bibl.SS.*, 2, 276-8. A modern English translation of the *apologia* may be found in Bruno Chenu *et al.*, *The Book of Christian Martyrs* (1990), pp. 55-60, from which the extracts above are taken.

St Anastasius I of Antioch, *Patriarch* (599)

Little is known about the life of this Anastasius. In 559 he became patriarch of Antioch in Syria and according to the main source, the historian Evagrius (*c.* 536-600), was a man of considerable learning and piety and a firm upholder of orthodoxy. He was a man of few words but had the gift of being able to comfort the afflicted. He spent twenty-three years in exile because he opposed the religious and political policies of the two emperors, Justinian I (527-65) and Justin II (565-78), but his friend Pope St Gregory I (3 Sept.) interceded for him, and he was restored by the emperor Maurice (582-602). Several of his writings have survived: there are five pieces from his controversies, "The Trinity," "The unlimited nature of God," "The divine plan for the Incarnation,"

"The sufferings of Christ," and "The Resurrection of Christ." There is also a pastoral letter of March 593 to the people of Antioch and four sermons, only two of which can be attributed to him with certainty. In all these writings Anastasius uses a clear style and form of logical argument that was to influence later Byzantine theological writers. He has occasionally been confused (for example, by the former edition of the Roman Martyrology) with St Anastasius, a hermit of Mount Sinai, who, however, lived a century later. He is sometimes called "Anastasius the Elder" to distinguish him from his successor of the same name.

Bibl.SS., 1, 1064-5; *E.E.C.*, 1, p. 36, with important bibliography. His writings are in *P.G.*, 89, 1289-1408.

St Beuno, *Abbot* (Sixth or Seventh Century)

Beuno is said to have been born and educated in Herefordshire, but the main centres of his influence were in north Wales. He founded a monastery at Clynnog Fawr on the coast of present-day Gwynedd. To judge from his influence on place names he probably founded other monasteries or churches, especially on the island of Anglesey and the Lleyn peninsula, although some of these may have been the work of his disciples. He died and was buried at Clynnog Fawr. A stone oratory was built over his tomb, remains of which were excavated in 1914. His relics were later transferred to a church at Eglwys y Bed where miracles were reported.

A Welsh Life was written in the fourteenth century. It may contain some historically true elements but most of it consists of far-fetched stories and conventional legends. The best known of these concerns that other famous saint from north Wales, St Winifred (3 Nov.), who may have been his niece; her severed head was restored to her body by Beuno; in another account she was brought back to life by him. The Life tells of two other occasions when he brought the dead back to life. For centuries afterwards, superstitious and magical practices survived in districts where his name had once been honoured. Lambs and calves with particular markings were dedicated to him and were supposed to prosper extremely well, while down to the nineteenth century sick people, especially children, were laid out all night on what was said to be his tomb in the hope of a cure.

His cult is not considered sufficiently well attested for his name to have been included in the new Roman Martyrology. Today he is known chiefly through St Beuno's, a Jesuit house near Holywell in north Wales, where Gerard Manley Hopkins studied theology and which is now a successful retreat centre.

The Life was published in a scholarly edition by A. W. Wade-Evans in *Archaeologia Cambrensis* 85 (1930), pp. 315-41; see also his *Welsh Christian Origins* (1934), pp. 170-6. See also J. H. Pollen in *The Month*, 80 (1894), pp. 235-47; Baring-Gould and Fisher, 1, pp. 208-21; E. G. Bowen, *The Settlements of the Celtic Saints in Wales* (1956), pp. 79-86; *O.D.S.*, p. 55.

St Maelrubha, *Abbot* (*c.* 642-722)

Maelrubha, or Malrubius, was born in 642 and became a monk in St Comgall's (11 May) monastery at Bangor in County Down. When he was twenty-nine he crossed to Scotland, probably spending some time on Iona before moving to Applecross in Wester Ross. There he set up a mission station with a church and monastery, and this became his base for the rest of his life. He preached and evangelized over a large area, including the Isle of Skye and as far south as Islay, and a large number of place names based on his are evidence of an influence that was second only to that of St Columba (9 June) among the Irish missionaries to Scotland. Loch Maree has an island church built by him, with a nearby spring long famous for its healing qualities, especially in cases of mental illness. He ruled Applecross for fifty-one years and died at the age of eighty, almost certainly from natural causes, although some accounts say he was martyred by Norse raiders. A mound near Applecross is said to mark his grave. His healing ministry lives on at Applecross, where there is now a centre for the treatment on cancer. The bark of the yew trees that were already seven hundred years old in his time yields a substance used in chemotherapy.

K.S.S., pp. 382-3; W. Reeves, "St Maelrubha: His History and Churches," in *Proceedings of Soc. of Antiquaries of Scotland*, 3 (1857-60), pp. 258-96; *The Irish Saints*, pp. 241-4.

St John I of Valence, *Abbot and Bishop* (*c.* 1070-1146)

John was born in Lyons about the year 1070 and became a canon of the cathedral there at an early age. He made a vow to join the monastery of Cîteaux, but then, unsure about his ability to stand the rigours of its way of life, he thought about making a pilgrimage to Compostela instead. It is said that a frightening dream or vision persuaded him to keep to his vow, and he joined the monastery, where he proved himself to be an exemplary monk. When the bishop of Vienne asked the abbot of Cîteaux for some monks to found a monastery in his diocese, John was among those chosen. He helped to found a new abbey at Bonnevaux, of which he became the first abbot in 1117, and he was later involved in founding four other houses of the strict Cistercian observance. In 1141 the bishop of Valence was driven from his diocese—he had alienated clergy and people and been excommunicated by the pope—and John was appointed, very much against his will, to replace him. He was bishop for five years and succeeded in restoring good order to the diocese in both spiritual and temporal matters. When he was accused of being too lenient to wrong-doers, he replied that those who had to judge others should remember they might not themselves do very well if faced with the same temptations. He died in 1146; his relics were destroyed in 1562 during the French Wars of Religion. His cult was approved in 1903.

An early Life by Géraud, a monk of Bonnevaux, was printed in Martène and Durand, *Thesaurus novus anecdotorum*, 3, pp. 1693-1702. See also *Vies des Saints*, 3, pp. 480-1; *Catholicisme*, 6, 437.

Bd Bartholomew of Cervere, *Martyr* (1466)

Bartholomew was born in Savigliano in Piedmont, where his father was lord of Ruffia, Cervere, and Rosano. He entered the Dominican priory there at an early age and was then sent to study in Turin. Here he excelled as a student and gained on the same day his licentiate in theology, a doctorate, and his admission to the teaching faculty. It was no surprise when he was appointed inquisitor—a position, according to the previous edition of this work, "fraught with considerable danger, owing to the number of determined heretics in Piedmont." Bartholomew seems to have been aware of the danger and when he was summoned to go to Cervere is reported to have said to one of his brethren after making a general Confession, "They call me Bartholomew of Cervere, although I have never been in the place. But I am going there today as inquisitor, and there I shall die." He was ambushed and murdered on his way to the town by some heretics. A cult started soon after his death and was confirmed by Pope Pius IX. He is one of three Dominicans from the priory at Savigliano who became inquisitors and suffered martyrdom—see, for example, Bd Antony Pavoni (9 April).

AA.SS., Apr., 2, pp. 955–6, gives a short account.

St Conrad of Parzham (1818-94)

Conrad Birndorfer was born in the Bavarian village of Parzham, the youngest of nine children of pious parents who were farmers. In his youth he developed a strong devotion to Our Lady; after his parents' death when he was sixteen he ran the family farm and also led a life of prayer and practical charity. In 1849 he joined the Capuchins as a lay brother and made his solemn vows in 1852. Shortly after this he was sent to the friary at Altötting, in Lower Bavaria, where there was a well-known shrine of Our Lady. For forty years he worked there as door keeper, meeting thousands of pilgrims and exercising a quiet ministry of prayer and counselling, able on occasion to read people's hearts and foretell the future. He impressed everyone by his humility and practice of the presence of God. He used to say, "The Cross is my book . . . one glance at it teaches me what I should do in every situation." His special devotions were to the Eucharist and Our Lady. In addition to his work at the friary he was heavily involved in looking after abandoned children. He became ill in 1894 and died on 21 April. As the previous edition of this work put it, "In its external aspects nothing could offer less of sensation or romantic interest than the life of this humble Capuchin lay brother." The process of canonization went forward very quickly; he was beatified in 1930 and canonized in 1934.

The decree of beatification contains a short biography—see *A.A.S.* 22 (1930), pp. 319-23. Several biographies were published to mark the canonization; see Fr Dunstan, *St Conrad of Parzham* (1934); Jérôme de Paris, *Un grand serviteur de Dieu et des Pauvres: St C. de Parzham (*1934); Imerio da Castellanza, *L'Ostiario di Dio: il santo portinaio San C. di P.* (1934).

22

SS Soter and Caius, *Popes* (*c.* 174, 296)

These two popes have traditionally been venerated as a pair although there is nothing to link them together. They have also been venerated as martyrs, but there is no reliable evidence that either of them suffered martyrdom, and the Roman Calendar of 354 does not list them as martyrs. There is no doubt, however, of their existence, and the dates of their pontificates are reasonably certain.

Soter succeeded St Anicetus (17 Apr.), probably in the year 166, and reigned until about the year 174. The *Liber Pontificalis* says he was an Italian from Campania. During his reign he sent a letter to the bishop of Corinth, St Dionysius (8 Apr.), along with some charitable gifts, and we have fragments of the bishop's fulsome reply—see the entry for St Dionysius. It seems that it was while Soter was pope that the celebration of Easter became an annual event in Rome.

Caius (more properly, Gaius) became pope in 283 in succession to St Eutychian (7 Dec.) and reigned until 296. According to tradition he was from Dalmatia and a relative of the emperor Diocletian, but these details are unlikely to be true. It is also unlikely he lived in the catacombs for eight years to escape the persecution under Diocletian, as the *Liber Pontificalis* recounts. We have no information about his pontificate, although it is clear it coincided with a period of peace and consolidation for the Roman Church (*O.D.P.*). He was buried in the cemetery of St Callixtus, where fragments of his epitaph giving his name as Gaius were found in the nineteenth century.

O.D.P., pp. 11, 24. See also *D.A.C.L.*, 2, 1736-40, and 6, 33-7.

St Leonides, *Martyr* (202)

Leonides was a prominent figure in the Church in Alexandria toward the end of the second century. He was married, with seven sons, the eldest of whom was the important writer Origen. Leonides was probably a Roman citizen and taught as a philosopher or grammarian in the city's famous theological school, which concentrated on spreading Christian beliefs to the cultured classes. He was arrested during the persecution launched by the emperor Septimus Severus (193-211) and imprisoned. Origen wanted to join him there and suffer martyrdom but was restrained by his mother, who hid his clothes. In a letter to

Leonides he urged his father to confess the Faith courageously and not to change his mind for the sake of his family. Leonides was beheaded in 202.

Almost all that is known about Leonides comes from Eusebius' *Ecclesiastical History*, bk. 6. See *E.E.C.*, 1, p. 480.

St Agapitus I, *Pope* (536)

Agapitus was the son of an aristocratic Roman priest named Gordianus and was an archdeacon at the church of SS John and Paul when he was elected to succeed John II in 535. He was a man of culture, with a library of the Fathers, and was a friend of the writer and statesman Cassiodorus (*c.* 490–580); together they had planned a university for Rome modelled on that at Alexandria. He was forceful and independent in character (*O.D.P.*). As a priest he had opposed the practice whereby a pope could choose his own successor, and as pope he took a hard line against converts from heresy holding office in the Church, upholding this view even when the emperor, Justinian, asked him to deal leniently with former Arians. He was already elderly, and his reign as pope lasted only eleven months, most of which time was taken up by a mission to Constantinople undertaken on behalf of the Ostrogoth king of Italy, Theodahad. The mission, designed to dissuade the emperor, Justinian, from invading Italy, was a political failure, but Agapitus was successful in upholding orthodox doctrine. He persuaded the emperor to remove from office the patriarch of Constantinople, Anthimus, a supporter of the Monophysite belief that Christ had only one, divine, nature. The pope then consecrated St Mennas (25 Aug.) as the new patriarch. Agapitus died in Constantinople, and his body was taken back to Rome and buried in St Peter's. He was described by Pope St Gregory I (3 Sept.) as "a trumpet of the gospel and a herald of righteousness."

P.L., 66, 35–80; *D.H.G.E.*, 1, 887–90; *O.D.P.*, pp. 58–9.

St Theodore of Sykeon, *Bishop* (613)

Theodore was born in the Galatian town of Sykeon in Asia Minor. His mother and aunt ran an inn that doubled as a brothel, until a cook arrived who was so successful in attracting customers that there was no need for the women to earn extra money by their prostitution. The cook was also a devout person and encouraged the young Theodore to visit the local churches, taught him how to pray, and introduced him to the practice of fasting. This early spiritual direction paid off, and Theodore became a hermit at Arkea, about eight miles from his home, where he lived in a cave attached to a chapel. His reputation for holiness attracted visitors, and he was reputed to have a special gift of exorcising evil spirits. To avoid the publicity he retired to the mountains and tried to live in a walled-up cave known only to one other person, but he had to be rescued and was found to be in ill health, dirty, and pest-ridden. He was ordained priest, apparently when still only eighteen, and then went on a pilgrimage to Jerusalem, where he was given the monastic habit.

On his return he took up an extremely austere way of life and is said to have lived in a series of cages suspended above a cave. All sorts of wonders were reported about him, and he again attracted visitors and disciples. For these he established a monastery, a guest-house, and a church. He was then chosen to be bishop of Anastasiopolis, very much against his will, and ruled the see for about ten years before obtaining permission to resign. To judge from the contemporary Life, his years as bishop seem to have been marked mainly by wonders and miracles; we have no details of his episcopal *acta*, except that he had trouble with the villages that were part of the diocesan estates. These had been let out to lay landlords who maltreated and oppressed the people, and Theodore tried to persuade them to act justly. He resigned so that he could spend more time in prayer and in order to look after his monks, who seem to have fallen into rather lax ways while he was away. Eventually he settled near Heliopolis. He was called to Constantinople and received with great honour by the emperor, whose son he cured. The rest of his life he spent in his own monastery, working miracles and giving advice and help to the many who visited him. He died in 613. Throughout his life he had had a particularly strong devotion to St George and was responsible for popularizing his cult.

A contemporary Life by a disciple is trans. in E. Dawes and N. H. Baynes, *Three Byzantine Saints* (1948); despite what Baynes calls its "portentous rhetoric" it gives an excellent picture of life in the Asia Minor of the time. For a full study, see A. J. Festugière, *Vie de Théodore de Sykeon*, 2 vols. (1970). See also *O.D.S.*, pp. 453–4.

Bd Wolfhelm, *Abbot* (1091)

Wolfhelm was from a noble Rhineland family and was educated at the cathedral school of Cologne. After his confirmation he decided to consecrate himself to God and became a canon at the cathedral. He soon gave this up and instead moved to Trier, where he received the habit at the abbey of Saint Maximinus in 1036 or 1038. Such was his reputation for learning, however, that he was asked by the archbishop to return to Cologne, where he became a monk in the abbey of Saint Pantaleon, where his uncle was abbot. Shortly after this he was elected abbot of Gladbach and then of Siegburg. It is said that he found the cares of office too heavy and so retired to the monastery at Brauweiler, to the east of Cologne, where he remained until his death, but this seems unlikely, as he became abbot there in 1065 and was an active and able administrator. He defended the rights of his abbey and was involved in appeals to the emperor and the pope to recover lands taken by the archbishop of Cologne. He built up a reputation as a theologian and was involved in a number of the controversies of the day, especially that concerning the Eucharist, with Berengarius of Tours.

His views are clearly expressed in a letter to the abbot of Gladbach in which he uses biblical passages to prove that in the Eucharist we have the whole living body of Jesus. Elsewhere he argues against the idea of a conflict between pagan and Christian philosophy: both should be studied, as we can learn something of the truth from both. As a monk he was noted for his devotion to the Rule and his love of the scriptures—he was insistent that all under his charge should read and study them as much as possible. He divided his time between prayer and action and was clearly a leading figure in the eleventh-century German Church, whose rights he was determined to uphold. It is unfortunate that we have so little detail of his life or work as an abbot; although his writings were considerable, not very much remains. He died at an advanced age on 22 April 1091. His cult was popular, and miracles were reported at his tomb in the abbey church, but it has never been officially approved, and his name does not feature in the new Roman Martyrology. His relics have been lost or destroyed.

A Life written by a monk of Brauweiler about the year 1120 is in *M.G.H., Scriptores*, 12, pp. 180-95. See also *P.L.*, 154, 405-34; *Bibl.SS.*, 11, 1342-4.

Bd Francis of Fabriano (1251- *c.* 1322)

Francesco Venimbeni was born in 1251 in Fabriano in the Marche region of Italy. After a devout and studious childhood he joined the Franciscan Friars Minor at the age of sixteen and soon gained a reputation for his holiness and learning. At the end of his novitiate he went to Assisi to gain the Portiuncula indulgence and met Brother Leo, who had been secretary and confessor to St Francis (4 Oct.). It appears that it was Leo who persuaded Francis to write a learned defence of the indulgence. In 1316 and from 1318 to 1321 Francis was guardian of a new house in his home town of Fabriano. He gave the money he inherited toward the building of a library, the first Franciscan building of its kind. He wrote a series of sermons, which is no longer extant, and a *Chronicle* that deals with the key events and dates in the establishment of the Order in Fabriano; unfortunately this exists only in fragmentary copies. He had a strong devotion to the Holy Souls and was an eloquent and effective preacher; he persuaded three of his nephews to abandon the world and become Minorites like himself. He died about the year 1322 after a lingering fever. His cult started soon afterwards and was approved in 1775.

A Life was written by Dominic of Fessis, one of his nephews; see *AA.SS.*, Apr., 3, pp.984-90. See also *Bibl.SS.*, 5, 1155-6.

ST GEORGE (over page)
Red cross on silver field, the badge of the English from the time of Richard the Lionheart and the arms of the Order of the Garter.

23

ST GEORGE, *Martyr* (*c.* 303)

St George is one of the most popular Christian saints ever to have existed and has been venerated at different times in every Christian tradition, Eastern and Western; he finds a place, too, in Islamic hagiography that gives him the honoured title "prophet." He is best known as the slayer of the dragon and saviour of the maiden, but although this story exists in a number of different medieval literary versions and artistic representations, it is without any historical foundation and does not seem to have existed before the eleventh century. It may have resulted from a misinterpretation on the part of the Crusaders of an image in Constantinople of the emperor Constantine destroying the devil in the form of a dragon or serpent. The legend owes its widespread popularity at least in part to its inclusion in the *Golden Legend,* written about 1260; the work was later translated and printed by William Caxton, thus adding to its popularity in England.

There is in fact every reason to believe that George was a genuine martyr who suffered at Lydda (modern Lod in Israel) before the time of Constantine and perhaps during the persecution of the emperor Diocletian, which started in the year 303; the Coptic account of his death puts it in the year 307. Little more can be said with any certainty despite the very detailed *acta*. These are "full beyond belief of extravagances and of quite incredible marvels" (Thurston) and describe how George, an officer in the Roman army, gave his goods to the poor at the outbreak of the persecution and openly confessed his Christianity before the court. When he refused to sacrifice to the gods he suffered terrible tortures, described in graphic detail and supposed to have lasted seven years; at one stage a magician brought in to poison him was converted and himself died a martyr, and Our Lord appeared and restored George to health—indeed, George was resurrected from the dead three times, and himself raised from the dust seventeen people who had been dead for several centuries! Then fire destroyed the pagan priests and their temple, and the local governor was also killed by fire from heaven after he had had George beheaded. These *acta*, dating probably from the end of the fifth century, exist in a great variety of versions in several languages, witnessing to the popularity of the martyr, but were so outlandish that they were treated with scepticism even by those used to exaggerated tales about the saints; some of the accounts were condemned as unorthodox.

A cult existed at least from the middle of the fifth century, when his name was listed in the *Hieronymianum* martyrology, while in the Eastern Church he was referred to as the "great martyr" and invoked as patron of the Byzantine armies. There was a monastery dedicated to him in Jerusalem in the fifth century, and pilgrims to the Holy Land between the sixth and eighth centuries speak of Lydda as the main place associated with his cult and the resting-place of his relics. The Coptic Church, however, claims these were transferred to Egypt and finally placed in the church dedicated to him in Old Cairo. It is often said he was from Cappadocia and that his *acta* were compiled there, but there is no evidence for this: "the compiler of the *acta* confused the martyr with his namesake, the celebrated George of Cappadocia, an Arian intruder into the see of Alexandria and opponent of St Athanasius (2 May)" (Delehaye). According to some accounts, George's mother was a Cappadocian named Policronia.

How he came to be regarded as the chief patron of England is unclear. He was known there from at least the eighth century, and Bede mentions him in his martyrology, though without giving him any particular importance because he had no traditions that were sufficiently reliable and orthodox to base an account on. The Irish martyrology of Oengus (early ninth century) refers to him under today's date as "George, a sun of victories with thirty great thousand," a reference perhaps to the many thousands said to have been converted as a result of his exploits. The *acta* of his martyrdom were translated into Anglo-Saxon by Abbot Aelfric (*c*. 955-1020), though in a modified form— Aelfric claimed he had a reliable source and could tell the difference between true ands false traditions; the latter he attributed to "heretics." Some pre-Conquest churches were dedicated to him (for example, at Doncaster, in 1061). It is assumed that it was the Crusaders who increased devotion to this military martyr. The chronicler William of Malmesbury reports that St George and St Demetrius (8 Oct), "the martyr knights," were seen assisting the Crusaders at the seige of Antioch in 1098, and it may have been King Richard I (1189-99) and his knights who brought back stories of George's power as a patron, for the king placed himself and his army under George's protection. In 1222 a national synod at Oxford included his feast among the lesser holidays, but it was not until 1415, after the battle of Agincourt, that it was included as one of the major feasts of the year. Meanwhile, Edward III (1327-77) seems to have introduced the battle cry "St George for England" and in 1348 founded the Order of the Garter with St George as its patron. It was about this time that the emblem of the red cross on the white background began to be used extensively by English armies. Over 160 medieval churches were dedicated to him in England. During the seventeenth and eighteenth centuries (until 1778) his feast-day was a holiday of obligation for English Catholics, and Pope Benedict XIV (1740-58) recognized him as the Protector of England.

George also became the patron saint of Venice, Genoa, Portugal, and Catalonia, and his cult was strong in Russia and Ethiopia. He was one of the Auxiliary Saints, or Fourteen Holy Helpers, who from the fourteenth century were popularly thought to have especially effective intercessory powers. At various times he has been the patron saint of armourers, soldiers, knights, archers, and, through a pun on the Greek form of his name, even of farmers (*O.D.S.*). His intercession was also sought by individuals suffering from plague, leprosy, or syphilis. The reforms of 1969 removed his feast-day from the universal Calendar but allowed it to be celebrated by national Churches.

For critical accounts of the legends and *acta*, see H. Delehaye, *Les Légendes grecques des saints militaires* (1909), pp. 45-76, and H. Thurston in the *Catholic Encyclopaedia*, 6 (1909), pp. 453-5. *Bibl.SS.*, 6, 512-32, also discusses the sources and archaeological evidence and has a range of illustrations from different periods and a very useful section on the iconography of the saint. See also *O.D.S.*, pp. 197-8; *The Coptic Encyclopedia*, 4 (1991), pp. 1139-40. W. H. C. Frend, "Martyrdom in East and West: The Saga of St George of Nobatia and England," in *S.C.H.* 30 (1993), pp. 47-56, discusses an early Egyptian form of the legend and its associated iconography.

Given the popularity and subject matter of the legends, it is not surprising that George features very frequently in various forms of art. The oldest known representation is a sixth-century fresco in Egypt, now, unfortunately, beneath the Aswan dam. There is a statue of him on the front of the cathedral at Chartres, and a beautiful one by Donatello in the Bargello, Florence, showing George as a young warrior with a rather apprehensive look on his face; the fight with the dragon is carved on the base of the statue. The well-known painting of him by Ucello in the National Gallery, London, includes a massive dragon with large wings and a very slim maiden, while George is depicted as a very young man. Youthfulness, indeed, is one of the commonest characteristics in depictions of the saint—see, for example, the painting by Mantegna in the Academy in Venice. Another painting by the same artist, now in the Louvre, is the *Madonna of Victory with SS George and Michael*. He is paired with St Michael again in a painting by Raphael, also in the Louvre. Another painting of him by Raphael in the National Gallery of Art, Washington, shows him slaying the dragon, and this is also the subject of the painting by Rubens in the Prado, Madrid. In England his conquest of the dragon is the subject on a number of misericords, and in Westminster Abbey there is a figure of him in full armour, with the dragon under his feet, on the grille in Henry VII's Chapel. It is interesting that the legend of St Mercurius (25 Nov.), another Eastern soldier-martyr, was sometimes attributed to St George in English iconography as well as elsewhere. Finally, there are a great number of Byzantine images of the saint, and his life and legends were a frequent subject for Russian icon painters.

St Ibar, *Bishop* (*c.* 500)

Ibar may have been one of the missionaries in Ireland before St Patrick (17 Mar.): he features in the Lives of some of these and is said to have been a vigorous opponent of Patrick, on the grounds that the latter was a foreigner. There is other evidence, however, that he was one of Patrick's disciples. He is best known for his connection with the island of Beg-Eire (or Becc-Eriu) in Wexford harbour, now known as Beggery Island. This had a monastic settlement of some sort, perhaps with a school attached, and it grew to be an important foundation. Some of the Irish annals give the date of his death, apparently at an advanced age, as 499; others put it in 500 or 501. His cult was strong in the Wexford area, and people still visited a church on Beggery Island at the end of the seventeenth century hoping for cures. The martyrology of Oengus (early ninth century) speaks of "the light of bishop Ibar who has smote heresy's head; a splendid flame over a sparkling wave, in Becc-Eriu he departed."

No Life of Ibar exists, and his cult is not considered definite enough for his name to be included in the new Roman Martyrology. The best summary of the evidence is in Kenney, *Sources for the Early History of Ireland* (1929), 1, pp. 310–11. See also *The Irish Saints*, pp. 195–6, the source of the Oengus quotation above.

St Gerard of Toul, *Bishop* (935-94)

Gerard was born in Cologne in 935 and educated at the cathedral school there. He had intended to go on to the priesthood, and when his mother died suddenly from being struck by lightning he decided he had to devote himself to a life of prayer and penance, for he was sure (rather curiously) her death was a punishment for his sins. He became a canon at the cathedral and in 963 was chosen to be bishop of Toul in Lorraine. This involved him in a considerable amount of civil administration in addition to his pastoral duties, but he kept up his life of prayer and penance as well as devoting time to the study of the scriptures and the lives of the saints. One of his aims was to make Toul a centre of learning, and he persuaded some Irish and Greek monks to settle there, with the result that it became noted for its scholarship. He rebuilt the cathedral in Toul, enlarged the ancient monastery at Saint-Evre, and completed his predecessor's foundation at Saint-Mansuy. He was an accomplished preacher and had a reputation for his charity to the poor, especially after his work during a famine in 982 and the epidemic that followed. He was responsible for founding the Hôtel-Dieu, the oldest hospital in the city. He went on pilgrimage to Rome in 984 and died in 994. There is no doubt Gerard was the best known and most venerated of the bishops of Toul.

His canonization is interesting because it was one of the first to be performed by a pope. A monk of Saint-Evre, Widric, wrote a Life of Gerard sometime between 1027 and 1049 at the request of the bishop of Toul, Bruno. In 1050 Bruno became Pope St Leo IX (19 Apr.) and called a synod of bishops to meet in Rome that same year. Widric's Life was used to support a request for the canonization. It may be that the pope did not want to appear too ready to canonize a predecessor, and he hesitated. The assembled bishops were then told about a vision a monk attending the synod had of Gerard in glory, and they declared, "the same Lord Gerard is a holy man numbered by God among the saints, and he ought to be numbered and venerated among the saints by men also" (*P.L.*). This was enough for Leo, and he issued a Bull of canonization; among other things this said Gerard had been the object of great popular devotion in Toul—Widric had said the same but had added that Gerard had not been treated as a saint in liturgical services. Leo returned to Toul to translate Gerard's body to a new altar he consecrated for the purpose. It is a

165

little strange that Leo had done nothing about this for the twenty-two years he had been bishop there, and it may have been part of a move by a reforming and centralizing pope to give control of the making of saints to the papacy: even though Gerard had been the object of popular devotion he was not considered a saint until Leo had said so.

Widric's Life is in *M.G.H., Scriptores,* 4, pp. 490–505. For the canonization see *P.L.*, 143, 644–7, and E. W. Kemp, *Canonization and Authority* (1948), pp. 62–4.

St Adalbert of Prague, *Bishop and Martyr* (956-97)

Wojciech (Vojtiekh) was the youngest son of Duke Slavnik of Libice in Bohemia and was born there in 956. He was sent for his education to St Adalbert (20 June), archbishop of Magdeburg in Germany, who gave him the name Adalbert at confirmation. When the archbishop died nine years later Adalbert returned to Bohemia and was ordained by Bishop Thietmar of Prague. Thietmar died in 982, and Adalbert, although still under the canonical age, was elected to succeed him. His biographers describe him at this time as amiable and rather worldly; clearly he was not expected to cause any problems as a young bishop, and his German education would mean he was acceptable to the German emperor, whose friendship the duke of Bohemia had to cultivate. Once he was bishop, however, he changed, somewhat in the manner of Thomas à Becket, and became a much more serious and religious person. He had been much moved by hearing Bishop Thietmar on his death-bed blame himself for his failure to lead a holy enough life, and Adalbert is reported to have said on that occasion, "It is easy to wear a mitre and carry a crozier, but it is a terrible thing to have to give an account of a bishopric to the Judge of the living and the dead." It is possible he was influenced also by the reformed Cluniac monks he had met in Magdeburg, by St Majolus (11 May), the holy abbot of Cluny, and by St Gerard of Toul (23 Apr., above), a saintly bishop, both of whom he met at his consecration. A note of caution is necessary here: both his main biographers were Benedictine monks and shared a bias toward monasticism. They may have overstated the influence of this on Adalbert, and it is interesting that they hardly mention his pastoral work as bishop and cannot wait to get him out of Prague and into a monastery. Whatever the reasons for his changed character, and however marked it was, he entered Prague barefoot and was received enthusiastically by Boleslaw II of Bohemia and the clergy and people of the city.

Despite assiduous preaching and visitations Adalbert was unable to make much impression on his people; the secular clergy opposed his reforms, and eventually, in 990, he left Prague for Rome, where he became a monk in the Benedictine monastery of SS Boniface and Alexis. Given what we know of his character and later missionary determination, it is unlikely he just abandoned his diocese because of a lack of immediate success. It seems that conditions in

Bohemia were not as bad as his biographers make out, and the main reason for his leaving was political. Sometime between 987 and 990 there had been a war with Poland in which the Polish duke had been successful and the Slavnik family had refused to back Boleslaw. Moreover, it appears that Adalbert did not leave Prague with the idea of becoming a monk, and it was only when he came under the influence of a Greek abbot, St Nilus (26 Sept.), in Rome that he decided to do so. He did not remain in the monastery for very long, however, as in 992 Boleslaw requested the pope to order his return to Prague in order to win the support of the powerful Slavniks. Adalbert agreed on condition he receive full support for his work from the civil authorities. It is interesting that his first act on his return was to establish a Benedictine abbey at Brzevnov, whose church he consecrated in 993. He was soon back in Rome, however, this time because he had excommunicated the killers of an adulterous noblewoman who had taken refuge in a convent on his advice; he was determined to uphold the Church's right to grant sanctuary. It is likely that the whole incident was manipulated by opponents of the Slavniks, almost all of whom were subsequently murdered, and Adalbert left Prague for good.

In Rome he was elected prior of the abbey. He was again ordered back to Prague by the pope, at the request this time of St Willigis (23 Feb.) of Mainz, his metropolitan, who was there with the emperor Otto III. Adalbert suspected, quite rightly, that he would not be allowed back because he was a Slavnik, and so he took the precaution of getting from the pope permission for a roving missionary brief. He travelled by way of Mainz, where he met the emperor again, and they had long discussions. He then settled in Poland (now ruled by Duke Boleslaw the Great) and toward the end of 996 planned an evangelizing mission to the non-Christian Prussian peoples to the north. He established another Benedictine abbey, at Miedrzyrzecze in Poznania, perhaps seeing in the monks the best means to consolidate and develop any missionary success he might have. In the early spring of 997 he set out with two companions to preach in Prussia, being accompanied as far as Gdansk by Duke Boleslaw's soldiers—it was to the duke's political advantage, of course, to have the Prussians converted. They met with immediate opposition, being regarded as Polish spies, and when they refused to give up their mission they were murdered, on 23 April. Traditionally the site of their death is said to have been not far from Königsberg (present-day Kaliningrad), but it seems more likely to have been somewhere between the Nogat river and the estuary of the Vistula river, east of Gdansk. Adalbert's body was found and buried at Gniezno, to the east of Poznan; in 1039 it was moved by force to Prague. His cult spread very quickly throughout western Europe—as Dvornik says, he combined early medieval Europe's two great ideals, martyrdom and monasticism. His cult was actively promoted by Otto III and Boleslaw the Great in the interests of Polish unity, and also by the abbey of SS Boniface and Alexis in Rome. Traces of it can be found in Kiev in the Ukraine and in Germany and Hungary, and

Gniezno became the first permanent bishopric in Poland in 1000, when Otto III visited Adalbert's shrine. Four separate accounts of Adalbert's life were written during Boleslaw's time, and this literature inspired further attempts to evangelize the eastern peoples—see, for example, St Boniface (Bruno) of Querfurt (19 June), who also gained a martyr's crown in Prussia, in 1009. Adalbert is credited with the composition of hymns in Czech and Polish and seems to have favoured the use of a Slavonic liturgy similar to that of SS Cyril and Methodius (14 Feb.) in the areas he evangelized.

Adalbert was an important figure in the history of central Europe. He was friendly with the German emperor, Otto III, and seems to have shared his ideal of renewing the Roman Empire and unifying the more remote parts of eastern Europe. Adalbert sent missionaries to the Magyars and visited them himself, while St Astrik (12 Nov.), first archbishop of Hungary, was a friend and disciple and probably a monk at Brzevnov. If at times it is difficult to distinguish the political from the religious in his life, that is only to be expected and reflects a period when the distinction would not have been understood.

Two contemporary Lives, by Boniface of Querfurt and John Canaparius of Rome, are in *AA.SS.*, Apr., 3, pp. 176-207. See F. Dvornik, *The Making of Central and Eastern Europe* (1949), pp. 97-135, for an excellent account of Adalbert's life and importance. See also *The Cambridge Modern History of Poland*, 2 vols. (1950), 1, pp. 22-3, 30, 66-8; *O.D.S.*, pp. 3-4.

Adalbert is depicted in various roles: as a bishop, as a Benedictine monk, as a martyr. The oldest representation seems to be one in the church of San Bartolomeo in Rome, in which he appears as a bishop with the *pallium*. The twelfth-century bronze doors of the cathedral in Gniezno (Gnesen) contain scenes from his life, including his receiving the crozier from Otto II and his murder with an axe.

Bd Giles of Assisi (1262)

Giles was a native of Assisi at the same time as St Francis (4 Oct.), whom he admired but was too diffident to approach. When he heard that two of his friends, Bernard and Peter, had become disciples of the saint he overcame his hesitation and asked if he, too, might join them in their life of poverty. He received the habit in 1209. He accompanied the saint on his early preaching campaigns and then went on pilgrimage to Compostela in Spain. He developed the habit of always trying to do some work in return for the alms he received, and when he was sent to Rome on his return from Compostela he earned his living there by manual labour, chopping wood and drawing water. It is said of him that when he was invited to dine by the cardinal bishop of Tusculum he accepted on condition that he could work in the fields to repay the hospitality; when it was too wet to do so he worked in the cardinal's kitchen. He spent the years 1215-9 as a hermit at Favorone near Assisi. After a visit to the Holy Land he went to Tunis to preach to the Saracens, but the mission was a failure and he received no encouragement from the local Christians, who feared his proselytizing would bring reprisals by the Muslims.

He spent the rest of his life in Italy in Fabriano, Rieti, and Perugia. He had little formal learning but was approached for advice by many people, and the short sayings attributed to him display a deep spirituality combined with shrewd insight. Their impact often turns on Italian usage, and this can make it difficult to appreciate them fully. His spiritual life developed to the point where he experienced frequent ecstasies, and in 1226 he had a vision of Our Lord, which he described as his fourth "birth"—the others being his birthday, his Baptism, and his taking the habit. He died in Perugia in the year 1262. He had been particularly dear to St Francis, who called him "a knight of the round table." His cult was approved in 1777.

Sources for his life are numerous. Two forms of an early Life, written perhaps by Brother Leo, exist. See R. Brown, *Franciscan Mystic: The Life of Bl. Giles of Assisi* (1962). The best Italian ed. of the sayings is N. Vian, *B. Egidio di Assisi, I Detti* (1923).

Bd Helen of Udine (1396-1458)

Helena was a member of the Valentini family of Udine in north-eastern Italy. At the age of fifteen she married Antonio dei Cavalcanti and for the next twenty-five years lived a happy married life with a large family. Then the death of her husband caused her to change her way of life completely, and she became a tertiary of the Hermits of St Augustine, devoting herself to prayer, charitable works, and penance. She took a vow of perpetual silence that she observed all year except at Christmas, but it is not clear what this involved, since the account written by her sister Perfecta, who lived with her, shows that she continued to run the household in a normal way. That account also relates how she was troubled by temptations to suicide and by physical attacks that seemed to have no human explanation, and how she was consoled by visions and ecstasies and enjoyed a gift for healing. She was bed-ridden for the last three years of her life and died on 23 April 1458.

There are two Lives, the longer and earlier of which claims to be derived from an Italian original, but neither gives an impression of being particularly reliable; see *AA.SS.*, Apr., 3, pp. 247-58.

Bd Teresa Mary of the Cross, *Foundress* (1846-1910)

Teresa Adelaide Manetti was born on 2 March 1846 in Campo Bisenzio near Florence. When she was eighteen she gathered together a group of young women to live communally and work as teachers of the poor. Ten years later, in 1874, she opened a free school and established an Institute of Carmelite Tertiary Sisters. Over the years she opened further schools and kindergartens, and her Institute was approved in 1904 with the title "Sisters of the Third Order of St Teresa of Jesus." Their way of life revolved around adoration of the Blessed Sacrament, the care of children, especially orphans, and missionary work. In the last years of her life her Sisters began to work abroad, and they set up houses in Lebanon and the Holy Land. Her own spirituality was strongly Carmelite in its inspiration, and she was motivated by an all-consuming love of Christ and a desire to save souls. In a prayer she wrote: "To suffer, to suffer, always to suffer. Do what you like to me, it is enough that I save souls for you." The daily source of her spiritual energy was her devotion to the Blessed Sacrament and Our Lady. Like her famous patron, St Teresa of Avila (15 Oct.), she faced opposition and slander before her ideas were accepted and had to endure spiritual dryness and the "dark night of the soul" in her interior life. She also suffered physically from a very painful cancer, yet people who visited the convent to ask for her help commented on the atmosphere of joy and peace that surrounded her and on her balanced approach to their problems. People would wait for hours to ask her for advice and comfort. She died on 23 April 1910 and was beatified in 1986.

A.A.S. 79, pt. 1 (1986), pp. 465–7, for the papal homily at her beatification. See also *N.S.B.* 2, pp. 104–5; B. Baldi, *La Serva di Dio, Madre T. M. della Croce* (1937).

Bd Maria Gabriella Sagheddu (1914–39)

Maria Gabriella was born in Dorgali in Sardinia on 17 March 1914. By all accounts she was a headstrong, independent, proud young person, although she also shared other traits said to be characteristic of her people, including a sense of duty, an intense loyalty, and—for women—an unshakable purity. When she was eighteen her favourite sister died, and this "meeting with the cross of Christ" changed her life: she put herself under the guidance of a spiritual director and joined a branch of Young Catholic Action, taking on the teaching of the catechism to young children, while at the same time devoting as much time as she could to prayer and works of charity. At the age of twenty-one she decided to dedicate the rest of her life entirely to God by becoming a Trappist nun in the abbey at Grottaferrata, near Rome.

Her life as a nun was dominated by two ideas: gratitude for the mercy God had shown her in calling her to such a life, and an anxiety to respond as totally as possible to whatever graces he gave her (Piccardo). Her particular apostolate was to pray for and dedicate all her spiritual activity to the cause of Christian unity, because, as she put it, "I feel the Lord is asking it of me." She knew nothing of the history of the divisions in the Church and had probably not even heard of ecumenism. It was an unusual and, it must be said, not a very popular cause among Catholics at the time, but for Maria Gabriella it was simply a question of wanting "everyone to turn to God and for his kingdom to be established in every heart." Her favourite text for meditation was the Gospel of St John, especially chapters 17 to 20, where Jesus prayed that all his followers might be one. Her own spiritual life was based on a faithful living out of the strict Trappist Rule with its silence and daily denials of self. She fell ill for the first time in her life when she was twenty-three and died after fifteen months of suffering on 23 April 1939, Good Shepherd Sunday, with its Gospel message that there would be only one flock and one shepherd. She was beatified in 1983.

A surprisingly large number of studies of Bd Maria Gabriella have been published: see list in C. Piccardo, *Bibl.SS.*, Suppl. 1, 1205-7, which also prints a photograph. Mention may be made here of G. Zananiri, *Dans le mystère de l'Unité: Marie Gabriella Sagheddu* (2d ed., 1983); G. Cabiddu, *Lettere di "Una figlia scappata da casa,"* (2d ed., 1983); B. Martelet, *La petite soeur de l'unité, Marie Gabriella* (1984).

24

ST FIDELIS OF SIGMARINGEN, *Martyr* (1578-1622)

Mark Roy was born in Sigmaringen in Hohenzollern and went to the university of Freiburg in Breisgau, where he gained a doctorate in philosophy in 1603 and then taught while studying for a degree in law. In 1604 he was appointed private tutor to a small group of young aristocrats who wished to do a "grand tour" of several universities in western Europe. This post seems to have lasted about six years, and Mark not only guided the young men's studies but gave them an example of religious devotion and generosity to the poor. On his return to Germany he was awarded a doctorate in civil and canon law in 1611 and began to practise at Ensisheim in Alsace. He earned the nickname "the poor person's lawyer," but he soon gave up his practice, disillusioned by the deceitful tactics of his colleagues and wishing to devote himself to the religious life. He was ordained priest and then joined the Capuchins, taking the name Fidelis in religion.

He is said to have had a fear of being lukewarm in religion and was heard to say, "Woe betide me if I should prove myself but a half-hearted soldier in the service of my thorn-crowned captain!" (*B.T.A.*). He began his ministry by preaching and hearing Confessions and soon gained a name for his holiness and dedication, his fasting, and intense life of prayer. He spent the years 1614 to 1618 studying theology at Constance and Frauenfeld and was appointed guardian successively of the Order's houses in Rheinfelden, Freiburg, and Feldkirch, and was effective not just as a superior but also in preaching in the locality and converting Protestants. He was particularly devoted to the care of the sick, many of whom he was reported to have cured during an epidemic. The bishop of Chur in eastern Switzerland heard about his reputation and asked the Capuchin superiors if Fidelis and a group of monks could be seconded to preach to the people in the Grisons Canton who had reverted to Protestantism in 1608 and were in revolt against the Austrian Habsburgs. Permission was granted for him and eight other monks to take on the mission, and the new Roman Congregation, *De Propaganda Fide*, officially appointed Fidelis leader of the project.

The mission, as the first of its kind in that part of Europe, was obviously a dangerous one, but at first it met with considerable success, and a number of Swiss leaders were converted. It was not long, however, before opposition began. Fidelis and his companions were seen as agents of the hated Habsburgs, intent on taking over the Swiss cantons, and he does seem to have had the protection of Austrian soldiers at least on some occasions. The Catholic Reformation was at its height, and the Habsburgs were its main proponents, using political, military, and religious means to further Catholicism and win back those regions of Europe that had gone over to Protestantism in the sixteenth century. He was warned his life was in danger and signed his last letter, "Brother Fidelis, who will soon be the food of worms." On 24 April he preached at Seewis and was in the middle of a sermon on the text, "One Lord, one Faith, one Baptism," when he was shot at. He was not hit, but the shooting caused a general disturbance. A Protestant offered Fidelis shelter from the crowd but he turned it down, saying his life was in God's hands; he tried to take the road from the town but was attacked by about twenty armed men. When they demanded he give up his Faith he said, "I came here to enlighten you, not to accept your errors" and was killed. He was canonized in 1746 and was honoured by *Propaganda* as its proto-martyr in 1771, when his feast-day was extended to the universal Church. It is interesting that the Bollandists in the seventeenth and early eighteenth centuries did not include him in their *Acta Sanctorum* because they could not find evidence of a definite cult. He is one of the patron saints of lawyers. A work he wrote while still a novice was published in 1746 as *The Spiritual Exercises*; later editions bore the title *Exercitia Seraphicae Devotionis* ("Exercises of Angelic Devotion"). The work is a collection of prayers, methods of meditation, and spiritual maxims taken from his reading.

A very scholarly Life of Fidelis was published in 1896 by F. della Scala, *Der hl. Fidelis von Sigmaringen*; this has been the basis of more popular accounts. See, for example, B. Gossens, *Der heilege F. v. S. Eine Lebensbeschreibung* (1933). See also *N.C.E.*, 5, p. 910.

There is an idealized painting of Fidelis by Tiepolo in Parma in which he is depicted as "the crusher of heresy."

St Anthimus, *Bishop and Martyr* (303)

Anthimus was bishop of Nicomedia in Bithynia, where the Roman emperors had one of their favourite residences. The persecution of Christians under Diocletian (emperor from 284-305) began in 303 and was particularly severe in that part of the empire. The historian Eusebius reports that a zealous Christian tore down the imperial edict ordering the destruction of churches and sacred books, and from then on Christian clergy were called on to offer incense to the Roman gods whenever they appeared in public. Anthimus was beheaded for refusing to do so. Eusebius goes on to say that the local Christians were blamed for a fire that broke out in the emperor's palace, and very large numbers of them were executed on the orders of the emperor when the persecution was extended to include laypeople. There seems to be some confusion about whether Anthimus had already been beheaded before this. In some calendars eleven fellow-martyrs are associated with Anthimus. Letters said to have been written by the bishop to encourage SS Indes and Domna (formerly 28 Dec.), martyred with those blamed for the fire, are not authentic. The emperor Justinian (483-565) built a magnificent basilica over Anthimus' tomb.

Eusebius' account is in *H.E.*, bks. 8 and 9. A late Greek text of the supposed *acta* of St Anthimus is given in *AA.SS.*, Apr., 3, pp. 487-91. See also *Bibl.SS.*, 2, 60-1. Part of the text of a work on the Church attributed to the saint is in *Studi e Testi* 5 (1901) but is almost certainly not authentic.

St Mellitus, *Bishop* (624)

Mellitus was a Roman abbot sent by Pope St Gregory the Great (3 Sept.) to England in 601 as head of a second group of missionaries who were to assist St Augustine (27 May). Bede gives us the text of a letter from the pope to Mellitus giving advice on how they should deal with the English: pagan temples should be turned into churches whenever possible, and days of sacrifice replaced by festivals in honour of the martyrs while the animals are killed for the people to feast on, for "if the people are allowed some worldly pleasures in this way they will more readily come to desire the joys of the spirit." Mellitus worked for three years in Kent and was then appointed by St Augustine to be bishop of the East Saxons. He baptized King Sabert and many of his subjects, and King Ethelbert, Sabert's overlord, built a church dedicated to St Paul in London and made it Mellitus' see, so he was the first bishop of London. He visited Rome in 605 and attended a council there. When King Sabert died in 616, his three sons, who had not been baptized, reverted openly to paganism. They still demanded from Mellitus, however, the Blessed Sacrament, or "fine white bread" as they called it, and when he refused they banished him from the kingdom. He went to France but was soon recalled to Kent and succeeded St Laurence (3 Feb.) as archbishop of Canterbury. We know very little about his rule as archbishop, but Bede tells us, "Although he became crippled with gout, his sound and ardent mind overcame his troublesome infirmity, ever reaching above earthly things to those that are heavenly in love and devotion. Noble by birth, he was even nobler in mind." He died in 624.

Bede, *H.E.*, 1, 29-30; 2, 3-7.

St Egbert of Iona (*c.* 640-729)

Egbert was a native of Northumbria who became a monk at Lindisfarne and then went to Ireland to study. While he was there, there was a serious epidemic in 664 that killed his Anglo-Saxon companion, and he made a vow that if he survived he would spend the rest of his life as a missionary away from his native country. He was ordained priest and decided to evangelize Friesland and the north of Germany, but he was persuaded by a vision that this was not God's plan for him and had to be content with inspiring St Wigbert (13 Aug.), St Willibrord (7 Nov.), and others to work in those regions.

Egbert went instead to Iona, in Scotland, the last bastion of the Celtic way of calculating the date of Easter, to persuade the monks there to adopt the Roman practice instead. He spent the last thirteen years of his life there, and tradition says his reputation for learning and holiness enabled him to succeed, so that the very day he died was the first time the Iona monks celebrated Easter in line with the rest of the Western Church. Too much importance has been attached to this Easter controversy, and it is at least possible that it was not Egbert's arguments that converted the monks but the passage of time and a general realization there was little point in being different; the Irish Church itself had been following the Roman practice for about a century. Moreover, Bede says the community on Iona held to their own custom in this matter only "until the year of Our Lord 715," when Egbert, "most learned in the scriptures and renowned for lifelong holiness," arrived there and persuaded them to change; the tradition that it was only on Egbert's death Easter was kept on the correct day seems to come from another part of Bede that is somewhat ambiguous. The *Anglo-Saxon Chronicle* says the change on Iona occurred in 716.

Bede tells us that Egbert led a life of "great humility, gentleness, purity and uprightness . . . [and was] indefatigable in teaching, firm in administering reproof, and generous in distributing whatever he received from the rich." He also says Egbert was a bishop but does not mention his see, and he was more usually venerated as a confessor.

Most of what we know about Egbert comes from Bede, *H.E.*, bks. 3 and 4. See also *K.S.S.*, p. 331.

St Mary Euphrasia Pelletier, *Foundress* (1796-1868)

Rose-Virginie Pelletier was born in 1796 on the island of Noirmoutier off the coast of Brittany, where her parents had taken refuge during the revolutionary wars. Her father, a doctor, died in 1806 and her mother in 1813, so she was sent as a boarder to a convent in Tours and there found out about the "Convent of the Refuge." This belonged to an Institute founded by St John Eudes (19 Aug.) in 1641 to rescue prostitutes and protect young women in danger, known as the Institute of Our Lady of Charity of the Refuge. Its Sisters took a fourth vow, "to be always zealous in the saving of girls and penitent women." Rose-Virginie joined the Tours convent as a novice in 1814, taking the name Mary of St Euphrasia in religion, and in 1826, still only twenty-nine years old, was elected superior. Her first act was to set up the "Magdalen Sisters" for older reformed prostitutes to join as a religious way of life combining prayer and manual work.

In 1829 she was asked if a convent and refuge could be opened in Angers, and Mary Euphrasia herself went there to look after its establishment, taking five Sisters from Tours with her. She used a former refuge that had been dedicated to the Good Shepherd as the foundation of the new house and was soon successful enough to feel able to hand it over to others and return to Tours. Two years later, however, the Angers house was in danger of closing through a lack of resources, and the local bishop persuaded the bishop of

Tours to release Mary Euphrasia so that she could take over its running again. A rather painful controversy broke out between the two communities; in the end Mary Euphrasia was elected prioress at Angers and left Tours. By 1833 the house in Angers had been restored, and four new houses had been set up in different towns, each autonomous and under the control of the local bishop.

These events helped to convince Mary Euphrasia that it was not satisfactory for each convent of the Institute to be on its own, having to recruit and train its own Sisters and unable to call on central resources in times of expansion or crisis. She was determined to establish a centralized organization with a superior general in charge, and she went ahead with this even though she was accused of ambition and self-interest and was blamed for destroying the spirit that had kept the Institute going for so long. Some of the bishops also opposed her plans because they feared losing control of the convents in their dioceses. While, however, she was deeply humble in herself and reluctant to seek any publicity or question authority, people who knew her said that when it came to doing what she believed was God's will she was quite capable of taking over and running the country. She was essentially a woman of action; she left no writings on spirituality or education, and her book, *Conferences and Instructions*, published in 1907, was based on notes taken by the Sisters during conferences and conversations. Her view of education was optimistic: she recognized in every human being a child of God, loved by him, unique and always capable of improvement because it had within itself the means of reform (*Dict.Sp.*).

What she eventually established at Angers was a new Institute that became known as the Institute of Our Lady of Charity of the Good Shepherd—the famous Good Shepherd Sisters. She said of them on one occasion: "Having brought to birth all our young Sisters in the Cross, I love them more than life itself. And the root of that love is in God and in the knowledge of my own unworthiness, for I realize that at the age at which they are professed I could not have supported such deprivations and hard work." She obtained papal approval for the Institute in 1835, and when she died in 1868 from cancer it numbered 2,760 Sisters in 110 convents throughout the world, including the United States, Chile, and Australia. Its spirit was the same as that in the original Institute in Tours, and St John Eudes was still its principal inspiration, with his intense love of the Sacred Hearts of Jesus and Mary. The changes introduced by Mary Euphrasia were designed only to make the apostolate more effective; as she put it, "The habit we wear must be zeal, and that zeal must embrace the whole world." Her own spirituality was based on the works of seventeenth-century French writers, and her fundamental spiritual aim was to allow Jesus to grow in her to such an extent she would be fired with his love for souls and willing to suffer as he did for them. She was canonized in 1940. She left a correspondence of about fifteen hundred letters and the book already mentioned.

G. Bernoville, *St Mary Euphrasia Pelletier: Foundress of the Good Shepherd Sisters* (1959); Denise Pezzoli, *S. Marie-Euphrasie Pelletier, Lettres et entretiens* (1964); Marie Dominique Poinsenet, *Rien N'est Impossible à L'Amour* (n.d.); Marie-Euphrasie Pelletier: *Lettres* (1996). See also *Dict.Sp.* 10 (1980), 531-3; *Bibl.SS.*, 8, 1140-44; *N.C.E.*, 11, pp. 60-1, and 6, pp. 627 on the Good Shepherd Sisters.

There is a modern statue of her by Nicolini in St Peter's, Rome.

Bd Benedict Menni, *Founder* (1841-1914)

Angelo Ercole Menni was born in Milan on 11 March 1841. His parents, Luigi and Luisa, were fervent Catholics who gave him a religious upbringing, including a keen sense of his duty to help the poor and the sick. After leaving secondary school he worked for a short time as a clerk in a Milan bank, but he left when he was asked to falsify some records to cover up some financial fraud. In 1859 he volunteered to help with the wounded soldiers returning from the battle of Magenta (about twelve miles from Milan) and was occupied in taking them from Milan station to the hospital of the Brother Hospitallers of St John of God. The devoted care shown by the Brothers inspired Angelo to follow their example, and in the following year he became a novice in their Order, making his solemn profession in 1864 and taking the name Benedict in religion. The Order had been founded in the sixteenth century by St John of God (8 Mar.) in Spain, but because of anticlerical legislation in the 1830s its work had been severely limited throughout the Spanish Empire, and by 1850 it had ceased to exist there. A few months after his ordination in 1866 Benedict was chosen to go to Spain to re-establish the Order; he received this commission from Pope Pius IX in person: he was to restore the Hospitaller Order in its birthplace, stressing "a perfect common life marked by great poverty, chastity and obedience." It was an extraordinary mission for so inexperienced a young man, but the superior general had already recognized Benedict's intelligence, ability, and determination—what some would later call obstinacy. He spent some months in France, learning how the Order had been re-established there after the French Revolution, and arrived in Barcelona in April 1867, with little knowledge of Spanish and no material resources.

By October of that year, with the help of two Brothers, he had opened a hospital-refuge for poor and abandoned children, especially those suffering from malnutrition, scurvy, and rickets. In 1872 he was appointed superior of the Order in Spain, and the work of re-establishment seemed to be progressing. Unfortunately, in 1873 a revolutionary government abolished the monarchy and re-introduced restrictions on the religious Orders. Benedict became involved against his will in these political struggles; he was taken to be a Carlist, or supporter of the deposed Queen Isabela, and his life was threatened, but he was released on condition he left the country. He went to Marseilles and with some of the Brothers became members of the Red Cross so that they could return to Spain to look after those wounded in the civil war. A testimonial from the Spanish Red Cross declared, "During the war he carried everywhere both spiritual and physical assistance to the wounded without distinction or favour, and showing equal love and charity to both sides." The civil war lasted until 1876, when he was able to return to Barcelona to reorganize the original hospital-refuge, and from there he moved to Madrid, where he acquired a building and some land at Ciempozuelos, about twenty miles from the city, where he opened a psychiatric hospital. Other foundations followed, and hospital-refuges and psychiatric hospitals were opened in another seven Spanish cities, in Mexico, and in Portugal. In 1884 he obtained approval from Rome for the establishment of a joint Spanish-American province of the Order and was chosen as its first provincial, a post to which he was re-elected five times.

There was a serious outbreak of cholera around Madrid in 1885, during which Benedict showed outstanding courage and devotion to the sick. He went with small groups of Brothers to the areas most badly affected, and in many of the villages he was the only person with medical knowledge able to care for the cholera victims and give advice on matters of hygiene. For some time he had been concerned that all his helpers were men and that all the institutions he had been able to set up could care only for men. He approached a number of female Orders to see if they would join him in his work but was unsuccessful. When two women, María Josefa Recio and María Angustias Jiménez, approached him and asked if they could dedicate themselves to the care of the sick under his guidance, he sent them to Ciempozuelos, where they were soon joined by others. In 1881 he formally received the first novices, and in the following year some of the group made their religious profession. He gave them his own six-word motto: "Pray, Work, Suffer, Forbear, Love, Silence." This was the start of the Congregation of Hospitaller Sisters of the Sacred Heart of Jesus; it received official approval from the Holy See in 1901. By the time of his death he had opened thirteen hospitals for women in Spain, France, and Portugal. The Congregation is currently active in Europe, Africa (Ghana and Liberia), Asia (the Philippines), and Latin America.

Benedict led an extremely busy life, much of it taken up with negotiation, administration, and travel. He was also involved in a good deal of litigation, most notably in a seven-year civil case against him in Madrid when he was falsely accused of abusing a mentally-ill woman. The anticlerical press denounced him in banner headlines and published cartoons of him as a "perverted beast." In the end the judge dismissed the case for lack of evidence. He also faced considerable opposition within the Order. In 1903 he was appointed by the Holy See to be apostolic visitor of the Order, and in 1911 he became its superior general. He resigned from this post just over a year later because he felt he lacked the support of its members. To at least some extent this was true: the pope had appointed him without calling a general chapter, and it seems that some of the male members of the Order had resented his establishment of the Sisters, seeing in them a rival organization. He was also a keen anti-Modernist and as apostolic visitor had removed some members from office whom he suspected of doctrinal laxity. Opposition to him was so strong that in 1912 he was ordered to leave the motherhouse of the Order in Rome and stay with the Sisters at Viterbo, but then he was told to leave Italy altogether and live in France—but not in any of the Sisters' houses. He was finally deprived of a secretary (a stroke had disabled his hand), so that he could no longer write to the Sisters or Brothers. Even allowing for the difficult traits in his character it is hard to understand the bitterness of the campaign against him. In the last year of his life he began to suffer from senile dementia and finally died from a second stroke on 24 April 1914. His remains were taken to Ciempozuelos and buried in the local cemetery; from there, in 1924, they were removed to the church of the motherhouse of his Sisters. He was beatified in 1985.

In everything Benedict did he was inspired by an intense devotion to the Sacred Heart, and to Our Lady under the title of Our Lady of the Sacred Heart of Jesus. He told his Sisters to ask Jesus to inflame them with his divine love, and also to ask "the Queen of Love, the Immaculate Virgin," to do the same. He believed Jesus was present in the sick, and especially in the mentally ill; those who helped those who were "the least of my brethren," were serving Jesus directly. "Have no trust in yourselves," he wrote, "but trust in Jesus and throw yourselves into his arms," for, as he often said, "we are nothing and we can do nothing without God's help."

Benedict's correspondence with the Sisters of his Congregation was published in 1920, with a second edition in 1975 by José Gonzáles, *Cartas del Servo de Dios Benito Menni . . . por él fundadas.* See also F. Bilbao, *Biografía del R. P. Benito Menni . . .* (1939); José Alvarez-Sierra, *El Padre Menni y su obra* (1968). In English there are two useful pamphlets, G. Russotto, *Blessed Benedict Menni of the Hospitaller Order of St John of God* (1985), and Sisters of the English Province, *Blessed Benedict Menni, Founder of the Hospitaller Sisters of the Sacred Heart of Jesus* (1989); see also Mario Soroldoni, *Sanctity proved in Fire: The Chequered Life of Benedict Menni* (Ital. original, 1981; Eng. ed., 1985).

ST MARK THE EVANGELIST (over page)
Gold winged lion and nimbus on red field.

179

25

ST MARK, *Evangelist* (First Century)

Nothing is known for certain about the personal life of Mark, the author of the second of the Synoptic Gospels. Indeed, it may be we should not call the author of that Gospel "Mark" at all, for there is no reference to the name of the author in the text itself (unlike, for example, the letters of St Paul) and no reference to its author by name until the second century. The historian Eusebius, writing in the late third century, tells us what Papias had reported second-hand in the second century: Mark had been St Peter's "interpreter" and had written down accurately all that he had remembered. Building on this slender base, tradition assumed that every mention of a person named Mark or John Mark in the New Testament must apply to the evangelist, and so he was said to be the son of the woman in whose house the disciples often met (Acts 12:12), and the missionary companion of both St Paul and St Peter (Acts 13:5 and 1 Pet. 5:13).

According to Paul, John Mark was a Jewish cousin of Barnabas whom Paul did not rate very highly because he deserted him and Barnabas (Acts 13:13; 15:37-9); presumably Paul was later reconciled with him, as Mark was in Rome when Paul was in prison there (Col. 4:10). But whether the "John Mark" of Acts, the "Mark" of Paul's Epistles, and "my son Mark" of St Peter's first Epistle are the same person as the "Mark" who was supposed to have written the Gospel is not certain: the name Mark was a very common one at the time in both its Latin and Greek forms. On the other hand it is difficult to see why the Gospel should have been attributed falsely to an unknown person named Mark, as nothing was to be gained by such an attribution, and so it seems sensible to continue to refer to its author as Mark. Tradition has usually identi-fied the writer of the Gospel with the young man who fled naked during the arrest of Jesus (Mark 14:51-2), but there is no strong reason to do so. He was reputed to be the author of an apocryphal *passio* of St Barnabas (11 June), and a set of unreliable *acta* describe his own martyrdom at Alexandria during the reign of the emperor Nero. A late legend makes him one of the seventy-two disciples sent out by Our Lord, although Papias was definite Mark had neither been a disciple nor heard the Lord in person.

The text of the Gospel does allow us to say something about its author. He makes minor mistakes when it comes to the geography of Palestine (he puts Sidon south of Tyre, for example, in 7:31), and his fluency in Greek would support the suggestion he was not a native of that country. The fact that he translates Aramaic words and phrases (*e.g.* 5:41; 15:34) and explains Jewish customs (7:2-4) seems to indicate he is writing for a non-Palestinian audience, or at least a non-Jewish one. According to tradition the place of composition was Italy, and probably Rome, where the author was with St Peter. But there is also a second-century tradition that says the Gospel was written in Alexandria, where, according to Eusebius, Mark went after leaving Rome to become that city's first bishop. The language of the Gospel is *koine* Greek, the *lingua franca* of the eastern Mediterranean lands. With regard to the date when it was written, it is difficult to be precise. To a large extent it depends on the view one takes of the much-debated question of the order in which the three Synoptic Gospels (those of Matthew, Mark, and Luke) were written. The traditional order was questioned increasingly from the nineteenth century onward, and the commonly accepted view among scholars today is that Mark's Gospel was written first and was used in a form very similar to what we have by Matthew (21 Sept.) and Luke (18 Oct.). There has been something of a revival of the traditional view more recently, but it seems safer at the moment to opt for the priority of Mark and to date the Gospel around the years 65 and 70—the earlier date if Mark's close association with Peter in Rome is accepted, the later if the Gospel were written in, say, Alexandria before the destruction of the Temple in Jerusalem in the year 70.

Until fairly recently, the structure and teaching of Mark's Gospel have been taken to be straightforward and even simplistic. The work was said to be arranged as a continuous narrative and the outline of events to be similar to that given in the speeches of Peter and Paul reported in the Acts. This links in with the tradition mentioned above that Mark accompanied Paul on his missionary journeys and was Peter's interpreter or secretary. According to this view, Mark in writing his Gospel was giving his readers a straightforward report of the life and death of Jesus as he had heard it from the apostles. Because of this, it was thought the reader came closest to the historical figure of Jesus in this account, which lacked the theological sophistication and manipulation of the other evangelists. Mark was acknowledged to be a graphic storyteller and a faithful reporter but little else; even the Greek he wrote in was dismissed as unpolished and unsubtle. In recent years, however, little short of a revolution has taken place in the study of Mark's Gospel, and the result has been to portray the author as a creative editor, working on the oral (and, perhaps, written) accounts circulating in the earliest Christian communities about Jesus' teachings, death, and resurrection. The resulting Gospel is far from being a simple account and is, indeed, as theological in its purpose as Matthew and Luke. So, why did Mark write his Gospel?

It is important to note that Mark devoted a third of his narrative to a single week in the life of Jesus, the final week spent in Jerusalem and ending with his passion, death, and resurrection. Clearly, then, everything else in the account was to be read in the light of that week: if, for example, Mark depicted Jesus as a great worker of miracles (3:10; 6:56), this power had to be seen in the context of the apparent failure of the cross—wandering magicians were common at the time, and Jesus must not be confused with them. Nor must he be confused with the contemporary wandering philosophers: Jesus spoke many words of wisdom, and no doubt his sayings and parables were circulating among the early Christians, but, again, his wisdom could only be understood in the context of the folly of his death. Mark also made it clear that it was not just Jesus who was to suffer: in 8:34-7 he underlined the fact that those who were Jesus' followers would have to suffer persecution and continue to acknowledge their master publicly despite it. It has been suggested that persecution had already started when Mark was writing his Gospel, and so he found it necessary to warn the Christians that was what they should expect instead of the "theology of glory" offered by Paul (Achtemeier). Perhaps that was also why Mark had Jesus telling the disciples even he did not know the time of his glorious return to establish the Kingdom (13:32): they and the early Christians were not to be discouraged, or worse, when the period of suffering and the terrible fall of Jerusalem were not followed by the Second Coming. Overall, Mark was concerned to use his Gospel to put the events and sayings of Jesus' life, already circulating in a number of versions, into the only context that made sense of them and so to drive home to his readers that suffering was the essential characteristic of their master's, and their own, lives.

This need for the Christian to accept suffering as central to the Gospel message may help to explain another feature of Mark's account, the way it highlights the failure of the disciples to understand Jesus' teaching. On a number of occasions Jesus rebuked them for this failure (7:18; 8:17; 8:29-33) and complained about their lack of trust in him (5:35-41; 6:45-52). In particular they failed to understand Jesus when he foretold how he must suffer and die (8:31-9:9; 9:30-31; 10:32-45) and deserted him when his sufferings began (14:50). Mark's criticism of the disciples contrasts with the the way they are praised at the start of his Gospel for following Jesus so readily (1:16-20) and congratulated on their first teaching mission (6:30-1). It is also in contrast with the faith of outsiders who on first meeting Jesus trust him to grant their requests or pay him the respect that was his due: the father of the epileptic boy (9:18), the blind man Bartimaeus (10:46-52), and the woman at Bethany (14:3-9). Is Mark perhaps saying a first acceptance of Jesus, with his miracles and wise teachings, is often not too difficult, but a lasting acceptance, with the idea of suffering that entails, calls for an altogether deeper commitment?

Another feature of Mark's account is the way those who meet Jesus try to work out who he is. The scribes ask, "How can this man talk like that? . . . Who can forgive sins but God?" (2:7); the disciples ask, "Who can this be?" (4:41); the chief priests and scribes want to know his authority for acting as he does (11:28); and the high priest asks Jesus openly, "Are you the Christ, the Son of the Blessed One?" (14:61). Again, it was his suffering and death that made clear who Jesus was: it was while he hung on the cross that the centurion announced, "In truth this man was a son of God" (15:41). The overall picture of Jesus in Mark's account is of a person of unique power, sometimes acting as only God can act (for example, forgiving sin in 2:1-12, and claiming to be lord of the sabbath in 2:28); demanding and receiving obedience (for example, over the preparations for the entry into Jerusalem and the Passover meal in 11:1-6 and 14:13-16), and teaching with an authority that cannot be questioned (12:34); he teaches and performs wonders in a way that is reminiscent of the ancient prophets (6:15), and "even the wind and the sea obey him" (4:41). And yet Jesus forbids anyone to draw the obvious conclusion from these displays of power and authority; he rebukes the unclean spirit that cries, "I know who you are: the Holy One of God" (1:23-6), and after the transfiguration orders the apostles not to tell what they have seen "until after the Son of Man had risen from the dead" (9:2-9). Again, it is only in the context of his immediate death (chapter 15) that Mark introduces the title "king" to Jesus: he is indeed king, as he admits to Pilate (15:2), but a king whose throne is to be the cross.

Mark, then, was principally interested to portray Jesus in a particular theological way, and so his account should not be expected to be historical in a modern sense. He was not concerned with the chronology of what Jesus did or said, and a number of inconsistencies and even impossibilities in his narrative appear in trying to piece together a precise itinerary for Jesus' journeys (see the two sea-crossings in 4:35 and 5:21) or an hour-by-hour timetable of what Jesus did at a particular time (all the events between 4:35 and 6:2 appear to have taken place in two hours). Perhaps it was because he was a good storyteller that he was for so long taken to be merely telling a simple story of what happened: he uses a series of short, punchy sentences and puts in the sort of detail an oral storyteller might use—"that evening, after sunset" (1:32); "in the morning, long before dawn" (1:35); Jesus was asleep, "his head on the cushion" (4:38); John the Baptist's head was brought in "on a dish" (6:28). To make sure his readers understood the importance of certain points, Mark also uses the device of repeating things three times: there are three important prophecies of the passion (8:31-3; 9:30-2; 10:32-4); Jesus visits the sleeping apostles three times in the garden of Gethsemane (14:32-42); St Peter denies Jesus three times (14:66-72); the high priest accuses him three times before the Sanhedrin (14:60-4); and finally, Pilate tried three times to set Jesus free (15:6-15). Using these storytelling skills, Mark gathered together the various accounts circulating in the early Christian community, of which he was himself a part, "and assembled them into the narrative which he identified as 'the beginning of the Gospel of Jesus Christ, the Son of God'" (Achtemeier).

Both the Eastern and the Western Church venerated Mark as a martyr from at least the fourth century. There was a shrine outside Alexandria where his body, saved from the flames by some Christians, was said to be buried, and this had become a place of pilgrimage by the fifth century. But the main cult developed at Venice, where his relics were taken by two merchants in the early ninth century to avoid desecration by the Arabs. The resulting development of the cult was not straightforward, but from about the year 1000 it was taken up officially by the city of Venice and grew in popularity as the Republic prospered; the symbol of the evangelist, a winged lion, became the symbol of the city. Other places claim part of his body, including Rome and Clairvaux in France, while Reichenau on Lake Constance claims, apparently not without some historical justification, to have it all on the basis of a translation from Venice in the year 890. There seems to have been very little veneration of the saint in medieval England, and only five pre-Reformation churches were dedicated to him. As well as being patron of Venice, Mark is also patron of Egypt and of notaries, basket weavers, glass workers, and opticians; in addition, in 1951 Pius XII formally declared him to be the patron of Spanish cattle-breeders because there had long been a strong devotion to him among them.

C. S. Mann, *Mark, A New Translation with Introduction and Commentary* (1986), in the Anchor Bible series, has very detailed bibliographies. For a summary of recent scholarship, see M. D. Hooker, *The Gospel according to Mark* (1991). See also the article by P. J. Achtemeier in *The Anchor Bible Dictionary*, 4 (1992), pp. 541-57; R. H. Gundry, *Mark: A Commentary of His Apology for the Cross* (1993); J. Fenton, *Finding the Way through Mark* (1995); W. R. Telford, *Mark* (1995), in the New Testament Guides series. *Bibl.SS.*, 8, 711-38, has a good section on the cult and iconography and prints a wide range of images of the saint.

The use of the winged lion to represent St Mark (based on the visions in Ezek. 1:5-12, and Rev. 4:6-7) is very ancient and can be found in the late fourth-century mosaics in Santa Pudenziana and Santa Sabina, Rome, and in the sixth-century mosaics in Ravenna. The earliest representation of the saint in human form is in the catacomb of SS Marcus and Marcellianus (*c.* 340). His cult was extremely popular throughout the Christian world, and he features in every type of art—mosaics, frescoes, illuminated manuscripts (see, for example, the beautiful Lindisfarne Gospels), statues, and paintings. He was usually depicted as one of the evangelists, holding a book and a pen and with a lion by his side or at his feet. With the removal of his remains to Venice and his adoption as the city's patron, he became an obvious subject for Venetian artists, and the city abounds in popular and artistic images of him, from statues on street corners to major works of art. There are twelfth- and thirteenth-century mosaics in St Mark's telling the story of his life, and he appears elsewhere as the saviour of the city from plague and the patron of justice and the law (especially in the Doge's Palace). Works by major artists include paintings by Gentile and Giovanni Bellini (now in the Brera, Milan); one by Titian in the Basilica della Salute, Venice, in which Mark appears solemnly enthroned and surrounded by other saints; and three striking paintings by Tintoretto. These last illustrate a legend that a violent storm that accompanied the saint's martyrdom allowed Christians to take and bury his body (in the Academia, Venice); the removal of the remains from Alexandria to Venice (in the Brera, Milan); and the legendary intervention of Mark to rescue a Christian slave from torture and death (also in the Academia, Venice). From the sixteenth century onward, any painting that served to glorify Venice or one of its rulers would almost automatically include an image of St Mark: see, for example, the painting of the battle of Lepanto by Veronese in the Academia, and Titian's *Pala di Ca' Pesaro* in the Frari, Venice.

St Franca of Piacenza, *Abbess* (1218)

Franca Visalta was placed in the Benedictine abbey of St Syrus in Piacenza, in northern Italy, when she was only seven years old. She made her profession seven years later and already had a reputation for self-denial and obedience to the Rule. She was elected abbess in due course, but after a brief honeymoon period she began to meet opposition from the community because of her strict interpretation of the Rule and her refusal to allow any of the small departures from it that had become customary—what seems to have annoyed them particularly was her rigid attitude to the rules about food and fasting. In the end the nuns deposed her and elected the bishop's sister, who took a more relaxed view to the Rule. Franca was exposed to calumny and misrepresentation and also suffered severe interior trials, and the only solution was for her to move to another convent. Given her Benedictine vow of stability, however, this was not easily done, but eventually it happened through the efforts of a young woman, Carentia, whom she had advised to become a Cistercian novice. In gratitude Carentia persuaded her parents to build a new Cistercian abbey at Montelana, to which both she and Franca were transferred, Franca becoming its abbess. The community later moved to Pittoli, where they kept the strict Cistercian Rule in all its austerity. Franca was said to have spent most nights at prayer in the chapel, despite her failing health. She died in 1218, and her cult was approved for Piacenza by the pope, Bd Gregory X (1271-6; feast-day, 10 Jan.), a relative of Carentia.

AA.SS., Apr., 3, pp. 379-404, gives a letter from a contemporary Cistercian prior recounting a vision of St Franca, and a long Life by Bertram Recoldi, written in 1336.

BB Robert Anderton and William Marsden, *Martyrs* (1586)

Robert Anderton was born in 1560 on the Isle of Man and educated first at the grammar school in Rivington in Lancashire and then at Brasenose College, Oxford. He was a close friend of William Marsden, who had been born at Goosnargh in Lancashire, had attended the same school in Rivington, and had also been at Brasenose. Their subsequent careers were so linked it is easier to deal with them together. They went to Douai, where they were reconciled to the Church by a Jesuit, Fr Columbine, and entered the college at Reims in 1580. They were described as being "unassuming but full of life and spirit, and remarkable for their piety and zeal for sacred things." Robert Anderton was apparently a skilled Hebrew scholar. They were both ordained in Reims, Robert in 1584, William in 1585, and left together for the mission in England in February 1586. Very shortly afterwards they were arrested on the Isle of Wight and tried and condemned at Winchester for being seminary priests in England.

At their trial they made such strong protestations of their loyalty to the queen that it was felt they should be examined by the Privy Council, so they were sent to London. The Council, however, found their answers unsatisfac-

tory and sent them back to Winchester for execution. The Council also ordered the local sheriff to read out and exhibit a royal proclamation that gave a
brief account of their arrest and original trial and then went on to say the
Council had asked them what they would do in the event of a papal invasion of
England. Anderton had "postponed" his reply while Marsden had said he
"would do his duty as a priest." Both, moreover, had revoked promises apparently made at their trial not to interfere with the official religion of the country.
Therefore, the proclamation concluded, their execution should be carried out.
According to Anstruther, this was the only time a royal proclamation was
issued ordering the execution of a priest. They were hanged, drawn, and quartered at Newport on the Isle of Wight on 25 April 1586 and were beatified in
1929.

M.M.P., p. 114-5; Anstruther, 1, pp. 8-9, 218, on which the above account relies heavily.

Bd Peter de Betancur, *Founder* (1619-67)

Peter, whose full name was Peter of St Joseph, was born in Villaflor, on Tenerife in the Canary Islands, in 1619; some accounts give his place of birth as
Chasna on Tenerife, and others imply he was born in 1626. These accounts say
his family was descended from an original Norman conqueror of the Canaries,
John de Béthencourt, and hence the "Betancur" usually attached to Peter's
name. Whichever date of birth is the correct one, we know that in 1649 Peter
gave up working as a shepherd and left for the New World. After a short stay
in Havana in Cuba he moved to Guatemala, where he lived for the rest of his
life. He tried to become a religious but failed to get accepted as a novice and so
in 1652 became a Franciscan tertiary, following an austere way of life and
devoting himself to works of charity. His special devotion was to the Holy
Child of Bethlehem, and he developed an apostolate to the poor and founded
the hospital of Our Lady of Bethlehem with a school for poor children attached
to it. He also ministered to the slaves and the native peoples, who worked in
inhuman conditions and whose physical and spiritual needs were totally neglected by the Spanish settlers. His own health had never been good, and to
make sure his apostolate did not cease with his death he founded two secular
Institutes, one for men called the Brothers of Bethlehem, and the other for
women called the Sisters of Bethlehem; both followed the Rule of the Third
Order of St Francis. Peter died on 25 April 1667. His Institute was approved a
few days later, but was changed by his successor into a Congregation with
solemn vows following the Rule of St Augustine; this in turn was approved in
1687. A number of his ascetical writings were published in the eighteenth
century, and he was declared "Venerable" in 1771; he was beatified in 1980
under his full name of Peter of St Joseph of Betancur.

Bibl.SS., 3, 142-3. *A.A.S.* 73, pt. 1 (1981), pp. 253-8.

26

St Richarius (c. 645)

Richarius, or Riquier, was born at Celles near Amiens in northern France when most of the area was still pagan. When two Irish missionaries landed nearby and started to preach he saved them from being ill-treated or even killed by the local people, and in return they instructed him in the Faith. He went on to become a priest and began a very successful preaching campaign. At some stage he travelled to England, perhaps to extend his missionary work but especially to redeem some prisoners and take them back to France. His work became so well known that he was visited by the king, Dagobert I (629-39), whom he is reported to have admonished with the words: "He who has to obey will only have to render account to God of himself, but he who commands will also have to answer for all his subjects." Some accounts say he founded an abbey at Celles that followed the monastic way of life of St Columban (23 Nov.), but this is very unlikely, and he probably just founded a church there, with the abbey being a later foundation. As he grew older he wanted to lead a solitary life, and so he retired and spent the rest of his life as a hermit in the forest of Crécy, where he did found a monastic community; he had one companion, Sigobard, who was to write the first Life of him. The day on which he died can be fixed accurately as 26 April, but the year 645 is conjectural. The monastery of Forest-Montiers near Crécy was built on the spot where his cell had been; it was later amalgamated with that at Celles and renamed Saint-Riquier. The present town of Abbeville claims to derive its name from the abbey Richarius is said to have originally founded at Celles.

There is an ancient Life, written in rather barbaric Latin and contemporary with the saint; its text was re-discovered at the beginning of this century. See A. Poncelet, "La plus ancienne vie de saint Riquier," in *Anal. Boll.* 22 (1903), pp. 173-94. Charlemagne celebrated Easter one year at Saint-Riquier (Celles) and was accompanied by the learned Alcuin, who was persuaded to re-write this Life in elegant Latin because he was astonished such a great saint, "second only to the apostles in the miracles he worked," should have such a badly-written biography. See also H. Leclerq, in *D.A.C.L.*, 14, pt. 2, 2430-54; *Bibl.SS.*, 11, 155-7.

St Paschasius Radbert, *Abbot* (c. 790-865)

Radbert was a foundling adopted by the nuns of Notre-Dame at Soissons. He was educated at the monastery of St Peter and developed a particular interest in the classics. After several years he decided to become a monk and received the habit at the famous monastery of Corbie, a few miles to the east of Amiens, which had one of the best libraries of the period. Here Radbert began to study theology and laid the foundations for his later reputation as one of the outstanding theologians of his age. In 822 he accompanied the abbot, St Adelard (2 Jan.), on a journey to Saxony to help found a new monastery at Corvey and was later appointed novice-master at Corbie. He was elected abbot in 843/4 and attended the Council of Paris in 847, but he found administration uncongenial and was happy to resign his office in 849; from then on he devoted himself entirely to study and writing. At some stage he added the prefix Paschasius to his name, as it was the custom in France for writers to adopt a classical or scriptural name. He spent some years in the abbey of Saint-Riquier near Abbeville in northern France but returned to Corbie and died there on 26 April 865.

Among his works were a Life of Adelard, a commentary on the Book of Lamentations, and a commentary on the Gospel of St Matthew. It is generally accepted he also wrote the letter, *Cogitis me*, which is an important document in the history of the doctrine of the Assumption. He wrote it openly in the person of St Jerome (30 Sept.), but later writers assumed it had been written by Jerome himself. Radbert's most important work was on the Eucharist, *De Corpore et Sanguine Domini*, written in 831 and revised in 844 for the instruction of the monks in Saxony. This was the first doctrinal treatise on the True Presence: Radbert was clear that the body of Christ in the Eucharist was the body born of Mary, crucified on the cross and risen from the dead, and multiplied by God's power at each Mass. He described the presence as a spiritual one, but did not have the theological language or technique to define what he meant by this; he seems to have been close to the later doctrine of transubstantiation. The realism of his teaching was condemned by some contemporary writers, and in the ensuing controversy Radbert defended himself against the charge that he thought of Christ as present in the host in a spatial way, somehow reduced in size. He was not thinking, he argued, of a presence that could be measured, but it was a real presence of Christ's real body. He also taught that by receiving the host people became part of Christ's mystical body, the Church.

For his collected works see *P.L.*, 120. A short Life is in *M.G.H.*, *Scriptores*, 15, pp. 452-4, and four of his poems are in *M.G.H.*, *Poetae Latini*, 3, pp. 38-53. For a scholarly bibliography see *O.D.C.C.*, p. 1039, on which the above account of his Eucharistic teaching is based.

St Stephen of Perm, *Bishop* (*c.* 1340-96)

Stephen was born between 1340 and 1345 in the town of Velikiy Ustyug, about five hundred miles north-east of Moscow in an area inhabited by the Zyryani or Permyak people, who were still largely pagan. His family, however, was

Christian and of Russian origin, his father being a chorister in the local church. Stephen became a monk in the monastery of St Gregory Nazianzen in Rostov, where he had been educated. He was unusual among Russian monks at the time in that he knew Greek well and became expert in Byzantine theology; he also set about learning the language of the Zyryani in preparation for missionary work among them, something he had planned to do from an early age. The language was almost entirely oral, and Stephen had to create an alphabet for it so that the scriptures and liturgical books could be translated and made available to the people because he did not want their conversion to Christianity to include the imposition of Russian culture. He began his missionary work proper about the year 1379 and had considerable success, attracting people especially through the beauty and mystery of the liturgy. As an accomplished painter of icons he decorated some of the churches himself. In 1383 he was appointed the first bishop of Perm and began the work of setting up churches and schools and training a native clergy to carry on the work of conversion. As bishop he was not only the people's spiritual leader: he organized the distribution of food during times of shortage, protected them from unjust taxation by officials in Moscow and Novgorod, and even on one occasion led them into battle against an enemy tribe. He made a number of journeys to Moscow, and it was there he died on 26 April 1396. He was canonized by the Russian Church in 1549 and is considered to be its outstanding missionary. He is venerated by both Catholics and Orthodox, with the Catholic Church recognizing his canonization by the Russian Orthodox. Unfortunately, his work on the Zyryan language was unsuccessful, and his alphabet has survived only in a few inscriptions, while his attempts to avoid Russification through the development of a local liturgy and culture failed.

His life is known from an account by his disciple Epiphanius the Wise, who died in 1420; it is of genuine historical value despite the inclusion of some doubtful material. See R. Aubert in *D.H.G.E.*, 15 (1963), 1257-9; *Bibl.SS.*, 12, 8-9.

27

St Simeon of Jerusalem, *Bishop and Martyr* (*c.* 107)

Simeon (or Simon) was the son of Clopas (see Luke 24:18, and John 19:25) and a cousin of Our Lord. He became bishop of Jerusalem after the martyrdom of the apostle St James the Less (3 May), which took place about the year 62. There is some debate whether his episcopate started straight after that of St James or some time later after the fall of Jerusalem in the year 70; it seems more likely there was no interval and Simeon was bishop before and after the catastrophe. While he was bishop the Christian community left Jerusalem and took refuge in Pella on the far side of the Jordan. The historian St Hegesippus (see above, 7 Apr.) tells us how the emperors Vespasian (70-9) and Domitian (81-96) issued edicts against those who claimed to be descendants of David, but it seems Simeon escaped the subsequent searches and execution. He was arrested, however, during the reign of Trajan (98-117) and after suffering severe torture was crucified about the year 107.

Hegesippus witnessed the martyrdom and says that Simeon was 120 years old when he was executed "for being a descendant of David and a Christian." The patience with which he bore his sufferings won the admiration of the Roman governor, Tiberius Atticus. On the basis of his advanced age Eusebius says Simeon probably "saw and heard the Lord" and regarded him as an important figure in the history of the early Church. Many writers have identified this Simeon with the apostle St Simon the Zealot (28 Oct.), brother of St James the Less, but ancient tradition distinguished between the two, and it is better to treat them as two separate individuals. From at least the ninth century his feast was celebrated in the West on 18 February, while the Eastern Church kept it on 27 April. Various places (Brindisi, Bologna, and Brussels) claim to have his relics.

Eusebius, *H.E.*, 3: 11, 22, 32; and 4: 5, 22; *Bibl.SS.*, 11, 1103-4; *E.E.C.*, 2, p. 779; *B.T.A.*, 1, pp. 365-6, under 18 February.

St Asicus, *Bishop* (*c.* 470)

Asicus is venerated as the first bishop of the diocese of Elphin in Ireland. Some of the early Lives of St Patrick (17 Mar.) say he was one of Patrick's earliest disciples, a married man and an expert metalworker. It is not clear whether he was appointed bishop during Patrick's lifetime or afterwards, but he seems to have been unsuccessful or unhappy as a ruler and fled to live a life of solitude

190

on an island in Donegal Bay. Legend explains his flight as being due to his having told a lie, either knowingly or accidentally, but this may be based on a similar legend about the great St Antony of Egypt (17 Jan.). After seven years he was found by monks from Elphin who took him back to the diocese, but he died on the way at Ballintra about the year 470. The important *Félire* of Oengus (early ninth century) refers to him as "the royal bishop" and describes how he gave Communion to St Patrick. Tassach is commonly given as an alternative version of his name, but this is very doubtful, and Tassach more likely refers to a saint associated, not with Elphin but with Raholp in County Down, who was said to have given Patrick the Last Sacraments.

There is no early Life of Asicus. See *The Irish Saints*, pp. 30-1.

St Maughold of Man, *Bishop* (*c*. 498)

Maughold is known chiefly through the early Lives of St Patrick (17 Mar.). These relate how he was a bloodthirsty pirate or despot in Ulster converted by Patrick and banished from his native Ireland as a penance for his previous evil way of life. He sailed away without any idea of where he would go, and his tiny boat was driven by the winds to the Isle of Man, where he was received by two missionaries sent there earlier by Patrick. While they were alive he seems to have lived as a hermit in the north-east of the island, but on their death he was elected bishop by the people and continued the work of evangelization. He died about the year 498. Maughold is the Manx form of his name, and this appears in a number of place names in the Isle of Man; in Irish his name is variously given as MacCuill, Maguil, or Maccul. The former edition of this work said that the *Félire* of Oengus described Maughold as "a rod of gold, a vast ingot, the great Bishop MacCaille," but this appears to relate to a different Irish saint, bishop of Croghan in County Offaly, with his own commemoration on 25 April.

There is no early Life. See *Bibl.SS.*, 8, 440.

St Tutilo (*c*. 850-915)

Tutilo (or Tuotilo) was born in Germany about the year 850 and became a monk at the famous monastery of Saint-Gall in Switzerland, where he was a contemporary of Bd Notker (6 Apr.). He was an important figure in the Carolingian cultural renaissance and became famous for his artistic skills; he was said to be expert in architecture, painting, poetry, oratory, and metalwork. It was as a musician, however, that he excelled, and he was probably associated with his friend Notker in the composition of sequences to be sung during Mass; he also developed the use of tropes, or additional verses, to elaborate liturgical texts. He was much in demand outside the monastery and travelled to towns such as Metz and Mainz to work on artistic commissions, but he hated the publicity this brought him and did all he could to avoid it. He held a number of offices in the monastery, including master of the monastic school, sacristan, and cellarer. He died on 27 April about the year 915 and was buried in the chapel of St Catherine, which was later renamed St Tutilo's in his honour.

There are paintings attributed to him in Constance, Metz, Saint-Gall, and Mainz, but of his music and poetry only three elegies and a hymn seem to have survived. Most of the tropes traditionally attributed to him are of uncertain authorship, but five may be accepted as his, including the *Hodie cantandus est nobis puer* for use in the Introit for the third Mass of Christmas and the *Gaudete et cantate* for the Offertory on Easter Sunday. Two of the carved ivory bindings he made for Saint-Gall manuscripts survive.

Bibl.SS., 12, 721-2; *New Grove Dictionary of Music*, 19, p. 257; *B.T.A.*, 1, p. 696, under 28 March.

St Zita (*c.* 1218-78)

Zita (also known as Citha, Scytha, and, especially in England, Sitha) was born in Monte Sagrati, a few miles from Lucca in Italy, about the year 1218. When she was twelve she went into service in the house of a wealthy textile manufacturer named Fatinelli in Lucca and remained there for the rest of her life. She led a devout life and was much abused because of it by her fellow-servants until her obvious sincerity won their admiration. Eventually she was put in charge of the household. Later in life she was reported as saying, "A servant is not good if she is not industrious: work-shy piety in people of our position is sham piety." Her lowly calling and her exemplary hard work could well be the reasons why she became so popular a figure throughout medieval Europe: working people found in her someone they could try to imitate, while employers could promote devotion to her with enthusiasm. Miracles were reported of her while she was alive, mostly in connection with her generosity to the poor— her master's foodstore was miraculously replenished when she had given too much of it away, and his fur coat was returned by a mysterious beggar when that, too, had been given away. On another occasion it was said that a batch of loaves was prepared for her to cook when she had been too long at her prayers. As well as helping the poor she was always keen to care for prisoners and the sick. She died on 27 April 1278. Her remains were moved to the church of San Frediano in Lucca, which she had attended for most of her life and where they are still venerated. Her cult was approved for the whole Church in 1696, and her name was included in the Roman Martyrology in 1748. From early on she became patron of Lucca—Dante, among other writers, uses her name as synonomous with the city—and in 1935 Pius XI declared her to be the principal patron of domestic servants.

She was one of the most popular of minor saints in medieval England under the name Sitha, and an English version of the early Life dates from 1377, only five years or so after it was written in Italy. There was an important colony of Lucchese merchants in London, and it may be assumed they were primarily responsible for the introduction of her cult; its rapid diffusion was probably due to her popularity with the widespread servant classes. No English churches were dedicated to her; St Benet Shorehog's in London, however, had a chapel to St Zita and was commonly known as St Sithes before the 1350s, while a chapel in her honour existed in Norwich Cathedral from at least 1363, and St Albans Abbey also had an altar dedicated to her. Eagle, in Lincolnshire, claimed, probably reliably, to have some of her hair and a little toe, and seems to have been a place of pilgrimage.

A Latin Life was written in 1372 by Fatinello degli Fatinelli on the occasion of the introduction of her cause; it is preserved in the Fatinelli family archives; see *AA.SS.*, Apr., 3, pp. 497-527. There are a large number of popular Lives; see P. Lazzarini, *La perla delle domestiche: santa Zita vergine* (1952), and *Una vida ejemplar: s. Zita, patrona universal de las empleadas* (1962). See also *O.D.S.*, pp. 513-4. The most up-to-date account of her cult in England is Sebastian Sutcliffe, "The Cult of St Sitha in England: an Introduction," in *Nottingham Medieval Studies* 37 (1993), pp. 83-9, on which this account is largely dependent.

She was invoked especially by housewives and servants, and her intercession was thought to be particularly effective in finding lost keys—hence her frequent portrayal with a bunch of keys hanging from her belt, as on the painted screens at Barton Turf in Norfolk, Somerleyton in Suffolk, and Torbryan and Ashton in Devon. She is depicted in stained glass at Mells in Somerset (holding three loaves and a book), and in a wall painting in the abbey of St Albans. Altogether there are more than fifty pieces of fifteenth-century art surviving in English parish churches, from Cornwall to Northumberland, some showing her as a young maid, others as an older woman. She also appears in illuminated manuscripts, and her image was cast in lead as a pilgrim's badge. Occasionally it is difficult to know whether an image is of St Sitha or of St Petronilla, since both saints are shown with keys; they appear together on the screen at North Elmham (Norfolk) with their names.

Bd James of Bitetto (*c*. 1400-85)

James was born about the year 1400 in Zara in Dalmatia and so was sometimes called "the Slav" or "the Illyrian." When he was twenty he became a lay brother in the house of the Friars Minor of the Observance in his home town. In 1438 he accompanied the provincial to Bitetto, a small town about nine miles from Bari in southern Italy, and spent the rest of his life in the area, serving in several houses of the Order before settling in Bitetto itself. He gained a reputation for great holiness through humility, self-denial, and the practice of contemplation. A fellow-monk testified that he experienced levitations during prayer and had the gift of prophecy. For some years he worked as cook to the community at Conversano, where he was reported to have been so moved by the flames of the kitchen fire as a symbol of the divine love that he would often fall into ecstasy during his work. At Bitetto his main work was the begging of alms for the support of the Order. He distinguished himself in the care of the sick during the plague of 1482 and died in Bitetto about the year 1485. Many miracles were attributed to his intercession, and his cult was popular from the early sixteenth century onward. He was beatified by Pope Clement XI in December 1700 (not by Innocent XII, as some authorities state).

F. Gilardi, *Il beato Giacomo da Bitetto - Vita e Documenti* (1914), gives the material collected for the beatification. See also *Bibl.SS.*, 6, 350-1.

Bd Osanna (1493-1565)

Catherine Cosie was born near the village of Komani in Montenegro in 1493, the daughter of poor Orthodox parents. She seems to have spent her early years looking after the family's sheep and goats. There is a legend that she had two visions as a child, one of Jesus as an infant, the other of him crucified, and as a result persuaded her mother to take her to a Catholic church in Cattaro to venerate images of Our Lord there. Later she was allowed by her parents to enter the service of a Catholic family in Cattaro, where she was instructed in the Faith and at some stage converted from Orthodoxy. Seven years later, as the result of hearing a particularly moving sermon on Good Friday, she left to live as an anchoress in a cell attached to the local church of St Bartholomew. When she became a Dominican tertiary she took the name Osanna in honour of Bd Osanna Andreasi of Mantua (20 June), who had died a few years earlier in 1505. Many people visited her cell to seek her expert spiritual guidance, and it was said her prayers helped save the town from attacks by the Turks. She moved her cell to the church of St Paul, and a convent was built nearby by some of her disciples who wished to live as Dominican tertiaries under her guidance. She enjoyed a number of supernatural gifts but also had to put up with unjust accusations about her personal life. She died on 27 April 1565. Along with Bd Sibyllina Biscossi of Pavia (23 Mar.), she is credited with founding an apostolate uniting solitary contemplation with active spiritual guidance along Dominican lines. Her cult was popular with Orthodox as well as Latin Christians and was apparently uninterrupted from the time of her death until its official approval in 1928, when Pius XI spoke of her importance in the context of relations between the Eastern and Western Churches.

A.A.S. 20 (1928), pp. 39-42.; *Bibl.SS.*, 9, 1274-5.

28

ST PETER CHANEL, *Martyr* (1803-41)

Pierre Louis-Marie Chanel was born in 1803 in the hamlet of La Potière in eastern France, about fifty miles north-east of Lyons. He was the fifth of eight children and worked on his father's farm. There is some evidence that the farm had been church land confiscated at the time of the Revolution, and Peter, feeling guilty about this, wanted to make amends for the wrong his father had done in buying it by devoting his life to the service of the Church. A local priest, Abbé Trompier, was struck by his intelligence and piety and took him as a pupil in a small school he had started in Cras for boys with possible vocations to the priesthood. From there Peter went to the junior seminary in Belley, where he was greatly impressed by the missionary fervour of its rector, and then on to the senior seminary, where he was ordained priest in 1827. After a year as a curate in Ambèrieu he was appointed parish priest of Crozet, about ten miles from Geneva, a parish that had been neglected for some years. He stayed there for three years and in that time brought about something of a transformation in the people, persuading them of his good intentions and dedication largely through his devoted care of the sick.

For some time he had been thinking of becoming a foreign missionary, but the need for priests at home was such that his bishop could not let him go. In 1831, however, he was allowed to join the Society of Mary, or Marists, a Congregation of priests dedicated to missionary work being established at Lyons and Belley. His hopes of working abroad, however, came to nothing when he was appointed to teach in the junior seminary at Belley. He remained there for five years, and became vice rector. He accompanied the founder of the Congregation to Rome in 1833 to try to obtain approval of its Rule; this was finally granted in 1836, when the Congregation was given the vast area of Western Oceania as its main mission field. At last Peter was given a missionary appointment, to preach the gospel in the islands of the South Pacific Ocean— the vagueness of the appointment reflecting his superiors' lack of knowledge about the area.

A group of eight Marists sailed from Le Havre in December 1836 for Valparaiso, in Chile, and from there sailed to Tonga. In November 1837 they called by chance at the island of Futuna, one of the French Iles de Horn, between Fiji and Western Samoa. Peter was asked by the superior if he would like to stay and work there, and on agreeing was left there with a young Marist brother, Marie-Nizier Delorme, and a European trader who offered to stay with them as interpreter. The missionaries were apparently well received by the people, but there was underlying suspicion of the foreigners, and their superior had taken the unwise precaution of describing them to the local king as travellers who just wanted to learn the language and customs of the people—this did not help them when the people later learned their true intentions. Peter kept a diary, noting his slow progress in learning the language, the strange customs of the people, his journeys, and visits to the sick. The entries are marked by a realistic appreciation of the difficulties facing the missionaries and a patient willingness not to try to rush ahead too quickly, though his frustration is also clear: "How sorrowful is the lot of a poor missionary who cannot yet preach the truths of salvation!" It is clear Peter believed those who died without Baptism were destined for hell and regarded the local religion as wholly the work of the devil. The diary also brings out his determination and his complete trust in divine Providence. He and Brother Marie-Nizier gradually began to preach the gospel and by 1840 were making a little progress, baptizing a few dying children and some elderly adults.

The king, who had been their main protector, now began to turn against them. The change was brought about by a number of factors, among which was news of the advance of Christianity on the island of Wallis and the fears of the king and his advisers that they would lose their own standing. It must also be said that they had good reason to fear the advance of white influence: a group of European traders who lived on the island ill-treated Futunian women, interfered in the politics of the island, and cheated and stole in the name of trade whenever they could. French and British gunboats were already patrolling the Pacific and protecting these traders and other settlers at the expense of the islanders. A campaign of harassment began, directed principally at the small number of catechumens Peter was instructing, but when the king's son asked to be baptized his family were outraged, and the king ordered the missionaries to be killed. Peter was aware of the danger and said to someone who mentioned it, "It does not matter whether or not I am killed; the religion has taken root on the island; it will not be destroyed by my death, since it comes not from men but from God." On 28 April 1841 a gang attacked some catechumens and then went in search of Peter; he was clubbed to the ground and then killed with an axe. One account of his death says he died saying, "I am happy to die."

Within a year almost the whole of Futuna's population had accepted Christianity and been baptized. This was due in part to Peter's influence and the death of the king, but a modern biographer makes the point that the islanders also feared reprisals, especially when a French frigate appeared off the island early in 1842 to inquire into the priest's death and collect his remains; conversion may have had an element of self-protection (Graystone). Peter was canonized in 1954, and his feast, formerly celebrated only in Australasia, was extended to the universal Chuch. He is honoured as the proto-martyr of Oceania and of the Marists. His remains were returned to Futuna in 1977.

His writings, especially his diaries and letters, were edited by C. Rozier, *Ecrits de Saint Pierre Chanel* (1960); the same author's *Saint Pierre Chanel d'après ceux qui l'ont connu* (1991) is another key source. There are a number of biographies; see W. J. Symes, S.M., *The Life of St Peter Chanel, The Marist Missionary Martyr* (1963); Philip Graystone, S.M., *Saint Peter Chanel S.M., First Martyr of the South Pacific* (1994).

St Cronan, *Abbot* (665)

Cronan's father was Odran, from Munster, while his mother was Coemri, from Clare in Connacht. Cronan grew up in Clare and made his first monastic foundation at a place called Tullyroe or Red Hill and his second at Lusmagh near Banagher in County Galway, which he gave away to some monks who had nowhere to settle. He then moved to Roscrea in County Tipperary and settled on the shores of Lough Cree. The story is told that some travellers, hoping to find Cronan and obtain shelter for the night, failed to do so because the place was so wild and difficult to approach and spent the night in the open. Cronan was so upset by this lack of hospitality that he moved again, this time to an accessible site at Roscrea itself, saying, "I will not remain in a desert place, where the poor and travellers cannot find me easily; I'll be on the public road where they can do so readily. And in that place I'll serve my Lord Christ, the King of kings." From time to time he retired to the island of Monaincha in the lough to find solitude. He is usually said to have died in 665, but some authorities put his death between 600 and 620. Unfortunately, the eleventh-century Life of Cronan gives few details about him, and his cult is not considered sufficiently well attested for him to feature in the new Roman Martyrology.

The Irish Saints, pp. 132-4; Peter Harbison, *Guide to the National Monuments of Ireland* (1970), pp. 232-3, 235.
  Roscrea has some impressive remains. On Monaincha (not now an island, as the lough was drained in the eighteenth century) there is a small, fine Romanesque church with part of a medieval cross, with a figure of Christ on one side and what is taken to be Cronan on the other. Nearby is a round tower and the facade of another, twelfth-century, Romanesque church, named after St Cronan and with a statue of him above the doorway; the ruins of an old church stand by the original lakeside site.

St Cyril of Turov, *Bishop* (1182)

Although Cyril is one of the outstanding figures of the early Russian Church, we know little about him, since there is no early account of his life and he does not feature in the chronicles of the time. He was a native of Turov, near Minsk in modern Belarus, and was probably born in the early part of the twelfth century. He first became a monk in the monastery of SS Boris and Gleb in Turov and then lived for a time as a recluse in a tower, where he was visited by many pilgrims seeking his spiritual advice. In 1174 he was chosen to be bishop of Turov but we know nothing about his administration of the diocese.

His outstanding reputation rests on his writings: we have twelve of his sermons, twenty-four of the prayers he composed, an *Exhortation on the Monastic Life,* and a penitential. These show he was a keen proponent of Byzantine theology and traditions, but it is not clear how much Greek he could read, and his direct knowledge of the important Greek Fathers may have been limited. He was the most learned biblical scholar in the Russian Church of his day, but his interpretations of the scriptures were often over allegorical. In the ascetical ideals he put forward he urged mortification of the spirit through humility: "You are a piece of cloth, and you may be conscious of yourself only until someone picks you up; do not worry if you are then torn up for footwear." It was as a preacher, however, that he was most famous, and he was nicknamed "the Russian Chrysostom." He used a very oratorical style that has sometimes been criticized as being over rhetorical, with his sermons having little application to everyday life. The former editor of this work suggested that this lack of practical lessons in his preaching was because he was "carried away by the contemplation of divine mysteries," a judgment supported by the view that "from his writings one receives the impression of a man who stands very remote from life . . . and who is entirely elevated to the sphere of religious worship and thought. . . . He is a unique example of theological devotion in ancient Russia" (Fedotov). Cyril's prayers are more straightforward and are predominantly concerned with the author's sinfulness and need for forgiveness. It was to bring forgiveness and salvation that God became human and died on the cross, and this divine plan of salvation provides the theme for some of the finest passages in the sermons. Cyril returned to his monastery in 1179 and died there three years later.

See G. P. Fedotov, *The Russian Religious Mind* (1946), pp. 69-84, 136-41. See also *Bibl.SS.*, 3, 1322-4. He does not feature in the new Roman Martyrology but seems to be sufficiently distinguished to merit an entry here.

Bd Luchesio (1260)

Luchesio, or Lucchese, was born in Gaggiano in the Val d'Elsa near Florence about the beginning of the thirteenth century. As a young man he was wholly taken up with politics and moneymaking and made himself so unpopular owing to his violent support of the Guelph party that he left his native town and settled in nearby Poggibonsi, where he started working as a provision merchant and moneylender. Sometime in his thirties he underwent a religious conversion, perhaps brought about by the death of his children. He began nursing the sick and visiting the local prisons and gave away nearly all his possessions, keeping only a small piece of land to cultivate with his own labour. Shortly after this St Francis (4 Oct.) visited the town, and Luchesio and his wife, Bonadonna, received from him the habit and cord of the Third Order. According to a strong tradition, they were the first people to become Franciscan tertiaries, but there is some doubt about this, since Francis founded the Third Order in 1221, which would be rather early for Luchesio and his wife. They devoted the rest of their lives to works of penance and practical charity, sometimes leaving themselves with nothing to eat and relying entirely on divine Providence for their needs. Luchesio developed a deeply spiritual life of prayer and was said to experience ecstasies and also to have the gift of healing. An early account says that Bonadonna, knowing her husband had only a short time left to live, asked him not to die too long before her, so that she who had shared all his sufferings here might share all his happiness in heaven; apparently her wish was granted, and she died shortly before him in 1260. He was buried in the church of the Friars Minor in Poggibonsi, and there is strong evidence that a very popular cult began straightaway; this was approved in 1694.

There was a contemporary Life and account of his miracles, but all we have is a summary version written about a century later; there was a later Life by a Sienese Franciscan, apparently based on the earlier one but embellished with legends. See *AA.SS.*, Apr., 3, pp. 594-610; *Bibl.SS.*, 8, 230-4.

There is an interesting painting of him in the National Gallery of Art, Washington, by Filippino Lippi; he is one of a group, all tertiaries, around St Francis comprising St Louis of France (25 Aug.), St Elizabeth of Hungary (17 Nov.), and his wife, Bonadonna.

St Louis Marie Grignion de Montfort, *Founder* (1673-1716)

Louis Marie Grignion was born in Brittany in 1673 in the small town of Montfort; he later added the name of his birthplace to his family name. He was the eldest of eight children of Jean-Baptiste Grignion, a lawyer of modest means and strictly authoritarian outlook. Louis Marie was sent to the Jesuit school in Rennes for his secondary education and began to show two traits that were to mark him for the rest of his life: he found it difficult to get on with his companions, and he developed a preference for solitary prayer, especially to Our Lady. He decided he had a vocation to the priesthood and went to Paris in 1692. He did not have enough money to live in the seminary of Saint-Sulpice and so boarded in a number of poor student hostels, where conditions were so rough that he fell dangerously ill and needed hospital treatment to save his life. On his recovery he was able to enter the seminary and pursue his studies more successfully, although he was never very interested in theology itself and would have preferred to spend his time helping the poor and teaching their children the catechism, an apostolate he had started while at school in Rennes. His superiors admired his fervour and obvious devotion but were concerned at his awkward personality. He was ordained priest in 1700.

The next six years were very unsatisfactory ones for Louis Marie. He worked in Nantes, Poitiers, and Paris but aroused opposition wherever he went. Some of this was due to his own difficult temperament and what a modern biographer calls his "gratingly odd behaviour" (Papàsogli), but some of it was due to his insistence on carrying out an apostolate to the poorest, whether as a hospital chaplain or as a giver of open-air missions, and to the resentment of his fellow-priests. He was himself unsure of his apostolate and wrote: "I find myself torn between two desires. . . . On the one hand I feel a secret attraction to solitude and the hidden life, to fight against and destroy completely my corrupt nature which loves to be admired. On the other, I feel a great desire to foster the love of Our Lord and His Blessed Mother: to go in a simple and poor way to teach catechism to the poor in rural areas, and to stimulate in sinners a devotion to the most Blessed Virgin." It is interesting that in the same letter, written in the year he was ordained, he voiced his desire to found a Congregation: "Seeing the needs of the Church, I can't help praying continually and in tears for a small and poor company of good priests who will work under the sign and protection of the most Blessed Virgin."

In the hospital for beggars in Poitiers he shared the life of the poor patients and tried to organize the women who helped there into a religious community; when they refused, he picked out twenty or so of the female patients, all physically handicapped in some way, and organized them into an embryonic Congregation with a Rule, under a blind superior. Over the door of their community room he wrote the word "Wisdom," and this strange formation of a group of the poor and powerless may be taken as the start of his acceptance, as a guiding principle in his life, of the gospel tension between the wisdom of the world and the wisdom of the cross. It also marked his breaking away from traditional spirituality and his adoption of the way of a prophet: the living out of public acts and gestures that were exaggerated in order to make his points vivid and real (Papàsogli). Two middle-class women also joined the group before it was broken up by the hospital administration. There was considerable opposition to his interference in the organization of the hospital, and the bishop ordered him to give up his popular parish missions because the clergy objected to his evangelistic methods, so Loius Marie decided to return to Paris. He felt he was a failure—"I spoil everything I ever get mixed up in," he wrote—and had still not found his vocation; he needed a wider field to cultivate than just a poor hospital, but it was all he could find to do in Paris. When he had to give even that up, he lived for a time in a cupboard under the stairs and devoted himself to prayer and meditation. It was a time of great interior uncertainty and distress for him but also a time when his spiritual life developed and his understanding of the demands of the "wisdom of the cross" became clearer: "What wealth, what glory, what pleasure would be mine if all these things [his failures] would obtain for me that Divine Wisdom for which I yearn night and day." It was probably at this time that he wrote *The Love of Eternal Wisdom*, a key work in understanding his spirituality, putting into context his devotion to Our Lady and to the cross and upholding Wisdom as his main inspiration: "Since there is nothing more active than Wisdom . . . she will not allow those she loves to drift into lukewarmness and negligence. She inflames them; she inspires them to undertake great enterprises for the glory of God and the salvation of souls."

After another unsuccessful spell in Poitiers he left for Rome in 1706, hoping to obtain permission from the pope to work on the foreign missions, especially in Canada—a way of escape, no doubt, from the difficulties he met whenever he tried to work as a priest in France. Pope Clement XI was impressed by his zeal and sincerity but sent him back to work in France "always in perfect submission to the bishops"; he gave him the title "missionary apostolic," a boost for his confidence and a mandate, Louis Marie felt, for his work of giving parish missions and preaching to the poor.

On his return he settled in Brittany, an area where parish missions consisting of basic instruction and spiritual renewal had already been well developed. He worked successfully as a member of a mission team, itself an achievement for him, and gained a reputation for his ability to animate crowds of people and to be "powerful in word and act." But he could still alienate others and slowly distanced himself from the other mission-givers to work with a single companion, Brother Mathurin. On the whole he was well received by the parish clergy, although in some places he was refused permission to preach, either on account of the Gallican and anti-Roman tendencies of the local priest or the strangeness of his methods, though these were not unique to him. They included strong emotional appeals, the burning of irreligious books on great bonfires topped by effigies of the devil in the guise of a society lady, and the acting out of a sinner's death scene with the devil fighting for the dying soul. He urged the saying of the rosary, wrote popular hymns, some of which are still used, and persuaded people to give money and practical help to restore dilapidated churches and shrines. He preached in La Rochelle on a number of occasions and succeeded in converting a number of Calvinists there. As part of his concern for the poor he opened or refurbished a number of schools for poor boys in the town, helped by the local bishop, using as teachers the "brothers" who had been helping him in the catechetical work of his missions. Out of this grew the teaching Order of the Brothers of Christian Instruction of St Gabriel, for whom he probably wrote at least the draft of a Rule; they were initially known as the Brothers of Christian Instruction of the Holy Spirit.

As has been seen, for some years he had wanted to set up a company of like-minded missionary priests, but he still found it difficult to attract people to work with him. In 1713 he wrote the "Rule for the Missionary Priests of the Company of Mary," but at the time of his death had attracted only two priests and a small number of lay brothers to join him formally. He was somewhat more successful with the female branch, and in 1715 two of the original members of the Congregation from Poitiers, including the influential Marie Louise Trichet, joined him in La Rochelle along with a small group of local women, and he produced for them "The Primitive Rule of the Daughters of Wisdom," the beginning of a Congregation dedicated, like its founder, to helping the poor, and especially to the running of schools for them. Throughout his priestly life his dedication to the poor and his own spirit of poverty were evident in everything he did and explain in part why he stood out among the French clergy of his day, with his radical understanding of the gospel message. He also had a deep interest in the Church and understood its constant need for reformation; this was an abiding mission for him and his main inspiration in wanting to ensure there would be others of like mind to carry on his work after his death. When he died on 28 April 1716, however, neither Congregation was secure, and it was left to others to consolidate them and help them become worldwide institutions.

In addition to a large number of hymns, some letters, and the Rules, Louis Marie wrote some spiritual books and treatises, most of which were not meant for general publication. The first of these was *The Love of the Eternal Wisdom*, written, it seems, for his own use. In 1714 he addressed *A Circular Letter to the Friends of the Cross* to members of an association of that name, while *The Secret of Mary* was for a nun in Nantes. *The Admirable Secret of the Most Holy Rosary* gives the best picture of his popular preaching, although much of the work was borrowed from other authors. His best-known work is his *Treatise on True Devotion to the Holy Virgin*, or *True Devotion to the Blessed Virgin*—the title was added in the nineteenth century. The first part covers the doctrinal necessity of devotion to Our Lady and urges the reader to enter into a compact with her, to become her slave (a subtitle sometimes given the book is *The Slave of Mary*), so that one's whole being, spiritual and material, is put at her disposal. The language and, indeed, the basic idea of the book strike the modern reader as excessive and over emotional, but it was very influential during the nineteenth and first half of the twentieth century; its ideas and language were adopted, for example, by the founder of the Legion of Mary, whose *Manual* encourages all its members to adopt its practices in order to become true lay missionaries. Louis Marie's canonization in 1947 helped to increase interest in the book and gave its ideas an even wider circulation. As with all his writings, Louis Marie borrowed heavily from others in compiling *True Devotion*, and the book reflects the rather pessimistic view of humanity and the world current in much seventeenth-century French writing. The all-powerful God is to be feared by corrupt and sinful human beings, and this stress on God's otherness helps to explain the position given to Mary in Louis Marie's thought: she is human and so approachable by us, while she is also sinless and so acceptable to God. Because of her sinlessness, God has given her as a gift "the same rights and privileges that Christ possesses naturally." While the bestknown of his works, it is not the most important for understanding his spirituality and should be read in the context of his other writings.

The range of work of today's Montfort Missionaries (the Company of Mary) is wide. They operate in thirty countries, in some cases as missionaries helping young Churches to develop, in others continuing their founder's work of giving parish missions and retreats, running parishes in difficult areas, and organizing pastoral centres. The Congregation sees as its priority in all its work "evangelization in Montfort's own way." The Daughters of Divine Wisdom (sometimes called the "La Sagesse Nuns") are also active throughout the world.

There are some very good recent English publications: R. M. Charest, S.M.M., *et al.*, *God Alone, The Collected Writings of St Louis Marie de Montfort* (1987); Stefano De Fiores, S.M.M., and Patrick Gaffney, S.M.M. (eds.), *Jesus Living in Mary, Handbook of the Spirituality of St Louis Marie de Montfort* (1994); Benedetta Papàsogli, *Montfort, A prophet for our times* (1991). See also Louis Pérouas, S.M.M., *Ce que croyait Grignion de Montfort et comment il a vécu sa foi* (1973), and the same author's article in *Dict.Sp.*, 9 (1976), 1073-81; *O.D.S.*, pp. 344-5.

Bd Gianna Beretta Molla (1922-62)

Giovanna Francesca Beretta was born in Milan on 4 October 1922, the tenth of thirteen children born to Alberto and Maria Beretta; two of the children died in infancy and three died from Spanish influenza at the end of the First World War. The family moved to Bergamo in 1925, and Gianna, as she was always called, enjoyed a happy family life with parents who were devout and committed Catholics. At school she showed no more than average ability, and when the family moved to Genoa in 1937 on the death of the eldest daughter, her parents took her away from school and kept her at home. Under the guidance of the local parish priest she became involved in Catholic Action and began to attend Mass every day, so that when she returned to school the nuns saw in her a future novice.

Her father and mother both died in 1942 and in the same year Gianna decided to study medicine, first at Milan and then at Pavia. She continued her involvement in Catholic Action and began instructing young girls in the Faith. In the light of her later concern to discover what vocation God wanted her to follow, it is interesting to see her writing to these girls as follows: "Your earthly and heavenly happiness depends on carrying out your vocation. Whatever that vocation may be, it is a vocation to physical, spiritual and moral motherhood, for God has put in us a tendency toward life. . . . If in carrying out our vocation it should happen that we die, that would be the finest day of our life." While at university she took up mountain walking and skiing and developed an intense love of nature that was to remain with her for the rest of her life.

In 1949 she qualified in medicine and surgery and opened a clinic in Milan; three years later she began to specialize in pediatrics. It was about this time that she started to give considerable thought to her future career and wondered whether she had a vocation to the religious life or not. Her brother had become a Capuchin and was working as a missionary in Brazil, and it seemed to Gianna she could use her medical skill to great advantage on the foreign missions, as either a religious or a laywoman. She was advised that she probably was not physically strong enough to be a missionary, and in 1954, a Marian Year, she made a pilgrimage to Lourdes to ask Our Lady for guidance in making her decision. Shortly after her return she met and fell in love with Pietro Molla, an engineer, and took this as a sign that her vocation was to the married state. They were married in 1955.

Their first child, Pierluigi, was born in November 1956; the second, Maria Zita, in December of the following year; and the third, Laura, in July 1959. They were a loving and happy family, and Gianna seemed to her friends the ideal modern woman, developing her own career, devoted to her family, and enjoying a full life that included travel, mountaineering, and skiing. In July 1961 she became pregnant again. None of her previous pregnancies had been easy, but this time matters were much more serious when a uterine growth was diagnosed in September. Medical science at the time offered two solutions considered safe for the mother: a complete hysterectomy, or the removal of the growth and termination of the pregnancy. Gianna insisted nothing should be done that might harm the foetus, and so she was operated on just for the removal of the growth; this was successful, and the pregnancy continued, though with the danger that the stitches in the wall of her womb would split as it developed. Before the operation Gianna had said to the priest who attended her in hospital, "I have entrusted myself to the Lord in faith and hope, against the terrible advice of medical science, 'Either mother or child.' I trust in God, yes, but now I must fulfill my duty as a mother. I renew the offer of my life to the Lord, I am ready for everything, provided the life of my child is saved." After the operation she returned to normal family life and work at the clinic, but was obviously aware of the possible complications. Six weeks before the baby was due she said to her husband, "I beg you, if you have to decide between me and the baby, decide in favour of the baby and not me." Just before going into hospital in April 1962 she told a friend, "The birth will be difficult; they must save one or the other; what I want is for my baby to live." After a difficult labour the baby was delivered safely by caesarian section, but Gianna developed peritonitis and died a week later, on 28 April.

In the 1960s there was a considerable debate on the "mother or baby" issue, with the Church insisting that in no circumstances was it morally acceptable to do anything directly to harm a foetus in order to save its mother; in difficult cases, every effort had to be made to save the lives of both. Opponents of this teaching usually interpreted it to mean that in such circumstances the mother's life had always to be directly sacrificed to save that of her foetus. Gianna's desire to save her baby was clearly fully in line with the Church's teaching. She was not faced with having to make a sudden decision at the time of the birth, which in the event passed off reasonably normally, but took that decision seven months before, knowing the danger that the stitches might burst as the pregnancy developed. Popular ecclesiastical accounts of her death gave the impression that she made the correct moral decision at the time of the birth, and so she was hailed as someone who had died as a result of embracing the Church's teaching wholeheartedly. Opponents of that teaching, then and since, have argued that in praising Gianna's self-sacrifice the Church was continuing its tradition of undervaluing women's lives and seeing their main function to be merely reproductive. Some recent feminist writing has argued that Gianna's choice can be respected, but so also should the choice of a woman who chose to live to continue caring for her children and making a worthwhile contribution to society through her career.

Gianna was beatified by Pope John Paul II in 1994, the International Year of the Family. In the light of the above controversy, it is interesting to note that the official announcement of the beatification does not dwell on that aspect of her death. In describing what happened when the growth was discovered, it gives a factual account, but adds "this was the beginning of her 'holocaust.'" The word "holocaust," of course, may mean sacrifice but may also mean imposed suffering leading to death. Gianna is then described as a "woman of exceptional love, an outstanding wife and mother, a witness to the power for good of the gospel in everyday life. In holding her out as an example of Christian perfection, we wish to praise all courageous mothers of families, who give themselves totally to the family, who suffer in bearing their children, who are ready for any labour, any sacrifice, in order to hand on to others something better than they had themselves." This stress on her virtuous life rather than her sacrificial death is something of a change; Pope Paul VI had described her as "the mother of the diocese of Milan, who in order to give life to her child, sacrificed her own through a deliberate offering," the "deliberate" referring no doubt to the fact she lived for seven months conscious of the possibly lethal effects of the choice she had made. More recent Lives have tended to show that her final decision was the result of a whole life lived in an attempt to follow God's will as expressed in the Gospels and through the teaching of the Church.

A.A.S. 86 (1994), pp. 42-4, for the official decree of beatification. See also Fernando da Riese, *Per amore della vita: Gianna Beretta Molla, medico e madre* (1979); Giuliana Pelucchi, *Gianna Beretta Molla, Una vita per la vita* (1994); Pietro Molla and Elio Guerriero, *Gianna, La Beata Gianna Beretta Molla nel ricordo del marito* (1995); Antonio Sicari, *Il terzo libro dei Ritratti di Santi* (1993), pp. 143-56. Pelucchi's book has a series of photographs of Gianna at various stages of her life.

CATHERINE OF SIENA (over page)
Faith and charitableness:
red cross, gold heart, on black field.

29

ST CATHERINE OF SIENA, *Doctor* (1347-80)

Caterina di Giacomo di Benincasa was born in the Fontebranda district of Siena in 1347, the twenty-fourth of the twenty-five children of Giacomo di Benincasa and Lapa di Puccio di Piacenti. Her twin sister died shortly after being born. Her father was a wool-dyer of comfortable means, and it is said that Catherine inherited his piety and interest in caring for others, while from her mother she inherited her drive and determination. It is difficult to distinguish truth from pious legend in accounts of her childhood, but it does seem she was a lively, friendly, and devout child. When she was six years old she had what she later described as a vision of Our Lord: he was dressed in papal robes, sitting on a throne above the local Dominican church and surrounded by saints; he smiled and blessed her, but said nothing. Whatever the true nature of this vision was, it appears to have confirmed in Catherine a decision to dedicate herself entirely to God. At some stage she made a vow of virginity, and when her favourite sister died suddenly in 1362 she began to lead a life of penance and prayer.

Her mother tried to persuade her to marry, but Catherine refused and cut off her hair to make herself look less attractive. There were prolonged quarrels with her parents, and she seems to have been reduced to the status of a servant at home because of her obstinate refusal to follow their wishes for her. The following year another sister, the youngest of the family, died, and Catherine began a fasting régime that was to last in one form or another for the rest of her life, taking only bread, raw vegetables, and water for sustenance. At the same time, she was attracted to the *Mantellate,* a group of devout women who were members of the Dominican Third Order. They wore the Dominican habit but continued to live at home. Most of them were widows, and they concentrated on charitable work among the poor in the town; they did not take kindly to a strange teenager who seemed totally withdrawn and over pious. Catherine persisted, however, and about the year 1365 was admitted as a member. For three years after this she lived at home in solitude, speaking as little as possible and devoting as much of her time as she could to prayer. When she was twenty-one her spiritual life had developed so intensely that she experienced what she later described as a mystical espousal to Christ; she also felt called to abandon her solitary way of life completely and become active in the world: it was as though the three years had been a prolonged, unconscious novitiate to fit her for the very public life she was to follow from then on.

That call, however, was not at first a welcome one, since the spiritual union she had reached seemed a goal in itself—"to be alone with the Alone," as she put it—and she saw it as a contradiction of the espousal she had just experienced: "Why, sweetest bridegroom, are you sending me away?" she complained. She did not immediately see the link between loving God and involvement in external activity, something that was to be a cornerstone of her later teaching. Once she understood "the tender will of God," however, her new apostolate was fired by her love of God. This was so intense it drove her to become involved with others, to spread the message of God's love for us and our duty and need to love him in return. The dignity of each human person, created and loved by God and redeemed by the death of a loving Jesus, was the basis of Catherine's concern to help others physically and spiritually. She had a strong sense of society as a community held together by bonds of charity and helping its members to love God now and hereafter. During the famine of 1370 and the plague of 1374 she put all her effort into helping the ill and the dying, at the same time undergoing intense mystical experiences and increasing her fasting, so that after about 1372 she found it difficult to take solid food and often vomited when she tried to eat.

There was nothing unusual, of course, in women undertaking charitable work, but Catherine faced considerable opposition when she started to preach, a ministry traditionally carried out entirely by men. She had herself objected to God when she felt he was calling her to such a ministry: "My very sex, as I need not tell you, puts many obstacles in the way. The world has no use for women in work such as that, and propriety forbids a woman to mix so freely in the company of men." (*Legenda Major*, quoted in Fatula). Here Bd Raymund of Capua (5 Oct.), her confessor and first biographer, drew a neat parallel between God's choice of women such as Catherine and Jesus' choice of the unlettered apostles: both served to humble the pride of men, "especially the pride of those who regard themselves as wise and learned." He added that if men would listen humbly, "welcoming and heeding, with all due submission, the women" sent by God, the Church would benefit greatly. Whether the "wise and learned" did listen to her or not, Raymund reported that many hundreds of people crowded in from the mountains and the country districts around Siena just to see and hear her, "and when they heard her or even only had sight of her, their hearts were pierced." So many were converted that he could not cope with their Confessions, and so he obtained papal permission for three confessors to accompany her on her preaching missions. When the civil and church authorites tried to stop her preaching she drew inspiration from the apostles and from St Dominic (8 Aug.), "the fiery heralds of God's word who bore Jesus in their hearts and spoke his name like fire on their lips," as she wrote in a letter to a priest. Her determination to continue her preaching is clear in a letter to the authorities in Siena: "I would sacrifice myself a thousand times if I had the lives. . . . I *will* go and I *will* do as the Holy Spirit inspires me."

Catherine was so driven by her understanding of God's love that she refused to acknowledge any conventions or other obstacles in her way. The link between loving God and wishing to spread that love became so clear, so essential, in her mind, that she could not act differently: the more we know and understand God, the more we see he is "mad with love" for us and the more we want to love him in return. There is a passage in *The Dialogue* in which Jesus speaks to Catherine as follows: "You must love others with the same pure love with which I love you. But you cannot do this for me because I love you without being loved by you . . . you cannot repay me. But you must give this love to other people, loving them without being loved by them. You must love them without any concern for your spiritual or material profit, but only for the glory and praise of my name, because I love them." From the time she understood this onward, "the most intensely intimate of Catherine's prayer times would consistently and abruptly culminate in the imperative to go out to others in companionship and service. . . . Our love relationship with God cannot therefore rest simply in intimacy and union but must reach out as God reached and reaches out to humankind in Jesus, even, as Catherine never tires of repeating, 'to the point of death'" (Noffke).

According to Catherine, our efforts to return God's love have two results: we want to live according to his truth (for Catherine God is always "gentle first Truth"), and we lay ourselves open to being led by his love, personified in the Holy Spirit. The suffering and death of people from poverty was one example of a contradiction of divine truth, for it was evidence of human beings not sharing God's love for us but loving themselves selfishly, so she had to act. The condition of the Church in Catherine's day was another contradiction, because it was not as the spouse of Christ should be, and therefore she had to act. She began to see that her response to that demand had to involve her in more than preaching and works of charity: if God's love was to become the dominant force in the world, the Church itself would have to be reformed, and governments would have to be persuaded to live peacefully together. She might be only the pope's "poor unworthy daughter, the servant and slave of the servants of Jesus Christ," as she most often referred to herself, but she had to respond to God's love for her by doing whatever she could to bring about the necessary reform of Church and society. Anyone on fire with love for God and ardent for his truth had to re-fashion the fallen world, whatever the human cost and no matter how foolish the action appeared. This love was the constant theme of her sermons and letters, and hers was truly a ministry of love; the apparently ridiculous extremes to which she sometimes took that ministry make sense only in the light of her understanding of God as loving and demanding love.

In 1374 she visited Florence while the general chapter of the Dominicans was meeting. The purpose of her visit is not altogether clear, but there is no evidence for the traditional view she was called to answer suspicions that her sermons were unorthodox and even heretical, accusations made out of jealousy at her success as a popular preacher. It is more likely, knowing her desire to reform clerical life and convince the Dominicans to be more like their holy founder, that she saw the occasion as an opportunity to carry on her mission. One important result of the visit was the official appointment of Raymund of Capua to be her spiritual director. He was an able theologian and respected figure, and the two became close friends. The following year she was in Pisa, trying to persuade its leaders and those of neighbouring Lucca not to join an antipapal league that would start a war in Italy. Part of her tactics was to preach the value of a Crusade against the Turks, hoping to divert military energies and ambitions from Italy to the Holy Land. At the same time she sent Raymund with a letter to Sir John Hawkwood, the leader of a group of English mercenaries who were causing trouble in the Italian States, begging them to use their military skill in the service of the Crusade. "How cruel it is," she wrote, "that we who are Christians, members bound together in the body of holy Church, should be persecuting one another! This must not be; no, we must abandon all thought of that and rouse ourselves to thoroughgoing earnestness." This public activity did not interfere with her fasting and prayers, and at Pisa she received the stigmata, visible only to herself, as she prayed God it would always remain. Toward the end of 1375 she was back in Siena assisting a young political prisoner, Niccolò di Toldo, as he prepared to face execution. In a deeply moving letter full of visionary references to the saving blood of Christ, she described how she persuaded the prisoner to receive Communion, knelt with him at the block to comfort him, and received the severed head into her hands; she added, "With the greatest envy I remained on earth!"

While Catherine regarded peace between the Christian States as an important objective, it was the state of the Church and its need for reform that was her keenest concern. Like an Old Testament prophet dealing with God's chosen people, Israel, her attitude to the Church was a mixture of reverence, abhorrence, and frustration. It was the "sweet bride of Christ," "the body of the living Lord"; it was Christ himself on earth, and so reverence, love, and obedience were due to it, and action against the pope was action against Christ. At the same time, Catherine was fully aware of the abuses in the Church, the weakness and human ambition of its leaders, and the immorality of many of the clergy. In a letter to Pope Gregory XI she wrote, "Ah, what a shame this is! They ought to be mirrors of freely chosen poverty, humble lambs, giving out the Church's possessions to the poor. Yet here they are, living in worldly luxury and ambition and pretentious vanity a thousand times worse than if they belonged to the world! In fact, many layfolk put them to shame by their good holy lives." In *The Dialogue* she attacked the bishops for ordaining "'little boys instead of mature men,' 'idiots who scarcely know how to read and could never pray the Divine Office,' ignorant of Latin and unable to say even the words of consecration. They consider it beneath them to visit the poor; refusing to lift a finger to help, they stand by as others die of hunger" (Fatula).

Catherine knew there could be no lasting reform of the Church without the involvement and leadership of the popes. At the time their prestige was low; since 1309 they had lived in Avignon in France and were thought to be completely under French control. Some of them had tried to carry out reforms and had led personal lives above reproach, but they had failed to provide the leadership required to bring about a general reform. Catherine became involved in 1376, when Gregory XI placed Florence under an interdict, and fearing this would lead to economic hardship and war, she intervened on behalf of the city, travelling to Avignon to intercede with Gregory. She was politically naïve, however, and was duped by the Florentines, who quickly repudiated her and made their own peace with the pope. Catherine, however, had wider interests to pursue with Gregory. It is worth looking more closely at one of the letters she wrote to him before she left for Avignon. This shows her usual mixture of reverence for the representative of Christ on earth, a friendly familiarity—she often called him *Babbo* or Daddy—and the down-to-earth outspokenness one might use with an erring child. It also shows her conviction that her mission was divinely inspired. Her three themes are the evils in the Church he must remedy, the return of the papacy to Rome he must undertake, and the Crusade against the Turks he must organize. "I tell you in the name of Christ crucified," she wrote, "that you must use your authority to do [these] three essential things. You are in charge of the garden of holy Church. . . . Ah, *use* your authority, you who are in charge of us! . . . Plant fragrant flowers in this garden for us, pastors and administrators who will be true servants of Jesus Christ crucified, who will seek only God's honour and the salvation of souls, who will be fathers to the poor." On the question of returning to Rome and launching a Crusade, she urged Gregory: "Ah, my dear father! I am begging you, I am *telling* you: come, and conquer our enemies. . . . In the name of Christ crucified I am telling you. . . . Be a courageous man for me, not a coward." At the end of the letter she asked, "pardon my foolishness, father, and let the love and sorrow that make me speak be my excuse in the presence of your kindness. Give me your blessing. Keep living in God's holy and tender love (Noffke, *Letters*)." Gregory had already decided to return to Rome, and Catherine's pressure did no more, probably, than confirm his resolve and ensure it happened sooner rather than later. He left for Rome in September 1376, and Catherine travelled separately back to Siena, where she founded a convent of enclosed nuns to pray for the Church.

The year 1377 was a comparatively quiet year for her. She spent most of it at Rocca d'Orcia, about twenty miles from the city, preaching to the people and trying to make peace between local feuding families. At some point she learned to write (until then her letters had all been dictated) and began work on *The Dialogue*, based on a deep mystical experience in which God asked her to offer her life for the suffering Church. The pope then ordered her to Florence in another attempt to make peace between the city and himself; again her naïveté and trustfulness allowed the Florentines to take advantage of her for their own political ends. Gregory died in March 1378, and in the troubles that followed the election of Urban VI Catherine was almost killed by the antipapal party. She lamented the fact that she had only narrowly escaped martyrdom in the Church's cause. Urban was opposed by a powerful faction, and in 1378 an antipope was elected, starting the Great Schism that was to split the Church and western Europe until 1417. Reform seemed as remote as ever, and Catherine began to blame herself for the failure to bring it about—if only she had fasted more and prayed more intensely God would surely have granted what she desired. She wrote to Raymund, "Am I always, because of my faithlessness, to shut the gates against Divine Providence? . . . Lord, unmake me and break my hardness of heart, that I not be a tool which spoils your works." She blamed her "many sins" for the opposition to Urban, and her desire to do something to improve matters became urgent and extreme. She prayed, "Here is my flesh; here is my blood. . . . Let my bones be split apart for those for whom I am praying. . . . Let my . . . marrow be ground up for your vicar on earth, your bride's only spouse" (quoted in Fatula). Others blamed her for meddling in matters beyond her understanding and for her part in persuading Gregory to return from Avignon.

Urban called her to Rome to support his cause, and she set up a community there of the women and men who had become her "family." The pope, however, had no intention of supporting her, and even her friends seemed to let her down. Raymund was ordered to France on papal business but got cold feet and stayed in Genoa; Catherine upbraided him in her strongest language for refusing to accept the martyrdom he might have suffered. St Catherine of Vadstena (24 Mar.) refused to go to Naples to try to persuade its dissolute queen, Giovanna, to support Urban. Meanwhile Catherine heard from Siena that the "family" she had left there to continue her work had broken up only two months after she had left. Much of her effort in Rome went into calling together a "council" of holy people to help the cause of unity and reform. She attacked those who refused to join her there for the purpose, including the English hermit William of Flete, whom she admired very much, choosing him as her successor to lead her "family." William was reading the situation better than Catherine and believed her support of Urban was unbalanced and efforts to call a "council" bound to be fruitless. By this time, however, Catherine was beyond any weighing-up of human possibilities and considerations. If she could not persuade people by her letters and pleading, she could at least offer herself as a sacrifice to persuade God to save the Church. From the beginning of January 1380 she refused to take even water; by the end of the month she had suffered a complete physical collapse and experienced convulsions and coma. She gave up her complete fast and during the early part of Lent was able to drag herself to St Peter's for daily Mass, but toward the end of February she lost the use of her legs through paralysis. She wrote to Raymund saying, "My life is consumed and shed for this sweet Bride: I by this road, and the glorious martyrs with blood"; she felt the Lord take the vessel of her body and "re-fashion" it in self-giving for the Church (Fatula). Constantly during this period she seemed to those around her to be struggling with "demons" who mocked her failure and suggested she had all along been following her own will and not God's. She died on 29 April, aged thirty-three.

In the context of her extreme fasting and her desire to offer herself as a sacrifice for the good of the Church, how far was Catherine responsible for her own death? Was she, as some modern writers have argued, suffering from a form of anorexia, evidenced and caused by the quarrels with her mother over marriage and her desire to take on a man's role in a totally patriarchal society, to challenge the accepted male/sacerdotal authority of her day? There are, certainly, parallels between the stages of her gradual giving up of ordinary food and the turning-points in her relationship with her natural family, and her wish to break away from her parents' ideal of bodily beauty and expectations about marriage is clear enough. Yet many women of her day achieved such a break relatively easily by joining a religious Order and without even approaching the extremes of asceticism adopted by Catherine. Traditionally, Christian asceticism aimed at controlling bodily appetites and in that way liberating the person to concentrate on spiritual matters, and "control" and "liberation" are certainly key terms in the modern vocabulary of anorexia. That asceticism, however, was not directed at overcoming external obstacles but the one internal obstacle that mattered, self-will. In *The Dialogue* God warns against those who "have invested more effort and desire in mortifying their bodies than in slaying their selfish wills. . . . [The truly holy] have used mortification as the instrument it is to help them slay their self-will." The purpose of Catherine's (and other holy women's) fasting was different from that of the modern anorexic, although the eating/vomiting pattern she developed may have become similar when her fasting had gone so far her body could no longer tolerate food. The immediate purpose was control of her will, the long-term purpose was to become as like Christ as possible: "[These holy women] saw all humanity as created in God's image, as capable of *imitatio Christi* through body as well as soul. Thus they gloried in the pain, the exudings, the somatic disorders that made their bodies parallel to the consecrated wafer on the altar and the man on the cross" (Bynum). The more Catherine fasted the more she desired to receive Holy Communion, so much so the frequency of her reception caused a scandal. The spiritual satisfaction she experienced after Holy Communion spilled over into bodily satisfaction, or did away with bodily needs: "I feel so satisfied by the Lord when I receive his most adorable Sacrament that I could not possibly feel any desire for any other kind of food," she told her first confessor. There would seem to be more differences than similarities between this *anorexia mirabilis,* or holy anorexia, as it has been called, and the modern *anorexia nervosa.* She was not "image conscious," nor was she anti-male; indeed, her motivation was not negative but positive: Bynum argues that these women forged "religiously grounded" personalities devoted to the ultimate values of redemptive suffering—*imitatio Christi,* disinterested love, and charity toward others.

To concentrate on the public activity in her life that brought Catherine both notoriety and fame would be to present not just an incomplete picture but a particularly lopsided one. A central place must be found for her mysticism. She was not like someone following an active ministry who retired regularly to pray and contemplate; the very centre of her life was contemplative prayer and the special relationship with God it established. Just as her writings are not theological treatises, neither are her actions the result of a thought-out plan: hers was a lived theology growing out of her closeness to God, woven into her writings and actions because it was woven into her life. Everything she did was what she believed God was telling her to do, as she gave herself more and more to the "tender will of God" in imitation of Jesus' complete submission to the Father. An example of the integration between her contemplation and her actions is the way she often broke into prayer and experienced ecstasies as she was writing her letters (Noffke); her secretaries included these outpourings as they took down her dictation. Catherine would not have understood the difference between activity in God's cause and contemplation: she spoke rather of "love of God" and "love of neighbour," and it was the same love (Scott).

The richness of her mystical life is best seen in "my book," as she called it—what we now know as *The Dialogue.* The work was written between 1377 and 1378 for the instruction and comfort of her spiritual family. Catherine dictated most of it, often in a state of ecstasy, and then expanded and edited it herself. Raymund described it as a "book that contains a dialogue between a soul who asks the Lord four questions, and the Lord himself who replies to the soul, enlightening her with many useful truths." It is a complex work because Catherine's thought "follows a relentless pattern of 'layering' in which she restates her arguments frequently, but almost always with the addition of and integration of new elements" (Noffke). At the beginning of the book Catherine asks God a number of questions that he answers in detail. The largest section is taken up with expanding the multi-layered metaphor of Christ as the bridge, the link between earth and heaven and the only way for human beings to cross the abyss opened up by sin. He is the bridge because of his incarnation and his death on the cross. The bridge also provides an ascent from sin to the highest stage of the spiritual life, and the stages the soul passes through on this journey are described with a psychological sensitivity based on Catherine's own experiences. Another section deals with "The Mystic Body of Holy Church" and starts by praising the priesthood and the Eucharist and goes on to detail God's condemnation of priests and religious who live immoral and scandalous lives.

Other sections deal with the spirit of discernment, true and false spiritual emotion, truth, obedience, and divine Providence. "The whole of the Dialogue is more like a great tapestry to which Catherine adds stitch upon stitch until she is satisfied that she has communicated all she can of what she has learned of the way of God" (Noffke). The book stands alongside the great classics of writers such as St Teresa of Avila (15 Oct.) and St John of the Cross (24 Nov.), both, like her, declared Doctors of the Church for their mystical theology.

Catherine's personal mystical experiences were a key influence in her mystical theology, but there were other influences as well. She had not received any formal education and it is not clear how fluently she could read, yet she had digested ideas from many writers, from Augustine to Aquinas and a number of contemporary authors. She had also absorbed a great deal of the Bible, though she had never studied or even read it in any systematic way—she probably learned it through hearing rather than reading. Phrases and ideas from the scriptures abound in her writings and are woven into them so tightly that it is often difficult to know where a particular reference starts and finishes; they set her off on her favourite themes or open up new paths as she takes a scriptural image and develops it. Given her lack of theological training, it is amazing how she handles mysteries like the Trinity, the Incarnation and relationship of Christ to the Father, and the Eucharist, so deeply and so confidently in her local Tuscan dialect, never departing from a strictly orthodox teaching. No doubt we must allow for the help she received from long conversations on these matters with Raymund of Capua, and some of her teaching may have been tidied up when he reported it in his biography, but whatever she absorbed from others became her own and was coloured by her individual approach. Her acknowledgement of God's freely-given love was the motive force directing all her activity; that love was all the more extraordinary to Catherine when she considered her nothingness as a creature before God the creator. In one of her earliest spiritual experiences, God spoke to her in these words: "Do you know, daughter, who you are and who I am? If you know these two things you have beatitude in your grasp. You are she who is not, and I am the one who is. Let your soul be penetrated with this truth, and the Enemy can never lead you astray." This basic relationship of creature and creator is part of "God's truth," a many-stranded theme in Catherine's thought and including, as we have seen, God's plan for his creation. It also included the unity and trinity of God: her thought is fully and richly Trinitarian—see, for example, this passage from a letter: "In Christ crucified we find the Father and share in his power; we find the wisdom of God's only-begotten Son, which enlightens our understanding; we see and experience the mercy of the Holy Spirit by discovering the affectionate love with which Christ gave us the benefit of his passion" (quoted in Noffke). The blood shed in that passion was for Catherine a most potent symbol: it is life-giving, enlightening us in the darkness of sin. She wrote, "Oh blood, you dissolve the darkness and give us light so that we may come to know the truth and the holy will of the eternal Father!" (*ibid.*). The Church is a garden irrigated by Christ's blood, priests are the channels of that blood to the faithful through the sacraments, and it is for us both the proof and the fruit of God's love.

The rich complexity of Catherine's theology defies easy summary. She remains an intriguing figure, frightening in her intensity yet popular and accessible, modern in some of her insights and concerns but fully medieval in her assumptions. Throughout her active life she was a teacher, determined to instruct others in God's truth and love and to persuade them to follow the demands of that love beyond the limits set by human considerations, as she herself had done. In making her a Doctor of the Church Pope Paul VI declared that Jesus' statement, "My doctrine is not my own but his who sent me" (John 7:16), and St Paul's "The only knowledge I claimed to have when I was with you was of Jesus Christ and him crucified" (1 Cor. 2:2), could both be applied to her theology.

A popular cult of Catherine started immediately after her death and was fostered by her disiples and the Dominicans, who commissioned and distributed pictures of her and began to celebrate her feast on 29 April, with the permission of Raymund of Capua, who had become master general of the Dominicans. She was buried at first in the Minerva cemetery in Rome, and the tomb quickly became a place of pilgrimage. Later her body was moved into the church of Santa Maria sopra Minerva, where it is enshrined below the high altar; it suffered the usual medieval indignity of being partially dismembered for relics, by Raymund of Capua among others—he was responsible for her head being taken to Siena, where it is still venerated. Raymund finished his Life, the *Legenda Major,* in 1395; it was a carefully crafted biography and intended to help the cause of Catherine's canonization. Ironically, perhaps, this was held up by the very divisions in the Church she had tried to heal and did not take place until 1461 under the Sienese pope, Pius II. In the present century St Pius X (26 Aug.) made her the special patron of women involved in Catholic Action, and in 1939 she and St Francis of Assisi (4 Oct.) were declared to be the primary patrons of Italy. Finally, in 1970, Pope Paul VI made her a Doctor of the Church, a title never before granted to a layperson, let alone a woman.

Contemporary sources for the life of Catherine are plentiful. Bd Raymund of Capua, her director and friend from 1374, published his *Legenda Major* in 1395. Tommaso d'Antonio Nacci da Siena, known as Caffarini and one of her earliest disciples, expanded Raymund's work with his *Libellus de Supplemento*, which used notes from Catherine's first confessor; he later published a more compact work, the *Legenda Minor,* and compiled the *Processus* for the canonization, which contains statements from most of Catherine's disciples. A work entitled *I Miracoli* was published anonymously during her lifetime. Finally, there are twenty-six of Catherine's prayers (taken down by secretaries as she prayed, often in ecstasy) and 382 of her letters, as well as some written to her and to each other by friends and disciples. The balance between hagiography and history as we perceive it in these early writings about Catherine is not always easy to determine. The critical and controversial works of R. Fawtier, *Sainte Catherine de Sienne: Essai de critique des sources* (1921), *Les Oeuvres de Sainte Catherine de Sienne* (1930), and (with L. Canet) *La double expérience de Catherine Benincasa* (1948) gave rise to worthwhile studies and editions of works and letters: see especially G. Getto, *Saggio letterario su S. Caterina da Siena* (1939); A. Grion, *Santa Caterina da Siena: Dottrina e fonti* (1953); G. D'Urso, *Il genio di Santa Caterina* (1971). Recent English work includes an edition and translation of Raymund of Capua's *Life* by C. Kearns, O.P., *The Life of Catherine of Siena* (1980); Suzanne Noffke, O.P. (ed. and trans.), *Catherine of Siena: The Dialogue* (1980), *The Prayers of Catherine of Siena* (1983), and *The Letters of St Catherine of Siena*, 4 vols. (vol. 1 only, 1988)—the first full English edition of the letters in what promises to be a definitive scholarly work; see also K. Foster, O.P., and M. J. Ronayne (trans.), *I, Catherine: Selected Writings of Catherine of Siena* (1980). From a multiplicity of biographies and studies see A. Curtayne, *Saint Catherine of Siena* (1934); M. de la Bédoyère, *Catherine* (1947); Arrigo Levasti, *My Servant, Catherine* (1954); Mary Ann Fatula, O.P., *Catherine of Siena's Way* (1987); Noffke, *Catherine of Siena: Vision Through a Distant Eye* (1996), with a most comprehensive English bibliography; G. Cavallini, O.P., *Catherine of Siena* (1998). On anorexia, see R. M. Bell, *Holy Anorexia* (1985), and C. W. Bynum, *Holy Feast and Holy Fast: The Religious Significance of Food to Medieval Women* (1987). There are interesting articles, incl. one by Karen Scott, in *Atti del Simposio Internazionale Cateriniano-Bernardiniano* (1982). *B.T.A.*, 2, pp. 197-8, has a useful critical bibliography of older works, and see also *Bibl.SS.*, 3, 1000-44, and Suppl. 1, 284-90, on the doctorate.

Catherine was a favourite subject for painters and sculptors. She was often depicted with a book or pen and sometimes with a dove, the symbol of divine inspiration, but most often she was shown holding a lily; she was usually dressed as a Dominican tertiary. Her mystic espousal to Christ features in a number of paintings, and she is also depicted, wrongly, as accompanying the pope on his return to Rome. In 1471 Pope Sixtus IV forbade pictures of her showing the stigmata, because of a controversy between Franciscans and Dominicans about the truth of her claim to have received it; while Urban VIII lifted this ban in 1630 he stipulated the stigmata must not be shown bleeding. A fresco by Fra Angelico in San Marco, Florence, shows her holding a heart, while a painting by Bergognone (*c.* 1490), in the National Gallery, London, shows her with the Madonna and St Catherine of Alexandria, in which the child Jesus gives the ring of espousal to the latter and not to her. There is a sixteenth-century painting by Giovanni Antonio Sodoma in the church of San Domenico in Siena, which shows her in ecstasy. Another painting, by Carlo Dolci, in the Dulwich Gallery, London, shows her with a crown of thorns. The earliest portrait is a fresco in Siena from *c.* 1380 by Andrea Vanni, who knew her; a modern statue commissioned by the city of Siena in 1972 shows her holding an olive branch and a cross.

St Wifrid the Younger, *Bishop* (*c.* 744)

When St Bede (25 May) finished writing his *History* in 731 he said the diocese of York was ruled by a Bishop Wilfrid. To distinguish this Wilfrid from his much better known namesake, whose feast-day is on 12 October, today's saint is usually referred to as Wilfrid the Younger or Wilfrid II. He was educated at the abbey of Whitby under the rule of St Hilda (17 Nov.) and was a favourite disciple of St John of Beverley (7 May), bishop of York who made him his chaplain. As John grew older and retired more from his pastoral duties Wilfrid became in effect his coadjutor and was named as his successor. John died in

721, and Wilfrid became bishop in his own right. Unfortunately we know very little of his activities as ruler of the important diocese of York except that he seems to have had a special interest in education, and Bede merely says he was a man of "outstanding merit and holiness." In a poem about the saints of York, Alcuin praises Wilfrid for what he had done to beautify churches and for his energy in works of charity. In 732 he retired from active duty, like his predecessor, to spend his last years in a monastery, where he died in 744. His name appears in only one early calendar, and there is little evidence of a popular cult. In the tenth century the churches of both Canterbury and Worcester claimed to have the relics of the more famous St Wilfrid; it is likely that one of them had those of today's saint by mistake.

Bede, *H.E.*, 4, 23, and 5, 6; Alcuin, *Carmen*, 2, 1215-40; Stanton, pp. 185-6; *O.D.S.*, p. 494. See also C. J. Godfrey, *The Church in Anglo-Saxon England* (1962), pp. 257, 472.

St Hugh of Cluny, *Abbot* (1024-1109)

Hugh was born in 1024, the eldest son of the Count of Semur. He showed early signs of a vocation to the religious life and was allowed to enter the abbey of Cluny when he was fourteen. At the age of twenty he was ordained priest and within a year was elected prior; five years later, in 1049, he was elected abbot, an office he was to keep until his death sixty years later. His predecessor, St Odilo (1 Jan.), had started to reorganize and centralize the Cluniac system, and Hugh continued that work, becoming one of the truly outstanding abbots of the early Middle Ages. Every aspect of the Cluniac reform was expanded: elaborate monastic observance, splendid architecture, large numbers, and firm control of dependent houses. The Congregation grew from some seventy houses to at least twelve hundred, the community at Cluny increased from about fifty monks to three hundred, and its abbey church was rebuilt to become the largest church in Christendom (Knowles). While Hugh was abbot it was the most highly regarded monastery in western Europe, and smaller houses rushed to be affiliated to it and share its reforming spirit. That spirit was centred on the solemn performance of the divine office and liturgy, "carried out by a huge community in a great church amid the splendour of gold, silver and jewels, of vestments of silk and golden thread, illuminated by countless tapers and lamps" (*ibid.*).

As a great abbot Hugh was necessarily involved in matters outside his abbey. Soon after becoming abbot he attended the Council of Reims, called by the reforming pope St Leo IX (19 Apr.) to condemn simony and uphold clerical celibacy. He accompanied the pope back to Italy and in Rome took part in the synod that condemned the Eucharistic teaching of Berengarius of Tours. In 1057 he was at Cologne for the christening of the emperor's son, the future Henry IV, whose godfather he was. Shortly after this he was in Hungary as papal legate, negotiating for peace between the emperor and the Hungarian king, and in 1058 he attended Pope Stephen X on his death-bed in Florence. He served as papal legate to Toulouse and Spain. The accession of St Gregory VII (25 May) strengthened the links between Hugh and the papacy in the cause of reform, for Gregory had been affiliated to Cluny. During the bitter quarrel between the pope and the emperor, Henry IV, Hugh worked hard to bring about peace without giving up any of the Church's claims and played a part in persuading Gregory to absolve Henry from excommunication in the famous meeting at Canossa in 1077. Such was Hugh's standing that he was publicly praised and thanked for his services at the Roman synod of 1081 and at the Council of Clermont in 1095. St Anselm of Canterbury (21 Apr.) turned to him first for help and advice in his quarrel with the English king.

This involvement in church politics, and his frequent absences from Cluny on visitations of its many dependent houses, meant that Hugh was away for long periods from his abbey. The level of religious observance among his monks remained high, however, and he was remembered as an effective administrator and a sympathetic and wise leader in spiritual matters as much as in secular. For all his building and external activities, Hugh was genuinely interested in monastic reform and in spreading its true spirit throughout Europe for the good of religion. What he achieved at Cluny may be criticized: the system was too monarchical and dependent on having an outstanding abbot at the centre. Moreover, he admitted too many recruits and allowed them to become novices after only a few days' trial; it seems many of them had no true religious vocation. Under his capable but unstable successor the abbey faced discord and violence, and even though it was rescued later its style was heavily criticized by reformers such as St Bernard (20 Aug.), who saw little of the spirit of St Benedict in its splendour and power. Historians no longer believe that Cluny was the spearhead of the Gregorian reform of the eleventh century, but it played an important part in it, and Hugh's influence was always on the side of monastic and clerical discipline. St Peter Damian (21 Feb.) was a contemporary reformer with the strictest standards; after a visit to Cluny he wrote to Hugh, "When I recall the strict and full daily life of your abbey, I recognize that it is the Holy Spirit that guides you." A few of Hugh's writings survive.

Hugh died on 28/29 April 1109 and was canonized shortly afterwards, in 1120, by Pope Calixtus II, himself a monk of Cluny, mainly on the basis of the oral testimony of those who had known him. The speed of the canonization was a recognition of the value of the monastic reform Hugh had fostered. It was also a defence of the Cluniac system, which was coming under increasing attack by bishops who objected to its privileged exemption from episcopal control. By the time of Hugh's death the reform movement was coming to rely more on bishops than on great abbots and their monasteries, and the more austere Cîteaux and its imitators were replacing Cluny as the monastic model.

Sources for Hugh's life are numerous, and there are some early Lives; see F. Barlow, "The Canonization and the Early Lives of Hugh I, Abbot of Cluny," in *Anal. Boll.* 98 (1980), pp. 297-334. See also N. Hunt, *Cluny under St Hugh* (1967); H. E. J. Cowdrey, *The Cluniacs and the Gregorian Reform* (1970); D. Knowles, *Christian Monasticism* (1969), and *The Christian Centuries, 2: The Middle Ages* (1969).

30

ST PIUS V, *Pope* (1504-72)

Antonio Ghislieri was born of poor parents in Bosco, near Alessandria in northern Italy, on 17 January 1504. He spent his early years as a shepherd until he joined the Dominicans at the age of fourteen, taking the name Michael in religion. He was ordained priest in 1528 and spent the next sixteen years lecturing in philosophy and theology at the university of Pavia. His learning and zeal were responsible for his appointment as inquisitor for the areas around Bergamo and Como, and he carried out his duties so conscientiously that he was made commissary general of the Roman Inquisition in 1551 by Pope Julius III on the advice of Cardinal Carafa. When Carafa became Pope Paul IV he appointed Michael bishop of Nepi and Sutri in 1556, made him a cardinal in the following year, and inquisitor general in 1558. As a result, he was involved in some unfortunate cases of inquiry launched by the over zealous pope, the worst of which was the accusation of heresy against the wholly innocent Cardinal Morone. The new inquisitor general, however, was not severe enough for the pope and was himself under suspicion on occasions; he was accused of Lutheranism and denounced before all the cardinals as unworthy to wear the sacred purple and threatened with imprisonment in Castel San Angelo!

The next pope made him bishop of Mondoví, but when he opposed some of the papal policies, and especially the over indulgent nepotism of the pope, he fell from favour; a committee of cardinals was set up to supervise the Roman Inquisition, and Michael spent more of his time in his diocese, carrying out a full visitation to see what reforms were needed. He gained a reputation as a strict clerical reformer and was a living example of that reform in himself: his ascetical way of life and the poverty he practised so assiduously made him stand out from many of his colleagues in the College of Cardinals. It was not unexpected, then, that the reforming party, led by St Charles Borromeo (4 Nov.), supported his election at the next conclave in 1566, and he became pope, taking the title Pius V. As pope he had only one thing in mind: the salvation of souls. All his energies were directed toward that mission, and the value of every action and every institution was judged according to its needs (Pastor).

His programme of reform was that outlined or implied in the decrees of the Council of Trent, which had ended in 1563. Unlike so many earlier papal reformers, he started with Rome itself. The money traditionally thrown to the people after the papal coronation was given instead to the poor and to hospitals, while the traditional banquet for cardinals and nobles was replaced by gifts to poor religious houses. He reduced the size of his court and household, imposed a strict code of morality on its members, and tried to reform public life in the city by issuing decrees against blasphemy, prostitution, brigandage, and even bull-fighting. Contemporaries are supposed to have complained he was trying to turn the whole of Rome into a monastery (Kelly). A few days after his coronation he set up a commission to inquire into the state of the Roman clergy and took part himself in a pastoral visitation of the city that looked into the teaching of catechetics, the care of the sick, other charitable works, and the personal lives of the clergy. He urged the cardinals to reform their way of life and made those whose presence in Rome was not necessary return to their dioceses. When he chose new cardinals he refused to be influenced by political or family considerations and chose people on merit. There was one exception: he made his grandnephew a cardinal to counteract the actions of a particular group within the sacred college, but he gave him no special favours and made sure he was always under the pope's strict control. He oversaw the complete reorganization of six of the Curia's departments in the intersts of efficiency and to get rid of any possibility of corruption. Finally he set about the reform of the religious Orders in line with the decrees of the council: he insisted on strict enclosure and the choral recitation of the divine office. He laid down minimum ages for admission and profession and forbade religious to change from one Order to another on the pretext of seeking greater perfection. He suppressed the male *Humiliati* altogether when they refused to reform but in most cases found the religious themselves eager to accept change, and indeed many had already started to implement this.

As pope, Pius was the ruler of a substantial part of Italy and attempted to introduce refoms there as well as in the Church. Twice a month he heard complaints against courts and officials, and every week he received poor people and listened to their accounts of the abuses they had suffered. He tried to stop the brigandage that was rife throughout the Papal States, sometimes with some success but often using the wrong means and failing. He stopped imposing certain taxes and services and tried to deal with the problems created by money-lenders. He was, however, less interested in these reforms than in those that could be seen to relate more directly to spiritual matters, but charity demanded that he try to reduce his people's sufferings as much as possible.

If Pius was to be successful in implementing the decrees of the council across Europe and in winning back the areas that had adopted Protestantism, he needed the support of Catholic rulers. They, of course, had their own political agendas, and the days when they might have united behind the papacy in some sort of crusade were long gone, if indeed they had ever existed outside the papal imagination. France was experiencing a long period of religious wars and would not, in any case, have united with Philip II of Spain, its chief rival, in any cause. Philip regarded himself, and not the papacy, as the true champion of Catholicism in Europe and beyond; if Pius agreed with him, well and good; but if not, the pope was ignored or opposed. Pius either could not or would not understand the complexities of policy involved in many of these issues. In most cases his ill-judged interventions caused no permanent damage, but this was not always so. Misled by some English Catholics abroad, and in an attempt to help the Northern Rebellion of 1569 in its aim of making the unstable Mary Queen of Scots queen of England, he issued a Bull excommunicating Queen Elizabeth, deposing her, and freeing her Catholic subjects from any oaths of allegiance. The rebellion had already failed before the Bull was formally promulgated in 1570, and all Pius achieved was to put conscientious English Catholics in a quandary and give anti-Catholic elements in the government the perfect excuse to brand them all traitors and increase the severity of the persecution against them. Pius' zeal to crush heresy had clouded his judgment. It was the last time a pope tried to exercise the papacy's long outdated medieval claim of being able to depose a sovereign.

In a sense Pius was also medieval in his approach to another issue, the threat to Christian Europe from Islam. During the sixteenth century the Ottoman Turks had been extending their control over the Mediterranean, besieging Malta in 1564 and capturing Tunis in 1570. In 1570 they also took part of Cyprus, and their raids along the Adriatic coast of Italy increased in scale and severity. Pius saw it as his duty to unite the Catholic princes of Europe in a Crusade against Islam. He wrote to them (and to the ruler of Muscovy) but received little support; it was only the renewed success of the Turks in 1571 that persuaded Spain and Venice to join him in a "holy league." On 7 October the Christian forces under Don Juan of Austria won an outstanding naval victory at Lepanto. Pius attributed this to the intercession of Our Lady, obtained by the saying of the rosary, and saw it as only the beginning of a successful Crusade. In March 1572 he issued a Jubilee Bull offering indulgences to all who joined the crusading army or helped to equip it; he reckoned ten years of warfare would be all that was required to defeat the Turks completely and retake Jerusalem. But once the immediate danger was over the allies fell out, and the league was disbanded: there was no follow-up to the battle and a valuable chance was missed. The victory made Pius very popular throughout Catholic Europe, and he was fêted in poems and sermons as the new Joshua saving the chosen people (see Exod. 17:8-13). A large number of churches and chapels were dedicated to Our Lady of Victory, and in 1573 Pius' successor, Gregory XIII, established a feast of Our Lady of the Rosary to be kept on the first Sunday in October.

While the victory of Lepanto was the most famous event in Pius' reign and made him a legendary figure, it was for his work in implementing the decrees of the Council of Trent that Pius is remembered today. He urged observance of its decrees on bishops in other countries, putting special stress on their obligation to reside in their dioceses and make pastoral visitations, and he made use of papal legates to ensure their compliance. To help with the instruction of the faithful he published the *Roman Catechism* and promoted its translation into different languages. He turned his attention to the reform of the liturgy and issued a revised Roman Breviary in 1568 and a revised Roman Missal in 1570, imposing both of these on every diocese and all clergy except those religious with liturgies of their own at least two centuries old. This was the origin of the so-called Tridentine liturgy, which remained in force until the reforms of the twentieth century; it served to unite the Church and rectify many liturgical abuses, but it also forbade any liturgical change not sanctioned centrally by the Holy See. Given his earlier work with the Inquisition, it is not surprising that Pius saw in it an indispensable means for protecting the faithful from heresy, and so he increased its importance and standing and established the Congregation of the Index as a new department with extensive powers to control the publication of books. He regarded the Jews as enemies of the Faith; while allowing some to settle in ghettos in Rome and Ancona, he expelled most of them from the Papal States. Finally, he set up a commission of cardinals to deal with foreign missionary work in the Americas, Africa, and Asia, but most of its achievements took place only after his death.

No major area of the Church's life escaped his attention, and he was able to combine an interest in its immediate needs with a concern for the long term. Since the Second Vatican Council he has been widely regarded as the epitome of Tridentine narrowness and over zealous legalism. It may seem perverse to suggest he was trying to do the same as Pope John XXIII (1958-63), yet both popes saw the need for a radical restructuring of the Church to suit a radically altered situation: both responded to the needs of the Church in their day to create rather than just conserve. It was not Pius' fault that his model of the Church was taken as the only permissible one for four hundred years. He was himself the ideal of the Tridentine reformed clergy—ascetic, learned, and spiritually motivated in all his actions: "From the first day of his reign to the last every effort of Pius V had been devoted to the protection of the Church against the enemies of the Catholic Faith, to her purification from every abuse, to her spread in the lands beyond the seas, and to the defence of European Christendom against the attacks of Islam" (Pastor). Yet it would be as great a mistake to ignore the negative side of his fanatical Catholicism as to see in him an ideal figure, symbol of a united Church and hero of a conservative tradition.

Pius died on 1 May 1572 with the words, "Lord, increase my sufferings but also my patience" on his lips. His remains were moved in 1588 to a magnificent tomb in Santa Maria Maggiore, despite his wish to be buried in the church of the Dominicans in his birthplace, for which he had designed a rather grand tomb. He was beatified in 1672 and canonized in 1712. His feast was formerly celebrated on 5 May.

For the earliest Life see F. Van Ortroy, "Le pape saint Pie V," in *Anal. Boll.* 33 (1914), pp. 187-215. See also Pastor, especially 17 and 18 (1929); *O.D.S.*, pp. 400-2; *O.D.P.*, pp. 268-

9; *Bibl.SS.*, 10, 883-99, with very full bibliography; E. Duffy, *Saints and Sinners: A History of the Popes* (1997), p. 170, with a reproduction of a portrait. The best modern Life is N. Lemaître, *Saint Pie V* (1994).

He features in many paintings, especially in Rome, and is variously depicted as pope, as the saviour of Christendom, and, wrongly, as the founder of the feast of Our Lady of the Rosary. His tomb is decorated with a large statue showing him in pontifical robes and with a series of bas-reliefs illustrating his reign.

St Erkenwald, *Bishop* (693)

Bede tells us that St Theodore (19 Sept.), archbishop of Canterbury, chose Erkenwald (also Eorcenwald or Erconwald) to be bishop of the East Saxons, with London as his episcopal see; this was in the year 675. He goes on to say that the new bishop lived such a virtuous life before and after his consecration that heaven "still affords proofs of his virtues"; sick people were cured when placed under or near the litter in which the bishop had travelled, and chips of wood from the litter brought relief when applied to the sick.

Erkenwald was said to be of royal blood, and his name would indicate he was a member of the Kentish royal house; he was wealthy enough to have founded two monasteries before becoming bishop. One of these, for men, was at Chertsey in Surrey; the other was for men and women at Barking in Essex, where his sister St Ethelburga (12 Oct.) was abbess. As bishop he helped to restore peace between St Theodore and St Wilfrid (12 Oct.), but little is known of his episcopal administration. We know he enlarged St Paul's Cathedral and was respected enough to be able to persuade wealthy benefactors to grant large amounts of land for religious purposes. He seems to have established Christianity "on a firm footing in a diocese notorious for back-sliding" (Whatley), and he advised King Ine of Wessex when he was drawing up his very important legal code. His foundation at Chertsey claimed to have a papal charter granting it certain privileges that Erkenwald obtained when he went to Rome about the year 678, but the charter has been shown to be a later forgery, and there is no evidence that he made such a journey. Overall, "in Erkenwald, London possessed an influential bishop at a period of great importance for consolidating the position of the English church" (Whitelock).

When he died on 30 April 693, probably at Barking, his relics were claimed by the nuns there, by his former monastery at Chertsey, and, of course, by the clergy of London. In the end he was buried in St Paul's; in 1148 his relics were transferred to a new shrine behind the high altar, and in 1326 they were moved again to another shrine, which over the years was richly embellished by London patrons and pilgrims and became one of the glories of the cathedral and a favourite place of pilgrimage, where miracles due to his intercession were reported. He was the patron saint of medieval London and also featured in other parts of the country on rood-screens (for example, at Guilden Morden in Cambridgeshire) and in stained glass (in St Peter Mancroft, Norwich, and Wells Cathedral).

Bede, *H.E.*, bk. 4, ch. 6. Two eleventh- and twelfth-century accounts, *Vita S. Erkenwaldi* and *Miracula S. Erkenwaldi*, both originating at St Paul's, have been translated and edited by E. G. Whatley, *The Saint of London* (1989). See also D. Whitelock, *Some Anglo-Saxon Bishops of London* (1975), pp. 5-10; *O.D.S.*, pp. 160-1.

BB Francis Dickenson and Miles Gerard, *Martyrs* (1590)

Francis Dickenson was born in Otley in the West Riding of Yorkshire in 1565. He seems to have followed the Protestant religion for a number of years, at least to the extent of attending its services, before converting to Catholicism. He entered the English College at Reims about the year 1582 and was ordained in 1589. Miles Gerard was born in Wigan, Lancashire, in 1549. He entered the English College in Reims in 1580 and was ordained in 1583. In August 1589 he left for the English mission in the company of Francis Dickenson and three other priests. The captain of their ship would accept only two of them, and Miles and Francis were chosen by lot. Off the coast of Kent, however, they were shipwrecked in a storm and rescued by local people, who pillaged the wreck and took the two priests to Dover to swear allegiance to the queen as head of the Church. It is not clear whether they knew they were priests by what they had found in their luggage or because the crew told them so. It was not unknown for priests to be picked up by the authorities as soon as they landed, as the government had spies in the colleges abroad, and Miles Gerard at least was easily recognizable, since he had only one eye.

They both refused to take the oath and were taken to London for further examination. At first Francis gave his name as Laurence Leighley of Yorkshire and his age as twenty-one, while Miles used the alias William Richardson. Subsequent examinations discovered their true identities and the fact they were priests; this in itself was enough to condemn them for high treason, since the Act of 1585 made it a capital offence for priests ordained abroad since the beginning of the queen's reign to be in the country. Francis was tortured to extract a more damning confession, however, and admitted that he believed in the deposing power of the pope and would support a Catholic army against the queen should one land in England. It is not clear whether Miles was also tortured, nor how much was made of Francis' forced confession at their trial, for no details of this survive. Both were imprisoned in the Gatehouse early in 1590 but were not executed until April, at Rochester in Kent, the county where they had first committed their treason. The date of their execution is variously given as 19 or 30 April; Anstruther says the earlier date is more likely but the evidence is not clear-cut. They were beatified in 1929.

M.M.P., p. 162; Anstruther, 1, pp. 101-3, 130; C.R.S., 5, pp. 169-73. See also the general entries on the English and Welsh martyrs under 4 May and 25 October.

Bd Benedict of Urbino (1560-1625)

Martin, or Mark, Passionei was born in Urbino in Italy on 13 September 1560, the son of noble parents. He studied philosophy at the university of Perugia and law at the university of Padua; in both places he gained a reputation for learning and his virtuous way of life. He decided on a legal career and went to work in Rome in the court of one of the cardinals but found this did not satisfy him and so sought admission to the Capuchin friary in Fossombrone. His family strongly opposed his wish to become a religious, and he was not able to receive the habit until 1584, when he entered the friary in Fano and took the name of Benedict in religion. It looked for a time as though poor health would prevent him from being professed, but his novice-master was so impressed by his piety that he insisted on his being allowed to make his vows.

For three years Benedict was attached to the vicar general, St Laurence of Brindisi (23 July), and travelled with him on visitations in Austria and Bohemia. While he was on these journeys his missionary sermons won back large numbers of lapsed Catholics and were responsible for the conversion of many Protestants, although he is also said to have had difficulties with the local languages and to have returned to Italy because of this and his bad health. One of his key themes in preaching was the passion and death of Our Lord, upon which he meditated for an hour every day, lying face down on the ground. A favourite saying of his was, "They who hope and trust in God can never be lost." He wanted above everything else for people to be consumed with that fire of love that Jesus came on earth to set alight. He was also interested in the education of the young. In 1625, although he was very ill, he set out to preach the Lenten sermons at Sassocorbaro but was too weak to continue beyond Ash Wednesday. He was taken back to Fossombrone, where he died on 30 April. He was beatified in 1867. A number of short works by Benedict exist in manuscript: a treatise on the Franciscan ideal of poverty; a translation of part of St Augustine on free will; some poems, hymns, and letters; and four pieces consoling a relative who could not have children.

A number of studies were published for the beatification in 1867. See Eugenio de Potenza, *Vita del beato Benedetto* (1920), and *Il convento dei Capp. di Fossombrone e il b. B. da Urbino* (1936). See also *Bibl.SS.*, 2, 1189-91.

Bd Mary of the Incarnation (Marie Guyart) (1599-1672)

Marie Guyart was born in October 1599 in Tours, France. Her father, Florent, was a baker. At the age of seven she had a vision of Our Lord as a beautiful child who asked her, "Do you want to be with me?" and early in her teens she decided she had a religious vocation. Her parents, however, wanted her to marry, and so at seventeen she married Claude Martin, a master silk worker. They had one son, Claude, who was to become a Benedictine and his mother's first biographer, and then her husband died the following year, leaving heavy debts and a business in danger of collapse. Marie took it over and was able to make enough money to pay the creditors. She was urged to re-marry so that she and her infant son could be properly cared for, but she refused and in 1621 made a private vow of perpetual chastity. She worked for a few years in her brother-in-law's transport business and learned how to combine an active external life with an awareness of the presence of God and an interior life of contemplative prayer. In 1625 she experienced her first vision of the Trinity, and this was followed by one of Our Lord, who seemed to take her heart in order to enclose it in his own. In 1627 a second vision of the Trinity occurred during an ecstasy and ended with her spiritual marriage to Jesus. Her desire to become a religious developed during these years, and in 1632 she entered the Ursuline convent in Tours, leaving her twelve-year-old son in the care of her sister. In religion she took the name Mary of the Incarnation and was professed in 1633. Shortly after her entry she experienced a third vision of the Trinity that seemed to mark the height of mystical union with God, but at the same time she also experienced a spiritual dryness and various temptations that caused her intense anguish and were a sign of her union with the suffering Christ.

There was great interest at the time in the work of the French Jesuit missionaries in North America. The Ursuline Order was dedicated to educational work, and it was a logical extension of their apostolate to set up convents and schools to support and consolidate the work of the missionaries. Marie desired a share in this new apostolic work; in 1635 she wrote to her confessor: "I see the deplorable state of those who do not know these great truths and it seems to me that they are already plunged in hell, and that the blood of my Jesus has been shed in vain for them. . . . I swear . . . that if [God] wishes me to go to hell until the day of judgment, he will be doing me a great mercy, provided that he converts these poor people and that they come to know him." It comes as no surprise, then, that when a wealthy lady, Madame Madeleine de la Peltrie, visited the convent in Tours in 1639, Marie reacted enthusiastically to her plans for a school to educate the children of native American converts. Despite the fact that it would probably mean her leaving her son for good, Marie volunteered to go Canada. She left with another Sister for Paris, where arrangements were made for setting up the school; she then embarked for Canada and landed there in August 1639, settling eventually in Quebec. She was the first French missionary Sister to go to Canada and has been called "Mother of the Catholic Church in Canada." She worked with one of the Jesuit missionaries to draw up a Constitution for the new convent; the first school was opened in Quebec in 1639 and flourished despite opposition from the native Americans, illness, and lack of funding. A larger house was obtained in 1642, but in 1648 the whole enterprise was in danger of folding because the Iroquois were threatening Quebec itself. Marie and her companions were advised to return to Europe but stayed on to keep the work going. A fire destroyed most of the convent in 1650, and during the Iroquois War from 1653 to 1663 the community faced further threats of extinction. To add to these troubles, Marie began to suffer increasingly from serious illness; she offered herself as a victim for the survival of Christianity in Canada. Although she lived an enclosed life she was fully involved in catechetical and other missionary projects; as she wrote in her autobiography, "My body was in our monastery but my spirit could not be confined. The Spirit of Jesus used to carry me to the Indies, to America, to Japan, to East and West, to all parts of Canada and among the Hurons, to everywhere in the inhabited world where there were human beings whom I could see belonged to Jesus Christ." She studied the languages of the Iroquois, Hurons, and Algonquins and compiled dictionaries so that the catechism and scriptures could be translated. Her convent became a general "advice centre," from which she wrote thousands of letters dealing with the problems of the missionaries, sharing their worries, and encouraging them to persevere despite the loss of several of their leading figures through martyrdom in the 1640s.

Her letters also reveal much of her own spirituality, a spirituality that continued to develop, despite her apparent total absorption in external concerns, and reached the highest levels of mysticism. She experienced the continual presence of Our Lord and, from about 1651, that of Our Lady as well, and enjoyed special revelations and consolations. For her, God was always a God of love: she wrote, "He has never led me by feelings of fear, but always by a spirit of love and trust." When her son had doubts about the religious life, she wrote, "Why do you not want to become familiar with a God who is so good and so loving. . . . He is our spouse and as such, as St Bernard says, he demands that we love him in return." The person who enjoys this "sweet familiarity with God" in prayer will be led to show that love more and more in practical works. For Marie there was an essential unity between contemplation and action: if the former led to an increasingly close union with Jesus, it was his spirit that determined the latter. "It is true," she wrote, "the mixed life has its difficulties, but it is inspired by the Spirit of him who regulates it. . . . I never find myself closer to God than when I leave the peace and quiet for the sake of his love" to do some Christian act.

Her austere and penitential way of life, and the never-ending work she was doing to support the missionaries, led to a severe illness in 1654, but this did not prevent her carrying on with her apostolate. When she died on 30 April 1672 she was already being hailed as a saint. The process for her beatification started almost immediately but was held up by the suspicions about most mystical writings that resulted from the quietist controversies in France. It was not until 1911 that her virtues were declared heroic; she was beatified in 1980.

In addition to her many letters, on the orders of her spiritual directors she composed two "Relations," or accounts of her spiritual life, one in 1633 just after she had become a nun, and the other in Quebec in 1653-4 (written largely, it appears, at the request of her son); these are sometimes referred to as an autobiography. There is also a book of notes made during her retreats and including an exposition of the Song of Songs, and another called, "The holy school, or a simple explanation of the mysteries of the Faith." Her writings show the richness and variety of those from whom she drew spiritual inspiration: St Bernard (20 Aug.), St Gertrude (16 Nov.), *The Imitation of Christ*, St Teresa of Avila (15 Oct.), St John of the Cross (24 Nov.), and St Francis de Sales (24 Jan.).

The biography written by her son was published under the title *La vie de la vén. Marie de l'Incarnation, première supérieur des Ursulines de la Nouvelle France . . .* (1677); he published an edition of her letters in 1681 (2d ed., 1876). H. Bremond did much to rescue her from neglect in his *Histoire littéraire du sentiment religieux* (1922), 6, pp. 3-176. A. Jamet published a critical edition of her letters and other writings, *Marie de l'Incarnation, Ecrits spirituels et historiques*, 4 vols. (1929-39). See also F. Jetté, *La voie de la sainteté d'après Marie de l'Incarnation* (1954; Eng. ed., 1963); J. J. Sullivan (trans. and ed.), *The Autobiography of Ven. Marie of the Incarnation* (1964); G.-M. Oury, *Marie de l'Incarnation 1599-1672*, 2 vols. (1973); *N.C.E.*, 9, pp. 219-20. The above account relies on *Bibl.SS.*, 8, 1015-8, and the long article by G.-M. Oury in *Dict.Sp.*, 10 (1980), 487-507. Marie's letter of 1635 is quoted from the section on her in Bruno Chenu *et al.*, *The Book of Christian Martyrs* (1990), pp. 119-28. See also the entry for the North American Martyrs under 19 October and what is said there about missionary work with the native Americans.

St Joseph Cottolengo, *Founder* (1786-1842)

Giuseppe Benedetto Cottolengo was born in 1786 in Bra, a small town in Piedmont. He was the eldest of twelve children of middle-class, strongly Christian parents and was brought up by his mother to care for the poor and the sick. It is said of him that at the age of five he was found measuring the house because he wanted, when he grew up, to fit in as many sick-beds for poor people as he could. In 1802 he started studying for the priesthood at home because the seminary had been closed by the Napoleonic War, and he was eventually ordained priest in Turin in 1811. Initially he wanted to work in a country parish and devote himself to a simple pastoral ministry among the people, but he was advised by his fellow-priests to undertake further study and so signed up for a degree in theology at the university of Turin. He graduated two years later and returned to his home town, where he worked for two years before being appointed a canon in 1818 at the Corpus Domini basilica in Turin. He was to spend the rest of his life in the city and find his true vocation there. For eight or nine years he performed conscientiously the various duties of his ofice, especially preaching and hearing Confessions, and earned the nickname "the good canon" because he was always looking out for ways to help the poor. He was fascinated by the life of St Vincent de Paul (27 Sept.) and was beginning to think he should devote all his energy to the sick and the poor when something happened to convince him this was to be his vocation.

In 1827 a French family was passing through Turin on its way home. They had no money and the mother was very ill, but she could not get medical help because the ordinary hospital would not accept her as she was pregnant, and the maternity hospital refused her because she had tuberculosis. She was taken to a room provided by the city authorities for sick vagrants, and Canon Cottolengo stayed there with her until she died, trying to comfort her and her husband and children. On his return to the basilica he decided to open a house for the sick and the poor who were rejected by everyone else; he claimed the inspiration for this came from Our Lady as he was reciting her litany before the altar of the Madonna delle Grazie. To begin with he rented just two rooms in a house opposite the basilica: he had no grand, overall plan and left any further developments to divine Providence. He was, he said, only the labourer: "Providence can do everything and will decide what is to happen." Other rooms were rented and a young widow, Maria Nasi Pullini, got together a group of girls to help with the work. Neighbours, however, began to object as the number of sick people using the house increased, especially when an outbreak of cholera threatened parts of Piedmont, and so the city authorities closed the house. Some of the canon's colleagues at the basilica had also raised objections on the grounds that the undertaking was imprudent and was bringing them into disrepute. Joseph had no choice but to move; he chose a derelict area called Valdocco on the outskirts of the city, covered in scrub and dotted with hovels and rough drinking-places, and rented a small building. On 27 April 1832 he moved there with a single patient, a young man suffering from cancer, and within a few months he needed another building to cope with the numbers. This was the beginning of his "Little House of Divine Providence," which he put under the patronage of St Vincent de Paul and gave as its motto *Caritas Christi urget nos* ("The Love of Christ drives us forward"). He started new sections of the work to meet each new need: the incurably sick, the aged and infirm, epileptics, the mentally ill, sick and abandoned children— he turned no one away, arguing, "All the poor are our patrons, but those who seem outwardly to be the most disgusting and repellent are our dearest patrons, indeed, are our jewels." The "Little House" grew into a "little town," providing shelter, medical care, orphanages, homes for destitute girls, schools, and workshops. In all this he put his complete trust in Providence, believing God would help overcome the inevitable difficulties and enable him to find sufficient funds and helpers. He founded a confraternity of lay brothers, the Brothers of St Vincent, to do manual work and act as hospital porters; a Congregation of secular priests, Priests of the Holy Trinity, to help him in providing spiritual care; and a number of different Congregations of nuns, each dedicated to a particular function in the "Little House." The best known of these are the Sisters of St Vincent or "Vincenzine," or "Cottolenghine," founded in 1830 with the help of Maria Nasi.

In addition to his trust in providence, Joseph had a special devotion to Our Lady and made her patroness of the Institute. He stressed the importance of prayer, calling it "the first and most important of our works. . . . It is prayer that makes the Little House live." His own spiritual life was firmly based on the sacraments; he insisted on a proper and reverent performance of the liturgy and recommended daily Communion at a time when it was not at all usual. In caring for the sick and disadvantaged he was concerned with their spiritual and mental well being as well as their physical state: he wished to restore their confidence in themselves and their trust in other people and in God, and to help them find peace and stability. He regarded himself as "poor among the poor" and dressed and ate as they did, even though he enjoyed the trust and high regard of the king, Charles Albert, who made him a knight of the Order of SS Maurice and Lazarus, and of the pope who gave official approval to his work.

He died on 30 April 1842 and was buried under the Lady Altar in the main chapel in Valdocco. He was beatified in 1917 and canonized in 1934. Today his Sisters work in a large number of charitable institutions and hostel,s and the spirit of the "good canon" lives on in the Cottolengo Charitable Institute, which has branches in several parts of the world and continues to serve the suffering and the abandoned.

The above account relies heavily on J. Cottino in *Bibl.SS.*, 6, 1310-7. See also S. Ballario, *L'Apostolo della Carità, S.G.C.B. fondatore della Piccola Casa della Divina Providenza in Torino* (7th ed., 1944); V. Di Meo, *La Spiritualità di S.G.B.C.* (1959); E. Pilla, *Un gigante della carità* (1964); *N.C.E.*, 4, p. 368.

Bd Pauline von Mallinckrodt, *Foundress* (1817-81)

Pauline von Mallinckrodt was born on 3 June 1817 in Minden, Westphalia. In her youth she suffered severely from scruples and uncertainty about herself and her future, and she overcame these problems only by prayer and a strong belief in God's love and support. She grew up to become a talented, confident, and friendly person, and when she moved to Paderborn in 1839 she became increasingly involved in social and charitable work in the area, like many Catholic women of her class. She was particularly devoted to the care of the sick, the blind, and the children of the poor and was later to add schooling for the poor to her concerns. In order to give herself entirely to this work, in 1849 she founded the Institute of the Sisters of Christian Charity. It was not an easy time for the religious Orders in those parts of Germany controlled by Prussia, and it says a great deal for her determination, trust in divine Providence, and the firm foundation she gave her Sisters that they were able to survive and, indeed, flourish. When the motherhouse was closed down by the Prussian government in 1876 she moved it into Belgium where it remained until 1887; some of the Sisters went to Italy and Bohemia and later others went to America. Her spiritual life was based on a total giving of herself to God and a strong devotion to Jesus in the Blessed Sacrament and to Our Lady. Our search for God, she wrote, had to be constant and practical: "We must courageously and confidently look for God in our suffering brethren." By the time of her death in Paderborn on 30 April 1881 the Institute had forty-five houses in Europe and North and South America, with 492 members. Pauline was beatified in 1985.

She wrote an autobiography, which was published by B. Keller in 1889. See also M. E. Pietromarchi, *Madre Paolina di M., fondatrice delle Suore di Carità cristiana* (1951); *N.S.B.* 2, pp. 64–7; *Bibl.SS.*, 8, 588.

Alphabetical List of Entries

(Names are listed for those saints and blessed who have entries in the main body of the text. Those listed in the RM paragraph at the end of each day are omitted.)

Consultant Editors

DAVID HUGH FARMER. Former Reader in history at the University of Reading. Author of *St Hugh of Lincoln* and other biographical studies of saints. Author of *The Oxford Dictionary of Saints*. General consultant editor.

REV. PHILIP CARAMAN, S.J. Author of numerous biographies of saints and chief promoter of the cause of the Forty English Martyrs (canonized in 1970). Consultant on English Martyrs.

JOHN HARWOOD. Librarian of the Missionary Institute in London and course lecturer on the Orthodox churches. Consultant on Eastern and Orthodox saints.

DOM ERIC HOLLAS, O.S.B. Monk of St John's Abbey, Collegeville, Minnesota, and director of the Hill Monastic Manuscript Library in Collegeville, where he also teaches theology at St John's University. General consultant, U.S.A.

PROF. KATHLEEN JONES. Emeritus Professor of Social Policy at the University of York. Author of many books and articles on social policy and mental illness. Honorary Fellow of the Royal College of Psychiatrists. Translator of *The Poems of St John of the Cross* (1993). Consultant on social history and abnormal behaviour.

DOM DANIEL REES, O.S.B. Monk of Downside Abbey and librarian of the monastery library. Bibliographical consultant.

DR RICHARD SHARPE. Reader in diplomatic history at the University of Oxford. Author of *Medieval Irish Saints' Lives* (1991), *Adomnán of Iona. Life of St Columba* (1995), and numerous articles on Celtic saints. Consultant on this subject.

REV. AYLWARD SHORTER, W.F. Long experience of African Missions and author of many books on the subject. Former President of Missionary Institute, London, now Principal of Tangaza College, Nairobi. Consultant on missionary saints.

DOM ALBERIC STACPOOLE, O.S.B. Monk of Ampleforth Abbey. Fellow of the Royal Historical Society. Secretary of the Ecumenical Society of Our Lady. Editor of several works, including *Vatican II by Those Who Were There* (1985). Engaged on a study of St Anslem. Consultant on feasts of Our Lady.

DOM HENRY WANSBROUGH, O.S.B. Monk of Ampleforth Abbey, currently Master of St Benet's Hall, Oxford. Member of the Pontifical Biblical Commission. Author of numerous works on scripture and Editor of the *New Jerusalem Bible* (1985). Consultant on New Testament saints.

SR BENEDICTA WARD, S.L.G. Anglican religious. Lecturer at Oxford Institute of Medieval History. Author of numerous works on hagiography, spirituality, and mysticism. Consultant on Middle Ages and age of Bede.